W9-AQQ-866

Norton
ON ARCHIVES

THE WRITINGS OF

Margaret Cross Norton

ON ARCHIVAL & RECORDS
MANAGEMENT

EDITED BY
Thornton W. Mitchell

FOREWORD BY
Ernst Posner

WITH A NEW INTRODUCTION BY
Randall C. Jimerson

THE SOCIETY OF AMERICAN ARCHIVISTS
SAA
ESTABLISHED 1936

Chicago

SOCIETY OF AMERICAN ARCHIVISTS
527 S. Wells St., 5th Floor • Chicago, IL 60607-3922
312/922-0140 • fax 312/347-1452
info@archivists.org • www.archivists.org

© 1975, 2003 by the Society of American Archivists
All rights reserved. Printed in the United States of America.

ISBN 1-931666-04-0

"Margaret C. Norton Reconsidered," by Randall C. Jimerson, was previously published in *Archival Issues,* Vol. 26, No.1 (Midwest Archives Conference, 2001). It is reprinted here by permission of the Midwest Archives Conference.

CONTENTS

INTRODUCTION
TO 2003 REISSUE

WHEN THIS VOLUME was first published in 1975 it brought Margaret Cross Norton's writings to the attention of archivists around the world. Although Norton published several articles in the *American Archivist,* most of her writings had been buried in a variety of journals and printed conference proceedings with limited circulation, and were not widely available. Thornton W. Mitchell, a professional colleague of Norton's two decades earlier while she was State Archivist of Illinois, conducted an extensive search for her articles and reports, and brought them together in a single volume.

Norton on Archives brought Margaret Cross Norton to the attention of a new generation of archivists. Hers was an important voice for the profession to hear, once again, as it entered a period of new challenges and opportunities for growth and development. Not only had Norton been a pioneering woman in a profession initially dominated by men, but she challenged the prevailing view of archives as resources primarily useful to historians and scholars. Appointed as State Archivist of Illinois in 1922, Margaret Norton became a founder of the Society of American Archivists (SAA) in 1936, serving as vice president, president, and editor of the *American Archivist* during a distinguished career of more than three decades. In addition to her professional leadership she was an original thinker who wrote clear and direct prose.

When published by Southern Illinois University Press in 1975, *Norton on Archives* became an instant classic. SAA obtained the rights in 1978 and issued a second printing in 1979. For several years Norton and T. R. Schellenberg were the only American archivists whose writings offered a broad introduction to archival theory and practice. The issues that they debated in print continue to challenge new generations of archivists.

As the Society of American Archivists and other publishers began to expand the available literature on archives, *Norton on Archives* went out of print in the early 1980s. Many archival educators continued to assign Norton as required reading, but the volume became increasingly difficult to obtain. When publication resumed in March 2001, the volume became a standard text for many graduate courses in archival studies. Its continuing timeliness—several decades after Norton wrote her last article in 1956—reconfirmed its importance in American archival literature.

In order to create a cohesive volume from numerous and sometimes repetitive brief articles written by Norton, editor Thornton W. Mitchell exercised considerable leeway both in combining separate articles on similar topics into chapters, and in excising text that he considered redundant, rearranging sentences, and applying consistent rules of spelling and grammar. The result is a much more readable volume, but one that takes some liberties with the original texts.

For further inquiry into Margaret Cross Norton's career and her thoughts on archives and records management, one may also wish to consult her correspondence, reports, subject files, photographs, and other papers in the Illinois State Archives and the Society of American Archivists archives, now housed at the University of Wisconsin at Milwaukee. Most of Norton's papers at these two repositories were published on microfilm in 1993 as "The Margaret Cross Norton Working Papers, 1924–1958," by Robert E. Bailey and Elaine Shemoney Evans. Norton's correspondence, of course, also shows up in the papers of colleagues, friends, and acquaintances in several other repositories. There is no full biography of Norton, although a good overview of her career is presented in Donnelly Faye Lancaster, "Margaret Cross Norton: Dedication to the Development of the American Archival Profession" (M.A. Thesis, Auburn University, August 2000).

This new edition of *Norton on Archives* contains the full text of the original 1975 edition, including Ernst Posner's tribute to Norton and Thornton Mitchell's preface and introduction. In addition, the Midwest Archives Conference graciously permitted reprinting of "Margaret C. Norton Reconsidered," which is an analytical and interpretive essay rather than a full biographical or critical account of Norton's career.

As Richard C. Berner stated in his *American Archivist* review (July 1976) of the first edition of this volume: "Margaret Cross Norton is basic! Archivists everywhere are indebted to an admiring Thornton W. Mitchell for skillfully editing and bringing together these articles (1930–1957) and giving all of the younger [members] in the profession . . . the full benefit of her contributions to archival theory and practices. . . ." As one of the "younger members" to whom Berner referred when this volume was first published, I too am pleased to see that *Norton on Archives* is again available for another generation to appreciate. Margaret Norton continues to stimulate our thinking about archival issues, to challenge our assumptions, and to help us expand our professional boundaries.

RANDALL C. JIMERSON
Western Washington University
Bellingham, Washington
November 2002

MARGARET C. NORTON RECONSIDERED

By Randall C. Jimerson

Margaret C. Norton never shied away from controversy, but only a woman of strong convictions could have challenged the prevailing orthodoxy of the emerging archival profession in 1929. Her paper, "The Archives Department as an Administrative Unit in Government," which she presented to the American Historical Association's Conference of Archivists, called for nothing less than a reconsideration of the intimate relationship between archives and history. Despite modest progress in archival legislation in Alabama, Mississippi, and a few other states, she pointed out, "in reality only about a dozen states in the whole country [are] providing sustained and systematic care to their official records." Norton charged that the popular misconception of archives as nothing more than historical documents blocked progress for the profession, and that "the greatest handicap . . . to getting adequate support for archives work is the belief that archives work is just another function of the state historical society." From these premises, Norton concluded that, "The archivist should be a public official whose first interest is business efficiency, and only secondarily should

"Margaret C. Norton Reconsidered," by Randall C. Jimerson, was previously published in *Archival Issues,* Vol. 26, No. 1 (Midwest Archives Conference, 2001). It is reprinted here by permission of the Midwest Archives Conference.

be interested in history." Archivists should make their records accessible, Norton declared, primarily for the "practical ends of administration."[1]

The historians at the December 1929 Conference of Archivists received Norton's message, as she later recalled, "in stony silence." Only historian Milo M. Quaife of the Burton Historical Collection, who served as editor of the *Mississippi Valley Historical Review,* privately congratulated her. "Margaret, 'you done noble,'" Quaife told her. "You are way ahead of them and they don't know what you are talking about."[2] Norton continued to press her point. Six months after her AHA presentation, she gave essentially the same paper at the National Association of State Libraries meeting in Los Angeles, where it "was enthusiastically received."[3] Librarians "weren't so hidebound in the belief that archives existed simply for the benefit of historical researchers," Norton later speculated, and they welcomed her arguments.[4] Norton sought to redefine the nascent archival profession in the United States. "To most persons, including some archivists, the term archives still connotes merely musty, dirty files of loose papers and decayed leather folios of little apparent use, but vaguely believed to be of value because historians keep saying they are valuable," Norton declared.

---

1   William F. Birdsall, "The Two Sides of the Desk: The Archivist and the Historian, 1909–1935," *American Archivist* 38 (April 1975): 166–67; Donnelly Faye Lancaster, "Margaret Cross Norton: Dedication to the Development of the American Archival Profession" (M.A. Thesis, Auburn University, August 2000), 1–2; Thornton W. Mitchell, "Introduction," in *Norton on Archives: The Writings of Margaret Cross Norton on Archival & Records Management,* ed. by Thornton W. Mitchell (Chicago: Society of American Archivists, 1975), xviii. [See lv in this edition]

2   Norton to Birdsall, May 24, 1973, in *The Margaret Cross Norton Working Papers,* 1924–1928, microfilm edition (Springfield: Illinois State Archives, 1993), roll 3, frame 1206 (hereafter cited as: in MCNWP, 3/1206).

3   Ibid.

4   Norton to Birdsall, June 18, 1973, in MCNWP, 3/1239.

"The real function of an archivist, however, is that of custodian of legal records of the state, the destruction of which might seriously inconvenience the administration of state business."[5]

Even though Norton's views on the administrative importance of archives seemed to historians like heresy in 1929–still several years before the founding of the National Archives– they soon became, as Ernst Posner stated in 1964, "a generally accepted tenet of archivists in the United States." Norton's ideas "struck a new and significant note," according to Posner. "Although giving due credit to the work of the Public Archives Commission, Miss Norton felt that the emphasis it had given to the historians' stake in archival preservation was one-sided and that the time had come to stress 'proper care of archives as an administrative problem of state government instead of as a mere adjunct to the historical library field.'"[6] In an obituary tribute to Norton, Maynard Brichford, archivist of the University of Illinois, declared these presentations "landmarks in the archival campaign for professional recognition."[7] Norton had clearly articulated a new vision of archival identity, one that would link the profession more closely to centers of political influence and power and less to the scholarly world of the academic historian. It is a struggle for identity with which archivists still grapple. This article explores the origins and development of Norton's thinking on archival matters in order to examine, from a new vantage point, current professional debates about archival theory, the role of archivists in modern society, and the relationship between manuscripts and archives.

---

5 Norton, "The Archives Department as an Administrative Unit of Government," in *Norton on Archives,* 4.

6 Ernst Posner, *American State Archives* (Chicago: University of Chicago Press, 1965): 25, 30.

7 Maynard Brichford, "Margaret Cross Norton," *American Archivist,* 47 (fall 1984): 473–74.

REPUTATION

Through her influential writings, Margaret Norton continues to play a role in current professional debates. More than any other archivist of her generation, Norton exemplified the shift in professional focus from historical manuscripts to public archives. Philosophically linked with English archivist Sir Hilary Jenkinson, Norton has been at the center of many recent North American debates.

The Canadian debate about history and archives began in 1983 with George Bolotenko's castigation of Margaret Norton's "ringing tocsin" that archivists should, in his words, "beware the enemy, beware the historian-archivist working with documents." Bolotenko characterized Norton, in her efforts to separate archivists from their traditional historical orientation, as "shrill," "strident," "vociferous," and using "a language bordering on the venomous." According to Bolotenko, Norton sought to replace the archivist-historian with "the archivist as administrator or bureaucrat."[8] What was at stake, in his view, was the identity of the archival profession. In the debate that ensued during the next several years in the pages of *Archivaria,* archivists struggled to define the roles and identity of the archival profession. Bolotenko's critics charged that his views would doom archivists to being relics of the past in the technological revolution that required new approaches and perspectives. The danger was that archivists would become obsolete, doomed to irrelevance as antiquarians in modern society.[9] In supporting Bolotenko, however, Patrick Dunae stated that the "real villains" are "Miss Norton and her disciples." Dunae warned of the danger of technologically oriented

---

8   George Bolotenko, "Archivists and Historians: Keepers of the Well," *Archivaria* 16 (summer 1983): 5, 10.

9   See, for example, Carl Spadoni, "No Monopoly for 'Archivist-Historians': Bolotenko Assailed," *Archivaria* 17 (winter 1983–84): 291–95; Anthony L. Rees, "Bolotenko's Siege Mentality," Ibid., 301–02; Bob Taylor-Vaisey, "Archivist-Historians Ignore Information Revolution," Ibid., 305–08; and other articles in subsequent issues of *Archivaria.*

administrators replacing historical scholars in the archival profession's leadership. "Nortonians, now allied with a new generation of public administrators and technocrats, have more than anyone else endeavored to push archivy off its humanistic, historical, scholarly base," he charged.[10] Thus, even after her death Margaret Norton's views on the archival profession still stirred passionate debates about the nature of archives and the future of the profession.

As an American proponent of Sir Hilary Jenkinson's views, Norton figured prominently in more recent debates about archival theory and methodology. Luciana Duranti cited Norton as the American proponent of Jenkinson's "moral defense of archives," in her critique of T. R. Schellenberg's views on appraisal. In contrast to Jenkinson, Duranti stated, "Schellenberg's definition of archives was theoretically flawed, not because he built into it the elements of value and use for research purposes, but because he arrived at it on purely pragmatic grounds." Duranti faulted American archivists for such pragmatism and challenged them to develop "a methodology driven by archival theory rather than vice versa."[11] In a rejoinder to Duranti, Frank Boles and Mark Greene defended American pragmatism and the inductive process for establishing archival principles based on experience and utility.[12] Although not formally charged as a Jenkinsonian theorist, Margaret Norton was closely associated with the English/European camp in opposition to Schellenberg. The common perception has been that Norton aligned her views

---

10 Patrick A. Dunae, "Archives and the Spectre of *1984:* Bolotenko Applauded," *Archivaria* 17 (winter 1983–84): 286–90. Bolotenko and others continued this argument in subsequent issues of *Archivaria*.

11 Luciana Duranti, "The Concept of Appraisal and Archival Theory," *American Archivist* 57 (spring 1994): 338–39, 344. Duranti does cite Andrew Raymond and James O'Toole, who stated that Norton had established a "middle ground" between Jenkinson and Schellenberg, but she does not elaborate this distinction (p. 339).

12 Frank Boles and Mark A. Greene, "Et Tu Schellenberg? Thoughts on the Dagger of American Appraisal Theory," *American Archivist* 59 (summer 1996): 298–310.

with Jenkinson and European theorists in opposing the American historical manuscripts tradition and the dominant role of historians. A closer examination of her career and her unpublished writings, however, challenges this interpretation.

Although recognized as one of the most influential archival theorists and practitioners of her generation, Norton was at heart a pragmatist. She adopted European principles but adapted them to modern American circumstances. Almost single-handedly she nudged the American archival profession away from the domination of scholars and into an independent identity that included service to records as both historical documents and, more importantly in her view, as legal records vital within the domain of government administrators. She became one of America's greatest archival theorists (though she would have shunned the title), for her approach to archival problems was fundamentally pragmatic, based on experience and experiment rather than on abstract theory. Even her central professional vision, that archives are in their truest essence legal records of business transactions, derived from her personal experience on an essentially pragmatic basis.

CAREER

Margaret Cross Norton (1891–1984) served as the first State Archivist of Illinois, from 1922 to 1957. Her career was remarkable, particularly for a woman in fields still dominated by male leadership. In her thirty-five years at the Illinois State Archives, she developed an archival program that became a model for many other states; supervised planning and construction for an archives building that was only the third facility in the United States planned specifically for archival needs; and established the Illinois Archives as an integral part of state government. Generous with her time and advice, she worked closely with a broad group of historians, librarians, and scholars to define the emerging archival profession. As a founding member of the

Society of American Archivists (SAA), she served as its first vice president (1936–1937), as a council member (1937–1942), as president (1943–1945), and as the second editor of the *American Archivist* (1946–1949). In most of these positions she was the first woman to serve in such capacities.[13]

Norton's professional work, however, was not confined to the field of archives. She also held important leadership positions within the American Historical Association (AHA), the American Library Association (ALA), the Illinois State Historical Society, the Illinois Library Association, the Historical Records Survey, and the National Association of State Libraries. She served as secretary-treasurer of the latter organization for five years and as a longstanding member of the ALA Archives and Libraries Committee. She chaired the AHA Public Archives Committee for several years and was a member of its Committee of Ten, which recommended the formation of SAA, the first profes-sional organization for archivists. Norton thus served, informally, as one of the links between the archives profession and both the library and history professions.[14]

Many archivists have become acquainted with Norton through her prolific writings, edited by Thornton Mitchell in 1975 under the title *Norton on Archives*. As Richard Berner observed, Norton was "an influential writer on every aspect of archival administration."[15] But her influence on the profession during the 1930s and 1940s went well beyond her writings on archives and records management. Under her leadership the

---

13 Thornton W. Mitchell, "Introduction," in *Norton on Archives,* xv–xxi. [See liii–lix in this edition.] Donnelly Faye Lancaster, "Margaret Cross Norton: Dedication to the Development of the American Archival Profession" is the best available biography of Norton. For her role as a pioneering woman in the profession, see Michele F. Pacifico, "Founding Mothers: Women in the Society of American Archivists, 1936–1972," *American Archivist* 50 (summer 1987): 370–89.

14 Mitchell, "Introduction," *Norton on Archives,* xvi–xvii. [See liv–lv in this edition.]

15 Richard C. Berner, *Archival Theory and Practice in the United States: A Historical Analysis* (Seattle: University of Washington Press, 1983): 16.

Illinois State Archives became a model consulted by archivists in many other states regarding archival legislation, new buildings, and organization of new archival agencies.[16] Archivists from other countries also wrote to or visited Norton seeking advice and guidance, which she freely provided. Reading her monthly reports to the State Library provides a true sense of her whirlwind schedule of consultations, professional activities, and scholarship, all of which came in addition to the daily responsibilities of managing an active state archives program.

The breadth and depth of Norton's professional activities and interests are remarkable. She attended professional conferences several times a year, often driving hundreds of miles out of her way to visit other archives and libraries, and her monthly reports detail specific practices, techniques, and new technologies being developed and tested in these institutions. She read voraciously in the archival literature of her time, including translations of foreign reports and articles whenever they were available. As she recalled long after her retirement, "While I was archivist I kept a file of everything I could lay my hands upon which would illustrate the history of American archival thinking." When she first decided to become an archivist, one of her mentors, Professor Lucy Salmon of the Vassar College History Department, had advised, "Read everything you can find on the subject, and if the opportunity comes you will be ready."[17] Norton took this advice to heart and continued to study the professional literature throughout her career. When Clarence Walton, who was teaching a course on archives at Harvard in 1939, sent her a copy of his lecture notes, she commented, "His point of view is so different from mine that I found them quite disappointing. They do not indicate much knowledge of modern archival literature or theory."[18] For

---

16 Berner, 31; Norton, "Budget Justification Report," February 27, 1943, in MCNWP, 1/785.

17 Norton to William F. Birdsall, May 24, 1973, in MCNWP, 3/1203–1205.

18 Norton, Archives Division Report, August 1939, in MCNWP, 1/248.

Norton, such knowledge formed the essential foundation for archival practice.

Norton began her career as archivist after earning degrees in both history and library science, a combination that reflected the twin sources of the profession. After obtaining her bachelor's and master's degrees in history from the University of Chicago, she earned the B.L.S. from the New York Library School in Albany in 1915. During her first professional position as cataloger at Vassar College, she later recalled, "I was a complete misfit and decided library work was not for me, unless I could get into the historical library field."[19] As a cataloger she found "the work monotonous with little opportunity for originality."[20] The "turning point" in her career came when she attended her first American Historical Association meeting in Washington, D.C., in 1915 and heard an "illustrated lecture" by Waldo G. Leland, of the Carnegie Institution of Washington's Department of Historical Research. Leland spoke eloquently on European archives, the dismal condition of American federal archives, and the need for a national archives building. On the drive back to Poughkeepsie with Professor Lucy Salmon, Norton exclaimed, "Now that is what I want to do—I want to be an archivist!"[21] She would later call Leland "my archival godfather," stating that he had "first directed my attention to the possibilities of an archival career."[22]

With this goal in mind, she continued to study history at Chicago, although she never completed a Ph.D. degree. She also gained experience, briefly, as a manuscripts assistant at the Indiana State Library and as a cataloger at the Missouri State Historical Society in Columbia. In January 1922, Norton interviewed for what she thought would be an archival staff position at the Illinois State Library, but instead was hired as the first

---

19   Norton to Birdsall, May 24, 1973, in MCNWP, 3/1204.
20   Norton to Birdsall, June 18, 1973, in MCNWP, 3/1231.
21   Norton to Birdsall, May 24, 1973, in MCNWP, 3/1205.
22   Norton, Archives Monthly Report, October 1956, in MCNWP, 3/136; Lancaster, "Margaret Cross Norton," chapter 2.

archivist of the Illinois State Archives. Overwhelmed by her new responsibilities, she asked for three months to prepare.[23]

During this three-month period Norton traveled the country visiting most of the existing archives programs in the Mid-Atlantic states and New England. "I picked up an idea here and another there, but I think I got more about what not to do as what to do," she later recalled. In Albany, for example, she found that "like all archives of the period they were treated as static objects, meant for historical research–no modern records." In Massachusetts a fire started in the State House during her visit, but during her tour of the archives she witnessed an alarming indifference to the dangers posed to irreplaceable records. "To my horror, the archivist seemed not the least perturbed and instituted no procedure for evacuating the records in case the fire broke through," she recalled. Furthermore, the head of the Vital Statistics Department "told me scornfully that nobody used the archives but 'old fellows with tobacco on their beards . . . who were hunting up ancestors.'" At the Virginia State Library, she discovered, "the archives . . . were organized as merely historical manuscripts." This tour of archival horrors reached Connecticut, where "I was shown the archives clerks sorting the colonial laws by subjects! I had read the horror stories from the French National Archives which had also been arranged by subject and were then being resorted by provenance."[24]

In the nation's capital she visited Dr. J. Franklin Jameson, Waldo Leland's supervisor as director of the Carnegie Institution's Department of Historical Research. Jameson had been the first managing editor of the *American Historical Review* and a founder of the Public Archives Commission, and was currently leading the campaign to establish a national archives. Jameson impressed her greatly. "I think he was the one person in the country who understood the relation between archives and government," she recalled years later. "He said he did not

---

23 Norton to Birdsall, June 18, 1973, in MCNWP, 3/1231–33.
24 Norton to Birdsall, June 18, 1973, in MCNWP, 3/1235–37.

think he could give me much practical help, but that he did want to show me some 'horrible examples.'" Jameson asked one of his staff members to spend four days escorting the aspiring young archivist to visit scenes of archival neglect in the nation's capital, including the deplorable condition of U.S. census records, some of which "were destroyed by fire here a few months later."[25] Thus, even before assuming her first archives position, Norton had clearly imbibed the European principle of provenance, as well as a concern for modern records and preservation needs.

Although inspired by the American archival pioneers Leland and Jameson, Norton stated that the greatest influence on her thinking was English archivist Sir Hilary Jenkinson. She stated that "Hilary Jenkinson's *Manual of Archives* was my Bible."[26] The first edition was published the same year she started her new position as State Archivist of Illinois. "I purchased a copy immediately," Norton later recalled. "With its emphasis on the reasons for and explanation of provenance, it coagulated the impression I already had, that archives are fundamentally business records."[27] This would be the major theme of her professional career and of her own influential writings: that archives serve an essential role as legal records necessary for public administration.

ARCHIVIST-ADMINISTRATOR

The archival profession that Norton entered in 1922 had been shaped largely by historians who saw archives as essential sources for scientific history.[28] Private antiquarians and collectors had shaped the historical manuscripts tradition, as Richard C.

---

25 Ibid.
26 Norton to Birdsall, May 24, 1973, in MCNWP, 3/1206.
27 Norton to Birdsall, June 18, 1973, in MCNWP, 3/1239.
28 John Higham, *History: Professional Scholarship in America* (Baltimore: Johns Hopkins University Press, 1965), 92–116; Mattie U. Russell, "The Influence of Historians on the Archival Profession in the United States," *American Archivist* 46 (summer 1983): 280.

Berner termed it, focusing on archival records as sources for historical scholarship. By the early twentieth century, however, a competing public archives tradition had developed in the United States, based largely on the introduction of French and Prussian concepts such as provenance and original order. This latter tradition, which Norton soon embraced, focused on archives as official records that supported government functions and gave only secondary consideration to private research interests. As Luke Gilliland-Swetland has argued, these two traditions led to competing views of the archivist's role, as custodian or as interpreter of records. The conflict between these two paradigms dramatically shaped the subsequent development of American archival theory and practice.[29] Since Margaret Norton became an influential advocate for the public archives position, the source of her archival ideas deserves further exploration.

Margaret Norton was among the first American archivists to challenge historians' domination of the field. As she later wrote, "I was the first American archivist to insist that the archivist's first duty was to aid his fellow officials to give more efficient service on their records, rather than to devote all one's energies to the research scholar."[30] This shift of focus would lead to a reorientation of the archivist's role, from an academic to an administrative perspective. In commenting on papers given at the 1946 SAA annual meeting, for example, Norton concluded, "I would say that it is high time we archivists

---

29 Berner, chapters 1–2; Luke J. Gilliland-Swetland, "The Provenance of a Profession: The Permanence of the Public Archives and Historical Manuscripts Traditions in American Archival History," *American Archivist* 54 (spring 1991), 165–66. See also William F. Birdsall, "The American Archivist's Search for Professional Identity, 1909–1936," (Ph.D. Dissertation, University of Wisconsin-Madison, 1973).

30 Norton to Birdsall, June 18, 1973, in MCNWP, 3/1234. Norton, in fact, was not the "first" archivist to adopt this position, which had already been advocated by historians such as Waldo Gifford Leland and by a few archivists, including Arnold J. van Lear, but she quickly became the most articulate spokesperson for this perspective.

stopped trying to make other officials fall in with our own program, and to find out what they want and need from us."[31] Norton thus argued for an examination of archives users, which archivists would later call "user studies," but for her the primary clientele of archivists would be government officials rather than academic historians or private researchers.

Norton argued that archives were vital to government administration and that the archivist must become engaged in the daily work of governmental management. In 1938, for example, she harshly criticized the report of the SAA Committee on Archival Training:

> One might conclude from the report that the ideal archivist is a scholar sitting in a remote ivory tower safeguarding records of interest only to the historian. In reality the archivist is at the very heart of his government and the archival establishment is a vital cog in its governmental machinery. Archives are legal records the loss of which might cause serious loss to citizens or the government.[32]

Although insisting that archives must be distinguished from historical manuscripts, which originate from private sources, Norton recognized that archives also have historical importance. In her 1931 annual report for the State Archives, she explained that "archives, as papers having historical value, are historical manuscripts, but many historical manuscripts are not archives."[33] Thus the State Archives served primarily a legal and administrative purpose, but it maintained records that also had an historical significance.

Despite her position as a division head of the Illinois State Library, Norton gained practical experience by immersing herself in all aspects of archival work. A state archivist, Norton wrote, must understand "mechanical details" and be able to perform a broad range of functions, because he "frequently is the whole establishment so far as professional work is concerned. He must

---

31 Norton, Archives Monthly Report, October 1946, in MCNWP, 1/1348.
32 Norton, "Archival Training," December 10, 1938, in MCNWP, 4/398.
33 Norton in *The Archives Division of the Illinois State Library* (1931) in MCNWP, 1/068.

train his subordinates in the mechanical details even if he does not perform all the work himself." The state archivist's functions "are largely administrative rather than scholarly." Although he "also needs the technique of scholarship," she declared that, "Overemphasis upon pure scholarship and contempt for administration is unfortunate for the archivist because his whole career is tied up with other officials who have either an inferiority complex towards or a contempt for, (or both) the academic outlook on life."[34]

Thus Norton called for a separation between the historian-scholar and the archivist-administrator partly because this would lead to greater financial support for archives. The distinction may have been necessary on theoretical grounds, but practical reasons also existed for reducing archivists' academic outlook. In a 1940 paper on "Training of Archivists" she elaborated on this theme:

> Too many archivists in the past have looked upon an appointment as state archivist as an appointment to a lifelong subsidy for private historical research. . . . Archives work is administrative work. The archivist must reconcile himself to the fact that it is most important to the government that he serves that he be able to document an important lawsuit for the State or some citizen; and that the unexploited source materials in his collection must probably be laid before some other scholar who will have the time to write the book that haunts him. . . . Archivists today must subordinate their scholarly inclinations to administrative work.[35]

It was this dedication to the administrative purposes of archives that compelled Norton throughout her career to seek cooperation with government officials, to recognize the legitimate concerns of such officials for their own records, and to urge the archival profession to recognize the necessity for such cooperation. Archival records were not created for the benefit of scholars, but to meet the needs of current administration and future legal requirements.

---

34 Ibid., 4/398–99.
35 Norton, "Training of Archivists," in MCNWP, 5/377–78.

Archives could meet these requirements, Norton insisted, only if their integrity and authenticity were preserved. The archivist, therefore, must understand the legal requirements for evidence and authenticity. Besides Jenkinson's manual on archives, the second major influence on Norton's thinking was John Henry Wigmore's *A Treatise on the Anglo-American System of Evidence in Trials at Common Law,* commonly cited as "Wigmore on Evidence." In particular, Wigmore's discussion of "Authentication of Documents" emphasized that, as Norton summarized, "the custodian must handle the records in a manner that will not impair their value as evidence should they ever have to be produced in court."[36] Thus, protecting the integrity of archives was essential in maintaining their authenticity and legal value.

For Norton, the crucial element in defining a separate identity for the archival profession was drawing a clear distinction between the archivist's responsibility for protecting the legal and administrative nature of records and the concern of both historians and librarians for information retrieval and research. "The needs of the historian in front of the desk and the archivist behind the desk are different," she declared. "It is amazing how long it took both historians and archivists to realize that distinction."[37] Although some archivists concluded from this distinction that their interests should be more closely aligned with librarians, Norton likewise dismissed that view. After teaching the second archival course ever given in a library school at Columbia University in 1940, she wrote that, "while both librarians and archivists are engaged in preparing our materials for 'information

---

36 *Norton on Archives,* 27. "I find that even today few archivists have ever heard of this book," Norton complained in 1973. "Familiarity with the principles laid down there are very helpful to the archivist." Norton to Birdsall, June 18, 1973, in MCNWP, 5/377–78.

37 Norton to Birdsall, June 18, 1973, and October 26, 1973, in MCNWP, 3/1242 and 3/1263.

retrieval,' the philosophy and techniques of the two professions are quite different."[38]

In Norton's opinion these differences presented a fundamental problem in basing archival education on either history or library science. In looking back on her career in the profession, she wrote, "The question as to who should train the American archivist became the subject of acrimonious dispute between the history and library professions and all because both historians and librarians approached the subject from the standpoint of the man in front of the desk, both interested in the use of archives rather than the methods to be used by the man behind the desk in order to service the records."[39] Therefore, Norton concluded, the archival profession needed to establish a separate identity, one focused on the legal aspects of records and their usefulness for administration.

EXPERIMENTER

In her published writings, Norton clearly enunciated her views on the need to recognize the legal and administrative significance of records. Her archival theory was based on fundamental principles, following in large part the concepts expressed by Jenkinson, and she remained steadfast in urging her colleagues to recognize the distinction between historical manuscripts and archives. Through her unpublished writings, however, we see more clearly that she based her theory on pragmatic grounds and personal experience. In fact, one of the most compelling aspects of her approach to archival issues, particularly during the 1930s and 1940s, is her insistence on experimentation as the basis for developing archival theory. Rather than construct

---

38 Norton to Birdsall, May 31, 1973, in MCNWP, 3/1215. Solon J. Buck, director of publications at the National Archives, had taught the first course at Columbia in 1939. Berner, 105.

39 Norton to Birdsall, October 26, 1973, in MCNWP, 3/1265.

abstract theory based on some sort of cosmic view of the universe, she insisted that archivists not constrict their thinking and practice until sufficient experience, through trial and error, could disclose the best means of managing archives. Her emphasis on the administrative aspects of archives likewise derived from an essentially pragmatic basis.

Norton never lost sight of the need to balance theory with practical realities of the political situation. "The point is that we are dealing with facts as well as with theories," she wrote to University of Pennsylvania law professor Francis S. Philbrick, who had pointed out a discrepancy between what Norton said about keeping county records in the counties and the possibility of collecting such records in the state archives. "In theory, the records should remain in the county. In practice, it is better for the State Archives to take what they can get," Norton argued. "What I am driving at primarily is propaganda to make people see that county archives relate to them and to their business interests: Whether or not they are interested in history."[40] While never losing sight of archival theory and fundamental principles, Norton recognized that at times one must adjust to political realities and the necessity of working effectively with other public officials.

Throughout her early career, Norton urged archivists not to "put the universe into a straight jacket" by insisting on premature standardization of practice. In 1940 Norton complained that Ernst Posner wanted "uniformity of procedure" in archival training courses. "That's the Prussian in him," she declared. "I don't believe we are ready yet for uniformity—we need to do a lot of experimenting before we crystallize."[41] Two years later she declared that efforts to seek uniformity would "stultify progress in archives," and that "I think we should all be experimenting and exchanging the results of our experiments until enough experimentation has been made so that on the basis of wider

---

40 Norton to Francis S. Philbrick, February 2, 1940, in MCNWP, 5/346.
41 Norton, Archives Monthly Report, November 1940, in MCNWP, 1/433.

experience than any of us at present have, we could begin to pick out the better points of all our experiments and then to combine them into a permanent scheme."[42]

Norton recognized that experiments sometimes could fail, but that one could learn valuable lessons from such mistakes. Under her leadership the Illinois State Archives in 1936 prepared detailed cataloging rules and distributed them to other archivists. Only two years later she decided that this "hastily prepared little booklet" was an experiment that must be abandoned. She told an SAA round table on classification and cataloging, which she chaired, that this cataloging manual "is absolutely obsolete, and I hope all of you who possess copies will promptly throw them in the waste basket. Please do not follow that, because it is all wrong."[43] Thus, she was willing to admit that her ideas had changed and to encourage others to experiment and report on the results.

In reminiscing about professional conferences during these early years, Norton later recalled the excitement of "bull sessions" lasting until "2 or 3 o'clock in the morning."[44] "I, as a neophyte archivist, found them extremely helpful and inspiring," she declared. "We would discuss together what we had been doing, then go home and mull over these ideas, experiment with them, then go to the next conference eager to exchange more ideas. The American archivist had not yet developed a mature philosophy of archives. Had a manual . . . [on archival techniques] been published, American archival economy might have been saddled with impractical procedures hard to eradicate when experience disproved their efficacy later."[45]

Thus, theory would follow from practical experimentation rather than the other way around. For Norton the true test of archival methods was how well they worked and whether they

---

42 Norton to J. B. Speer, February 5, 1942, in MCNWP, 5/1368

43 Transcript of proceedings, SAA round table on classification and cataloging, October 25, 1938, in MCNWP, 4/151–52.

44 Norton to Birdsall, June 18, 1973, in MCNWP, 3/1242.

45 Norton to Birdsall, October 26, 1973, in MCNWP, 3/1263–64.

served the needs of a practicing archivist facing numerous daily challenges in managing voluminous modern records. As her close friend Helen Chatfield, archivist of the U. S. Treasury Department, wrote to Norton in 1945:

> These custodians have, in most instances, acquired whatever knowledge they have of record administration and discipline through their own experience, and there is not yet a body of systematized knowledge of the field. . . . In fact, it is safe to say that the development of this field of endeavor as a profession is merely in its infancy—with only slight glimmerings of a philosophy, and some rudimentary beginnings of a discipline becoming discernible."[46]

This sense of flux led many archivists of Norton's generation to a belief that trial and error would be necessary for a time to determine the best methods for the newly emerging profession.

Far from being an "ivory tower" theorist, Norton threw herself into the daily regimen of archival practice. In her monthly report for October 1946, she declared, "Archivists have got to get their hands dirty, but the young ones don't want to do so."[47] Often lacking trained staff assistants, Norton found that she routinely had to get her own hands dirty. With a clear sense of pride she stated: "Ernst Posner commented after an inspection trip many years later that I seemed to have done most of the work myself in the early days."[48] Posner later recalled that "by processing records and getting her hands dirty," Norton had acquired "an amount of practical experience unmatched at that time in most other state archival agencies."[49] In 1939 she had to take over processing of the governor's correspondence from an inefficient staff member. As she reported: "Although this work was somewhat time consuming and part of it perhaps too mechanical for executive time, it gave me a somewhat different

---

46   Helen L. Chatfield to Norton, March 11, 1945, in MCNWP, 6/373–74.
47   Norton, Archives Monthly Report, October 1946, in MCNWP, 1/1347.
48   Norton to Birdsall, May 31, 1973, in MCNWP, 3/1212.
49   Ernst Posner, "A Tribute to Margaret C. Norton," *Norton on Archives*, viii. [See xlvi in this edition.]

outlook on the laminating process."[50] A few months later she reported, "Most of my time this month has been given over to the petty interruptions of an executive, and to discussions with state officials regarding the transfer of records. My major piece of work was to index the 1939 session laws to bring down to date my index to State departments."[51] When some of her staff members left in 1946, Norton reported that she spent half her time on reference service and had to run "attic to cellar" all day.[52] Despite occasional complaints about routine or technical work, Norton throughout her career remained close to the daily activities of records transfers, reference requests, processing and indexing records, and other archival procedures.[53] Her experience thus provided insights into archival principles. Theory emerged from experimentation.

This concern for practical approaches to archives, rather than scholarly treatises on historical uses of records, led to one of the major confrontations of her career. As president of SAA in 1944, Norton privately complained to SAA secretary Lester Cappon that the *American Archivist,* under editorial leadership of Theodore Calvin Pease, published too many scholarly articles and that "the archivist of a small struggling archival agency . . . finds little practical help" in the journal. "However, I have yet to visit an archival institution in person where I did not come away with some really practical suggestion for a better means of doing some piece of work." She complained that "we archivists are all trying to impress each other with our scholarship. If this society is to be a vital organism, we must decide what kind of a society it is to be and what its functions shall be." She told

---

50 Norton, Archives Monthly Report, June 1939, in MCNWP, 1/224.

51 Norton, Archives Division Report, November 1939, in MCNWP, 1/292.

52 Norton, Archives Monthly Report, March 1946, in MCNWP, 1/1258; August 1946, in MCNWP, 1/1309.

53 Mary Givens Bryan of the Georgia Department of Archives and History noted that Norton's focus on details may have led her to neglect "the bigger aspects, which kept her from being a top administrator." Quoted in Lancaster, "Margaret Cross Norton," chapter 4.

Cappon that she planned to address this issue in a president's message: "Possibly I shall stir up a hornet's nest. Personally, I rather hope that I do. I think the society is strong enough now for us to be able to take off our coats, roll up our sleeves and do a little slugging. I am afraid we are going to settle down into a very stodgy institution unless we are very careful."[54]

Working behind the scenes, Norton gained enough support for changing the orientation of the journal that Pease stepped down as editor of the *American Archivist*. Having completed her term as president of SAA, Norton reluctantly agreed to accept the position of editor in 1946. As she wrote to the new SAA president, Solon J. Buck, "It never seems to be my fate . . . to be the clinging vine for which I believe nature intended me, or to be able to dodge responsibilities."[55] Editor Norton quickly set about to make the *American Archivist* a "lively professional journal" with a new technical section on practical issues. Her goal was to have "one scholarly article to three of the popular type for each issue."[56] Under her leadership the professional journal emphasized practical techniques over scholarship. This represents a further shift from the historical manuscripts tradition, with its emphasis on historical interpretation and scholarship, to the public archives approach to archival administration.

PRAGMATIST

Margaret Norton's emphasis on the administrative and legal values of records likewise derived from pragmatic concerns. In Hilary Jenkinson's writings she found theoretical justification for these views, but they emerged from her own experience rather than from an abstract conceptualization of archives. In examining her correspondence and reports, as well as a 1973

---

54 Norton to Lester J. Cappon, January 15, 1944, in MCNWP, 6/214–15.
55 Norton to Solon J. Buck, February 1, 1946, in MCNWP, 6/400.
56 Norton to Carl L. Lokke, May 4, 1946, in MCNWP, 6/608.

interview in which she reflected on her career, at least four practical reasons for her emphasis on archives as legal and administrative records can be discerned.

First was the need to develop an identity for the Illinois State Archives separate from other state agencies. This led Norton to emphasize the legal and administrative significance of the archives rather than its historical value. As she explained to Grace Lee Nute, curator of manuscripts for the Minnesota Historical Society:

> The chief difficulty I have found in getting funds for an archives establishment here in Illinois is that we have, as you know, a strong Historical Library. Therefore, we have to stress the fact that this is not an historical institution. Otherwise, the question immediately comes up as to why we need another building for historical purposes. Consequently, in all our publicity we stressed the importance of the building from the business angle.[57]

As Norton recalled in a 1973 interview, when she was beginning her career in Illinois the "soundest advice" she received came from Mrs. Jessie Palmer Weber, head of the State Historical Library, who suggested that she emphasize the benefits of the archives for state officials:

> She said, "When your appropriation comes up before the Legislature you are going to be asked, 'Illinois already has one historical agency; what's the use of another?'" She pointed out that my big job was to sell the State officials the idea that an archives department could be useful to them."[58]

Thus, one of Norton's reasons for emphasizing the business aspects of archives was the practical necessity of creating a distinctive identity and purpose for the archives, separate from the state's historical library.

A second practical reason for emphasizing the legal value of archives was that Norton believed state officials would not provide funding for the archives unless they could see the benefit to the

---

57 Norton to Grace Lee Nute, November 22, 1940, in MCNWP, 5/158.
58 Norton to Birdsall, May 24, 1973, in MCNWP, 3/1205.

state. This could be achieved more clearly, she reasoned, by emphasizing the legal necessity of creating and maintaining accurate records, rather than the more abstract concept of preserving state history. In writing to Charles Gates of the University of Washington Department of History in 1938, Norton agreed with Gates's opinion that archival training should be based more on political science than on history:

> Unless state officials are personally interested in history, they are apt to be rather condescending to the care of archives as histori-cal records. Our experience in emphasizing here the fact that records must be preserved because of their legal value certainly proves that that is the tack to take in order to get appropriations.[59]

This recognition that state funding required justifications based on practical grounds surely reinforced Norton's focus on the legal and business aspects of archives. One must be careful, however, to avoid the easy assumption that pragmatism alone influenced her thinking on these issues. It is much more likely that these practical arguments provided further justification for her archival theory, rather than that her theories derived wholly from practical considerations.

Theory and pragmatism melded together in Norton's efforts to secure broader support and recognition for the value of archives in modern society. Thus, the third reason for her emphasis on archives as legal and business records rather than as historical documents was her concern for public recognition of archives. In a 1939 letter to law professor Francis S. Philbrick, who served with her on the AHA subcommittee on archives, Norton wrote of her interest in gaining support of the Illinois Bar Association not only for the Illinois State Archives, but for all archival establishments:

> I feel quite strongly that archivists in the past have gone at the preservation of archives from the wrong angle. They have over stressed the value as historical documents, and under stressed the value as legal documents. In the seventeen years I have been here,

---

59 Norton to Charles Gates, February 25, 1938, in MCNWP, 4/869.

I have seen a marked change in attitude towards the necessity for accurate documentation. This I think will become increasingly manifest. Archives after all were originally preserved primarily because of their legal value. I feel that we should do everything in our power to enlist the support of the members of the Bar as the persons most vitally interested in the preservation of archives. It is important to everyone that the records upon which he may wish to base his claim of citizenship, his parentage, his rights to old age pensions and his real estate—but to name a few items—should be preserved, so that when the need for them arises the records may be found in a usable condition. After all, comparatively few people care very much for history, except perhaps from an antiquarian point of view. Everyone does or should care for archives as legal records.[60]

This might be construed as special pleading, to convince the Bar Association to support archives on the grounds of the legal value of records. But Norton did not adjust her arguments to fit the interests of her audience. She remained consistent.

Norton's concern for securing broader public recognition and acceptance of archives also can be seen in her 1940 report, "Program for Preservation of Local Archives," which she circulated to members of the AHA committee on archives. In this remarkable statement she articulated a concern for archival outreach and publicity, based on the legal value of local records for each citizen:

Ninety-five percent of all that we have written on behalf of the preservation of local archives has stressed the value of records as historical source material. . . . We must broaden the base of appeal if we are to preserve the local records for the historian of the future. . . .

Why are such records preserved at all? Fundamentally they are saved because the court says the deed to your property is invalid until it is recorded; your marriage is invalid and your children illegitimate if that marriage is not licensed and recorded by the county clerk; your rights as a citizen may be imperiled if you cannot produce acceptable birth records; your estate may not be distributed among your heirs except on court orders duly authenticated by its records. Present day candidates for social

---

60 Norton to Francis S. Philbrick, November 13, 1939, in MCNWP, 4/1341.

security benefits who were born in Illinois cannot produce official birth records because the birth records of that state go back only to 1878. . . .

Are archivists not missing an important source of support by a failure to capitalize on the value of local records to every American citizen? If we follow through along this line we shall shift the emphasis from the preservation of noncurrent and historical records to the preservation of those records which touch the present day lives of citizens, making the preservation of the historical records secondary in importance but not relenting in efforts to protect them too.[61]

Clearly the legal implications of archives could be used as a strong argument for funding and support of archives at all governmental levels. But it was the citizen's direct and personal interest in the legal protections afforded by records that provided the basis for these arguments, rather than an abstract appeal to government accountability or documentation of society.

The fourth pragmatic reason for Norton's emphasis on archives as legal records derived from her early personal experience. In seeking the source of Margaret Norton's emphasis on the legal aspects of archives, it is tempting to point to Hilary Jenkinson or other European archivists. Certainly Jenkinson influenced her thinking, but more by way of providing justification and credibility to ideas that Norton herself claimed to have developed on her own. She freely admitted that "in my day I have done plenty of brain-picking," but she bridled when an interviewer repeatedly asked her to explain the source of her archival theories. As she wrote to historian William Birdsall in 1973, "Your constant quizzing about who 'influenced my think-ing' on this and that subject reveals, I fear me, Male Chauvinism." Norton had spent her career being the first woman to hold numerous professional positions—from president of SAA to editor of the *American Archivist*—and she remained adamant about the independence of her thinking and about her

---

61 Norton, "Program for Preservation of Local Archives," January 1940, in MCNWP, 5/311-12.

role as a pioneering woman in what had been a male-dominated profession. Her theories of archives derived not from Jenkinson or other archivists, but from her own personal experience, she told Birdsall:

> [T]he major influence on my archival philosophy was absorbed unconsciously, but most emphatically, from my family background. At the time of their marriage, my mother was Deputy County Treasurer and my father Deputy County Clerk. . . . Occasionally my mother would park me in my father's office while she attended her club. To keep me out from under foot, I was encouraged to play in the vault. . . . In those days the public, chiefly of course, attorneys, had free access to the vault. In other words, I saw how and why records were being created, and how they were used. And I was subject to that atmosphere not only in the office but at home, for unlike most men, my father talked shop at home. He often issued marriage licenses there. . . . We had a copy of the latest Illinois Revised Statutes over which father pored by the hour. Is it strange, therefore, that to me archives have always been primarily records of official business?[62]

This personal experience with governmental records, from a very young age, gave Margaret Norton an inherent appreciation for the value and importance of archives that transcended an intellectual understanding. The archival theories of Jenkinson, Leland, and other influential archival writers of her era reinforced assumptions and predilections that she claimed to have assimilated from her parents. She thus gained at an early age a powerful appreciation for the daily significance of archival records and for the legal basis they provided for the rights of ordinary people.

AMERICAN ADAPTATIONS

By emphasizing her childhood experiences as the basis for her independent orientation toward archives, Norton also helped to establish an indigenous basis for the development of American

---

62 Norton to Birdsall, June 18, 1973, in MCNWP, 3/1234–35.

archives. She did adopt European principles, more fully than most of her contemporaries, but she continually sought to define a peculiarly American approach to archives. A crucial distinction, Norton believed, was the lack of ancient records in the United States in contrast with Europe. Illinois and many other states had few truly historical records, she wrote, but "one hundred years hence, possibly in fifty years, the materials now in our archives, will partake of the nature of true archives."[63] The techniques for managing modern records must differ from those for ancient records. "European archivists have been dealing with quite a different type of material from that which American archivists have to deal with," Norton stated at the 1938 annual meeting of SAA. "The European archivists hardly know anything has happened since 1800. Most of the archives most of us are handling date certainly past 1865, and largely past 1900."[64]

Archives in a democracy likewise differed from those in a highly centralized or monarchical country. Shortly after Ernst Posner immigrated to the United States from Europe, Norton wondered whether his knowledge of European archival theory could be transplanted easily. "Whether any foreigner, especially one accustomed to ideology of highly centralized states fully grasps the significance of the democratic implication with respect to American archives, I do not know," Norton wrote to Charles Williamson, dean of the Columbia University School of Library Service, who was considering hiring Posner to teach archives courses:

> In talking with foreign archivists, whom I have met, they have a way of saying, "of course, we get those records—that is the law." This I think is a result of the European monarchical idea that archives are the personal property of the sovereign, who may make any disposition of them by law which the central government sees fit; as opposed to the democratic idea that all records

---

63 Norton quoted in Lancaster, chapter 4.
64 Transcript of SAA round table on classification and cataloging, October 25, 1938, in MCNWP, 4/151.

are public records and belong to the community which created them, not to the central government.[65]

Thus, the political and juridical systems of Europe and America would require different approaches to archival administration. Norton accepted fundamental principles such as provenance, but did not believe that all European approaches could be adopted without modification.

Another critical distinction between European and American archives was the problem of voluminous records. "The Muller, Feith and Fruin *Manual on Arrangement and Description of Archives,* which has just appeared in translation, has proved disappointing to many because it is highly technical and does not describe methods," Norton wrote in 1940. "Americans are asking whether the principles for the classification of the rather simple archives described in the manual still hold."[66] In reviewing the Dutch manual for the *Mississippi Valley Historical Review,* Norton elaborated, stating, "the records described seem so simple as to have little analogy with our own bulky and complex filing systems." Although the soundness of the principles enumerated in the manual "have been proved correct by forty years of European and American tests," Norton concluded, "the next need is for a companion volume to demonstrate practical procedures for applying the principles to the complicated American record keeping systems of today."[67] Even when proposing to use Jenkinson's manual as the basis for her summer course at Columbia, Norton recognized that its emphasis on English archives would require some adaptations. "However, I like his approach to the various subjects which he takes up," she told Solon J. Buck, director of publications at the National Archives, "and I think when these are Americanized the outline will prove workable."[68]

65 Norton to Charles C. Williamson, November 13, 1939, in MCNWP, 4/364.

66 Norton, Archives Monthly Report, May 1940, in MCNWP, 1/366.

67 Norton, typescript review of *Manual for the Arrangement and Description of Archives,* May 1940, in MCNWP, 5/070.

68 Norton to Solon J. Buck, January 13, 1940, in MCNWP, 4/337.

In rejecting the American Library Association proposal for a manual on "the care and cataloging of archives," Norton also stated similar concerns to SAA secretary Philip C. Brooks of the National Archives staff. "I find that most of the available literature in English is based upon English conditions and I have to stop and translate what is said into American conditions," she complained. "What we need is writings based upon practical experience— not some librarian's rehashing of what has already been said many times."[69] Thus, Norton not only called for a new and specifically American approach to archives, she also stated that European archivists did not pay sufficient attention to methodology and practical solutions to archival problems and that American librarians did not properly understand archival methods. Once again, Norton the pragmatist overshadowed Norton the theorist.

In summarizing these issues in 1973, Norton elaborated on the distinctions necessary between European and American archival approaches:

> It was only natural to suppose that American archivists would copy the techniques of the European archival agencies which had been in existence so long. The few Americans who were familiar with European archival institutions were historians who had used them in research. So we find such men as [Samuel Flagg] Bemis enthusiastically urging American archivists to study paleography and medieval foreign languages. They failed to realize that the contents of European archives were entirely different from those of America. European archivists [were] concerned with old records—none dated later than 1800; whereas few states, except those of the 13 colonies, had any records at all earlier than 1800. The Europeans knew nothing concerning the problems of dealing with the ever-growing complexity of the records of rapidly growing governmental agencies.[70]

Far from being a Europeanist, Margaret Norton remained a quintessentially American archivist in her practical approach to solving the distinctive problems of modern records. Her

---

69 Norton to Philip C. Brooks, February 23, 1940, Society of American Archivists records, file 200/03/01, University of Wisconsin-Milwaukee.

70 Norton to Birdsall, October 26, 1973, in MCNWP, 3/1265.

approach focused primarily on governmental archives rather than private manuscripts, however, and in this respect she did emphasize the European custodial role rather than the American manuscripts interpretive role for archives and archivists.[71]

RESTORING BALANCE

In attempting to replace the archival profession's emphasis on service to historical scholars with a focus on administrative and legal needs, Norton may have taken a position as devil's advocate. Maynard Brichford claimed that she "sought to restore a balance that is lost when only scholarly research needs are considered." Brichford went on to state, "The view that administrative use should take precedence can be as misleading as the view that archives serve only scholarly researchers."[72] However, as Luke Gilliland-Swetland concluded, "the entire tenor of Norton's writings and activities" demonstrates a perspective different from "her contemporaries in the historical camp."[73] Were Norton's opinions deliberately confrontational or exaggerated?

Limited evidence from Norton's unpublished writings suggests that she did occasionally feel constrained by her official position in stating her public opinions and that she at times overemphasized her arguments to provoke discussion. Two comments made to historian William Birdsall in 1973 suggest the self-censorship required to maintain good relations with her supervisors. "As a member of the staff of the Illinois State Library I owed a loyalty to my institution which in substance was to pretend that all was perfect in an imperfect situation—which it wasn't," she told Birdsall.[74] This comment suggests that she could not criticize

---

71 Gilliland-Swetland, 165–66.
72 Maynard Brichford, "Academic Archives: *Überlieferungsbildung*," *American Archivist* 43 (fall 1980): 457.
73 Gilliland-Swetland, 165.
74 Norton to Birdsall, June 18, 1973, in MCNWP, 3/1243.

library management of the archives, including the impositions she faced in using library staff for archival work and in having to allow her own staff to prepare library exhibits and provide library reference service. But she also stated that some of her on-the-job decisions were based on political expedience rather than on archival principles. "You must realize that I had to conform to an official line which did not always correspond to what I might recommend to others," she confided to Birdsall.[75] This statement raises doubts concerning Norton's candor in discussing the archival situation in Illinois in her public writings, most of which were published in the "house organ," *Illinois Libraries.* Even in her professional correspondence with fellow archivists, historians, and librarians, Norton seldom criticized the problems she faced within the Illinois State Library.

It is doubtful, however, whether such constraints affected Norton's views on archival theory. More likely, this self-censorship related principally to putting the best face possible on the daily annoyances and power plays within the library. In one candid comment, however, Norton did admit that her views might sometimes be exaggerated for effect. At the 1940 American Libraries Association annual meeting, Norton and Roscoe Hill, chief of the Classification Division of the National Archives, debated the proper basis for classification of archives. In her monthly report to the Illinois State Library, Norton conceded, "Both of us probably overemphasized our points of difference deliberately, because we feel that the whole subject should be kept open to discussion until American archivists have had more experience with the subject."[76] It would be a mistake to read too much into this statement. But it does seem likely that part of Norton's unflagging insistence on the legal aspects of archives was a deliberate counterpoint to the prevailing view that archives should be regarded principally as historical sources. This lends credence to Brichford's belief that she was

---

75 Norton to Birdsall, June 6, 1973, in MCNWP, 3/1222.
76 Norton, Archives Monthly Report, May 1940, in MCNWP, 1/366.

attempting to restore a more balanced view of archives than the prevailing notion that they served an essentially historical or scholarly purpose.

If Norton emphasized the legal aspects of archives for pragmatic purposes, it is worth examining the extent to which such arguments succeeded. Although Norton seldom expressed complete satisfaction with her achievements and repeatedly felt that her efforts were constrained by the State Library administration or by a lack of staff, on the whole her efforts must be recognized as successful. "Norton brought the Illinois State Archives to the forefront of public archives," Richard Berner concluded. Norton not only exerted considerable personal influence on the development of the archival profession in the 1930s and 1940s, but she had "established a model public archives."[77] One measure of her achievement was the successful campaign for a new state archives building. From the beginning of her tenure as state archivist, Norton had lobbied for facilities adequate for archival purposes; the building dedicated in 1938 was only the third public archives building constructed in the United States for such purpose. "The Illinois State Archives, which under Margaret C. Norton had become an important center of archival work, moved into its new building in 1938, and its activities contributed significantly to a reorientation of archivists," Ernst Posner wrote in 1964. "The archives and records management program of the state of Illinois is known as one of the outstanding programs in the United States," Posner concluded. "The archives program of Illinois owes some of its characteristics and much of its national and international reputation to the leadership of Margaret C. Norton, who developed it to a high level of perfection."[78] This did not mean that she always received the appropriations or new staff that she requested. But the success of an archival institution can also be measured in its influence as a model for others, and in this respect, at least, Norton's success is beyond doubt.

---

77   Berner, 16, 31.
78   Posner, 30, 98, 101.

LEGACY

An examination of Margaret Cross Norton's personal correspondence and reports clearly indicates that the archival theory for which she is so well known did not originate in ivory tower musings on the meaning of life or the origins of records. Rather her "archival philosophy," as she called it, derived from daily experience, from experimentation, and from the realities of a life lived in service to the public. An appreciation for Margaret Norton as a pragmatic archivist dedicated to the needs of public officials enables us to see her as a bold and consistent advocate for the significance of records in administration of state government. Norton adopted European archival principles such as provenance and the moral defense of archives, but she adapted them to the requirements of modern American records. She pleaded for recognition of archives as legal records, but she also recognized their secondary importance for historical research.

Margaret C. Norton's perspective on archives as legal records must be acknowledged as an essential part of archival identity. But she also recognized that some archival records were historical documents and that the historical significance of archives must also be preserved. Norton's legacy needs to be reconsidered in light of her private writings and the practical reasons behind her archival philosophy. Although influenced by Jenkinson, she did not remain a strict Jenkinsonian in her views. She believed that archives are more than just historical sources, but she did not deny the historical importance of archives. Margaret Norton presented a more complex and nuanced theory of archives than either her advocates or her detractors have recognized. She deserves to be remembered for promoting European principles, but also for developing distinctively American adaptations. She espoused adherence to theory and principles, but she practiced experimentation and innovation. Above all she represents the ultimate triumph of American pragmatism and the emergence of a distinctive identity for archivists, free from the control of both historians and librarians. With a background in both of these disciplines, Norton proclaimed a separate identity as an archivist.

Although her influence moved archivists away from their reliance on historians and the traditions of the historian-archivist, Norton's views should not lead archivists to abandon their dual heritage. The profession must recognize both the legal and administrative identity of archives and their historical significance. Rather than pulling the profession apart into separate camps of historian-archivists and archivist-administrators, or of practitioners and theorists, Norton's legacy should remind archivists of their twin responsibilities. The continuing challenge for archivists is to balance these dual aspects of archives: to maintain both their legal and administrative integrity and their usefulness for historical research.

DEDICATED TO

Thornton W. Mitchell

1916–2003

Thornton W. Mitchell earned bachelor's and master's degrees from Stanford University and received his doctorate in American economic history from Columbia University. His forty-year career as an archivist and records manager included positions at the National Archives in Washington, D.C., and in California, Ohio, and Illinois. The last twenty years of his career were in North Carolina, culminating as North Carolina State Archivist, a position from which he retired in 1981. He was a Certified Records Manager and was a Fellow of the Society of American Archivists.

FOREWORD

A Tribute to Margaret C. Norton

BY ERNST POSNER

IN A LIMBO PERIOD OF MY LIFE which I spent in Sweden in 1939, I became one of the more assiduous readers of the reports of the Public Archives Commission of the American Historical Association and of the minutes of the Conferences of American Archivists. Among the distinguished names I encountered, the one that intrigued me most was that of Margaret C. Norton, for as a European I could hardly conceive of a "female" achieving such prominent status among her professional peers. And so I was eagerly looking forward to meeting her, which I did in the lobby of Carvel Hall during the Annapolis meeting of the Society of American Archivists in 1939. Ever since I have been her admirer and her devoted friend.

Margaret Norton did not have to be "liberated." Honors and recognition came to her naturally in the course of her career. Indeed, the significance of the role she has played in the evolution and maturation of archives administration in the United States can hardly be overestimated. It was she who was instrumental in "putting us on the right track" when as early as 1930 she warned against letting the historians preempt the field of archival care and preservation, pointing out that records are the product of governmental activity and primarily destined to serve governmental needs. Her words paved the way toward recognizing archives administration as an indispensable element of public service and hence entitled to full public support.

Miss Norton applied her convictions successfully to the Archives Department of the Illinois State Library of which she was the head. She did so, not by sitting at a glass-topped desk but by processing records and getting her hands dirty. She thus acquired, in addition to her theoretical insight, an amount of practical experience unmatched at that time in most of the other state archival agencies in which historical activities still tended to predominate. This experience is embodied in the articles on aspects of record and archives administration that over the years she contributed to *Illinois Libraries* and to other professional journals. They represent the yield of more than thirty years of her work and, systematically organized, they are the first American manual of archives administration. It would be entirely wrong to consider these articles as a mere historical monument, simply because in the meantime the profession has progressed into new fields of concern and endeavor. On the contrary, as one rereads Miss Norton's articles, one is struck by the timelessness of her understanding of the philosophical as well as the technical aspects of the archivist's work.

Never preaching and never dictating, she attacks the problems confronting the archivist, diagnoses their nature, and suggests how they may be dealt with. She does so with the modesty that is one of her characteristics and with the wisdom that reveals her judicious mind. Do not ask "the attorney general for opinions," she says. "Nine times out of ten he will say 'No' and it will be almost impossible to get that 'No' exchanged for a 'Yes.'" And is it not true that "Asking advice is the greatest form of flattery"? The words quoted stem from Miss Norton's masterful piece on "Organizing a New State Archives Department" (*Illinois Libraries*, December 1946), still prescribed reading for those put in charge of a nascent archival institution.

As the teaching of courses in archives administration is expanding in the United States, it seems our duty to make Miss Norton's writings more readily available than they are in the issues of *Illinois Libraries* and other journals. We would be hiding a valuable treasure if we would further delay publishing them in book form so that future generations can readily turn to this precious source. They are indeed the bequest to us of a wise lady, and they deserve an honored place in our professional literature.

PREFACE

In a period of twenty-six years, Margaret Cross Norton as state archivist of Illinois wrote several dozen professional articles. This compendium contains thirty of them, selected because they dealt with concepts, principles, and techniques of archival economy. They appeared originally in the *American Archivist*, quarterly journal of the Society of American Archivists; publications of the American Library Association; and *Illinois Libraries*, the publication of the Illinois State Library.

In a new and emerging profession, it was unusual that one person should write so extensively over so long a period of time. And since Margaret Norton wrote principally about her own experiences as the archivist of a state and as the administrator of a small archival establishment (as opposed to a large establishment such as the National Archives), her writings had unusual interest. Although her first article was published in 1930 and her last in 1956, they have a timelessness and currency that gives them a continuing value many years later.

Unlike less modest authors, Margaret Norton kept neither a bibliography nor a collection of her writings; for this reason they were searched out from a variety of sources. It was not, for example, until the project was well advanced that the editor discovered some of her writings for the American Library Association. Her writings in *Illinois Libraries* were easily determined by checking a complete set of the journal. In addition, such bibliographical aids as *Readers' Guide to Periodical Literature*, *International Index to Periodicals*, and *Library Literature* were checked for titles to her articles and names and issues of magazines in which they appeared. They were helpful but none was complete. It is believed, however, that all of her significant writings have been traced.

It was not an easy task to select the articles included in this collection. Several were omitted because they were outdated; others that were not selected described procedures and operations of the Illinois archives that have since been superseded. Others, like an interesting series on local government and records, were omitted because they did not deal with archival concepts and techniques. The valuable article, "The Illinois State Archives Building," was not included because it was reprinted in 1970 in *Reader for Archives and Records Center Buildings*, edited by Dr. Victor Gondos, Jr., and published by the Society of American Archivists.

The articles that were selected were carefully examined and were then assembled into thirteen chapters. Some of the articles were originally published as parts of a series and these fell logically into a chapter; those relating to a comparison between library and archival techniques that are included in chapter five are an example. Other articles were brought together because their subject matter was related. This arrangement into chapters, however, seems more logical and meaningful than reprinting the articles in the chronological order in which they were originally published.

Since the articles were written over a period of twenty-six years for several different publications, there were variations in style in the originals. They have, therefore, been edited to obtain consistency in capitalization and grammar. Modern rules of spelling and hyphenization have been used. In a few instances, the arrangement of sentences has been changed to make them easier to read.

The material omitted in editing has generally been indicated by ellipses. This has been limited to transitional paragraphs or sentences at the beginning or end of articles that were parts of series. Some reference and bibliographical citations that appeared in the body of articles were also eliminated. In some instances, phrases or sentences were left out to avoid dating an article or to make smoother reading. In *Illinois Libraries*, for example, the archives was almost always referred to as the "Archives Division of the Illinois State Library." This has usually been shortened to "Archives Division" or, where the references were frequent, it was occasionally changed to "state archives." When one or two words were eliminated from the original, ellipses were not always used.

Similarly, obvious errors were corrected without indication. It did not seem worthwhile to correct a typographical error and then to indicate in a footnote that a word had been misspelled in the original article. Typographical errors in quoted material were also corrected without indication; in the very few instances in which an apparent error could not be checked, the word *sic* was used.

All quotations and citations in the original articles have been verified and, where possible, compared to the sources. Whenever they could be located, the citations were checked against the same edition as was originally used. Miss Norton in the original articles occasionally cited references in the text of the article; without exception these have been changed to footnotes. Whenever it seemed necessary to do so, footnotes have been added although they have not been distinguished from citations in the originals.

This work would not have been possible without the help and cooperation of many people. Appreciation is expressed to Dr. Ernst Posner; Dr. James B. Rhoads, archivist of the United States; John Daly and Theodore J. Cassady, present and immediate past director, respectively, of the Illinois state archives and the members of their staff; Philip S. Ogilvie, state librarian, Mrs. Virginia Gibson, and the staff of the North Carolina State Library; the Library of Congress; the library of the National Archives; the library of the American Library Association; the library of the National Bureau of Standards; the North Carolina Supreme Court Library; the library of the University of North Carolina at Chapel Hill; and the D. H. Hill Library of North Carolina State University. Not only did these persons and institutions assist in collecting the articles used, but checking and verification of references and other editorial tasks could not have been accomplished without their help.

Maynard J. Brichford, university archivist of the University of Illinois at Urbana-Champaign, read the entire manuscript; C. F. W. Coker, my predecessor as North Carolina state archivist and now on the staff of the National Archives and Records Service, Washington, D.C., read several chapters. Both of them offered suggestions that strengthened the manuscript, and I am deeply indebted to these two friends for their help.

Appreciation is also expressed to the American Library Association for permission to reprint the copyrighted articles that originally appeared in various of its publications. The articles are specifically cited when they are reproduced in the text. I am also indebted to the honorable Michael J. Howlett, Illinois secretary of state and state librarian, for permission to reprint the articles that appeared in *Illinois Libraries* and for his support that made it possible to publish this compendium.

The Chicago Chapter of the American Records Management Association, as successor to the Chicago Filing Association, allowed me to reprint Miss Norton's article, "What the State Archives Can Do for the Business Man," which appeared in the *Chicago Filing Association Official Bulletin* for November 1940. My thanks is also expressed to the Society of American Archivists for permission to use Miss Norton's articles which appeared originally in the *American Archivist* and others of its publications.

Completion of editorial work and preparation of the manuscript for publication were made possible by a grant from the National Endowment for the Humanities, whose support is gratefully acknowledged. The endowment, of course, is not responsible for the results of its grant, and these edited writings of Margaret C. Norton do not necessarily represent the view of the endowment in regard to archival and records management.

This work was encouraged by the late Dr. Christopher Crittenden and by Dr. H. G. Jones, successive directors of what is now known as the North Carolina Division of Archives and History, while I was a member of their staff. They tolerated my continuing involvement in the project; it could not have been completed without their forbearance.

The manuscript was typed by Mrs. Peggy R. Hopson and Mrs.

Darleen M. Graham, both of whom contributed much more than their skill as typists. Copying from photocopies of articles for the most part, they brought many things to my attention that helped me to do a better job of editing.

I am deeply indebted to Margaret Norton for permitting me to edit her writings. She gave me complete leeway and she made no demands upon me. The arrangement of the articles and the editorial errors are my responsibility. My wife, Memory F. Mitchell, was patient with my frequent questions about editorial practices, and she and our sons put up with my preoccupation with the project over a long period of time. She read the entire manuscript and tactfully guided me away from editorial pitfalls into which I could easily have fallen; she is a much better proofreader than I! This compendium could not have been completed without her.

T. W. M.

Raleigh, North Carolina
January 1, 1975

INTRODUCTION

By *Thornton W. Mitchell*

ON APRIL 15, 1957, Margaret Cross Norton retired after thirty-five years of service as Illinois state archivist. The Archives Division of the Illinois State Library was established in 1921, and Miss Norton became its first head on April 1, 1922. A native of Rockford, Illinois, she received her bachelor's degree from the University of Chicago in 1913, followed by her master's degree a year later. Her undergraduate and graduate work were in history. She graduated from the New York State Library School, Albany, New York, in 1915 and was employed as a cataloger at Vassar College Library. In 1918, she became a cataloger in the Department of History and Archives of the Indiana State Library, although the early part of 1919 and the 1919–20 academic year were spent studying for her doctorate in history at the University of Chicago. Late in 1920, she became cataloger for the State Historical Society of Missouri, returning to Illinois as state archivist in 1922.

Few states had an archival program when Margaret Norton arrived in Springfield. Alabama, Delaware, Georgia, North Carolina, Pennsylvania, and Texas had agencies with archival responsibilities, and several quasi-public state historical societies served as repositories for archival materials. In addition, some state libraries were beginning to acquire and store permanently valuable documentary materials.

In Illinois, the secretary of state had long been legal custodian of the state's records. He had established a "Division of Archives and Index" in 1873, but it became concerned with current matters and did not develop along archival lines. Waldo Gifford Leland's "Report on the Public Archives and Historical Interest of the State of Illinois, with Especial Reference to the Proposed Education Building" in 1912 was epochal although his recommendations were not accepted. In 1921, the legislature rewrote the Illinois State Library Act, establishing an Archives Division as a part thereof. The legal authority of the Archives Division was broadened in 1925, but it was not until 1957 that the State Records Act created an independent archival agency as an operating division in the office of the secretary of state.

Nationally, the Public Archives Commission of the American Historical Association became largely ineffective after 1922 as its major interest—the establishment of a national archival agency—approached realization. Completion of the National Archives Building and the Historical Records Survey, both of which gave tremendous impetus to the development of state programs, were more than thirteen years in the future on the first day of April 1922, when Margaret Cross Norton became archivist of Illinois.

Margaret Norton attended a meeting of the Public Archives Commission for the first time in December 1923. Seven years later, in 1930, she became a member of the commission, continuing until it was replaced by the Society of American Archivists in 1936. A charter member of the society, she was its first vice-president, and in 1937 she became a council member. She served as fourth president of the society from 1943 to 1945, and in 1946 she began a two-year term as editor of the *American Archivist*.

In addition to her interest in the Public Archives Commission, Margaret Norton was active in the National Association of State Libraries, although she did not attend any of its meetings until 1929. Her activity was to be expected, since the Illinois archives functioned as a division of the Illinois State Library. Margaret Norton became secretary-treasurer of the National Association of State Libraries in 1933, and served in that capacity for five years.

Of greater interest, however, was her connection with various committees of the National Association of State Libraries and the American Library Association concerned with archival matters. A

Committee on Public Archives was established by the National Association of State Libraries in 1910 and reported regularly until 1918. By 1919, the committee apparently was discontinued although occasional reports on archival subjects were made to the association. In 1929, a report on archival developments was made at the annual meeting and in the same year an Archives Committee consisting of Charles B. Galbreath, Ohio, and George S. Godard, Connecticut, with Margaret Norton as chairman, was appointed. This committee apparently became inactive after a few years, but by the mid-1930s the Public Documents Committee of the American Library Association had become interested in archives and its interest resulted in the creation of an Archives and Libraries Committee in October 1935. Margaret C. Norton served as a member of the Archives and Libraries Committee from its inception, and in 1942 she succeeded A. F. Kuhlman as chairman. Although the committee continued, she served as chairman only one year; in 1948 its name was changed to the Archival and Library Materials Committee and it became concerned with the archives of the American Library Association. For more than ten years, Margaret Norton was one of the links between the National Association of State Libraries and the American Library Association on the one hand and the Public Archives Commission of the American Historical Association and the Society of American Archivists on the other.

The Public Archives Commission from its inception had been dominated by historians and its successive chairmen were distinguished and well-known scholars. The motive behind its movement for a national archival establishment was to insure the preservation of valuable records for historical research. Although she was trained as a historian—and as a librarian—Margaret Norton dissented from this emphasis on the scholarly justification for an archives. Approaching the matter from a pragmatic point of view, she foresaw that the development of a national archival program would be followed by the development of state programs, some of which would be difficult—if not impossible—to justify solely on scholarly grounds. At the meeting of the Public Archives Commission held during the American Historical Association annual meeting at Chapel Hill, North Carolina, in December 1929, she emphasized the necessity of making archival material accessible for the "practical ends of administration." She later described her Chapel Hill paper as a "dud"; but the impact of her remarks to a group of historians who had struggled for thirty years to justify an archival establishment solely on the grounds of its service to the historical profession can well be imagined. Six months later, at the Los Angeles meeting of the National Association of State Libraries, she gave substantially the same paper. In it, she was the first to suggest that the archivist had something to contribute to efficient government. She restated her position before the newly established Society of American Archivists and the National Association of State Libraries in 1937 and the theme was repeated in other, later writings.

The mid-1930s were doubly important, professionally, to Margaret Norton. After its organization in 1922, the Archives Division was housed in one of the stacks of the Illinois State Library in the Centennial Building. In 1934, the state arsenal located adjacent to the capitol grounds burned, destroying some of the soldiers' bonus and World War I records of the Military and Naval Department. Responding to the outcry of patriotic and veterans' organizations, the 1935 General Assembly appropriated money to build a state archives building. Additional funds were obtained from the federal Public Works Administration, and construction began in March 1936. The building was accepted January 16, 1938, and was occupied soon thereafter. It was dedicated during the Second Annual Meeting of the Society of American Archivists on October 26, 1938. Into the building was introduced the concept of the "departmental vault," a space assigned to various state officials and agencies in which permanently valuable material of too recent date to be transferred to the archives was to be kept. Although these areas were intended to replace conventional vaults in agency offices and the Archives Division was supposed to control the material placed in them, in practice they erected a dual system for the housing of permanently valuable records and placed control over a major portion of the archives building in the hands of the agencies themselves.

The departmental vault system, however, had one major advantage. As an intermediate step between custody by the agency of origin and by the Archives Division, virtually all valuable records were placed physically in the archives building although custody of some of them could not be transferred because of legislative or other restrictions. Records of the closed federal land offices of Illinois, for example, were in the custody of the auditor of public accounts in his departmental vault in the archives building. They could not be transferred to the custody of the archivist until enabling legislation was passed in 1957.[1] Similarly, over a period of years virtually all of the permanently valuable records in the departmental vaults have been turned over to the custody of the archivist.

Although planning and construction of the Illinois archives building was a major achievement, of much greater impact on Margaret Norton's professional career was the reorganization of the Illinois State Library which began in 1938. The secretary of state, as state librarian, was authorized to appoint a "Superintendent of Library Divisions," but he did not do so until 1935 and the heads of the three library divisions, including the Archives Division, reported directly to him. In 1935, the superintendent of library divisions position was filled in order to supervise expenditure of a state aid fund for libraries. With the completion of this task and removal of the Archives Division to its own building, reorganization of the library started and in 1939 the State Library Act was rewritten. The "Superintendent of Library Divisions" became "Assistant State Librarian," and the Archives Division became an operating division of the library with Margaret Norton reporting to the assistant state librarian.

Of greater significance, however, was the fact that *Illinois Libraries*, which had been a publication of the Library Extension Division, in 1938 became the official publication of the Illinois State Library; Margaret Norton, as a division head of the library, was expected to contribute to it regularly. Several short notes and comments relating to the archives appeared throughout 1938. The January 1939 issue contained a separate section on "The Archives of Illinois," which appeared regularly under that name until February 1942. Beginning with the March 1942 issue the name was changed to "Illinois Archival Information," and in these two sections Margaret Cross Norton made a significant contribution to the archival literature of the United States.

Margaret Norton wrote infrequently for "Illinois Archival Information" after 1947 and many times used the writings of others in the section. During 1949, a series of documents were reproduced in *Illinois Libraries* and in 1950 and 1951 "Illinois Archival Information" was devoted to a nine-part checklist of Illinois published documents. After 1952, the archival section began to appear even less frequently, and as Margaret Norton approached retirement she wrote less and less. One of her articles appeared in the January 1954 *Illinois Libraries*, and she did not write again until October 1956, when her final article was published.

These articles Margaret Norton later called "pot-boilers" which, she claimed, were "written to meet a deadline and in the wee-small hours after a fatiguing day's work." Some of the articles were calendars or descriptive lists of records in the Illinois state archives; some were reproductions of significant documents; others were reprints either of National Archives papers or publications or of papers by other members of the archival profession. A surprising number of them, however, were discussions of archival problems and techniques, and although she borrowed heavily from other sources in some instances, many were devoted to areas of concern to the profession and to solutions she had developed. Margaret Norton wrote with great facility and she wrote well. It is not surprising, therefore, that many of the articles she wrote for *Illinois Libraries* are still pertinent and that some which have become outdated because of the technical equipment discussed are still valid insofar as the discussion of the concepts governing the use of that equipment is concerned.

When Margaret Norton retired, several of her friends urged her to write a book that would be helpful to the operations of a "small" archives. Pointing out that she had had to write professional articles for too many years, Margaret Norton preferred to travel and to sit in her home on the shores of Lake Springfield and watch the rabbits. After several unsuccessful attempts to persuade her, Ernst Posner and the editor agreed in 1964 that her writings and ideas should not be lost. The project of bringing together those of her articles that related to archival principles began in 1964 and proceeded sporadically until late 1968 when personal considerations made it possible to concentrate on the project. This volume, then, represents an effort to bring together the writings of a pioneer in the archival profession, writings that have largely become unavailable but that still have pertinence to the field.

Norton

ON ARCHIVES

>─┤◄►─○─◄►├─◄

1

The Scope and Function of Archives

1 / THE ARCHIVES DEPARTMENT AS AN ADMINISTRATIVE UNIT IN GOVERNMENT

SINCE 1900, there has been organized and sustained agitation for the creation of departments to preserve the important archives of the state and federal governments in this country.[1] Practically every state has legislated the necessary machinery for the care of its records. In ten states, the archives work is delegated to the state library as in Connecticut and Illinois; in about ten states to some elective state officer, usually to the secretary of state as in Massachusetts, or else is left to the various state departments; in fourteen states there is a separate board or historical commission; in practically all other states—Kansas, for instance—the state historical society has authority to accept the custody of state archives. Successful work is being done by the states in each field. . . .

⋐ PART 1 OF THIS CHAPTER, "The Archives Department as an Administrative Unit in Government," was first published in National Association of State Libraries, *Papers and Proceedings, Thirty-Third Annual Convention, Los Angeles, California, June 23–27, 1930,* pp. 44–48. (Reprinted from *Bulletin of the American Library Association,* September 1930.) Part 2, "Scope and Function of a State Archives Department," was first published in National Association of State Libraries, Papers and Proceedings, 1936–1937, Fortieth Annual Convention, New York City, June 21–25, 1937 (Springfield: n.p., 1936 [1937]), pp. 15–20.

As state librarians, we are concerned with the state archives situation. Despite an ever growing mass of constructive legislation, there are in reality only about a dozen states in the whole country which are really giving sustained and systematic care to their official records. To say that this is due to inability to get adequate appropriations is to beg the question, for appropriations are being had for other state departments no more worthwhile.

The explanation for this slow material progress can be laid directly to the popular misunderstanding as to the real definition of the term archives. To most persons, including some archivists, the term archives still connotes merely musty, dirty files of loose papers and decayed leather folios of little apparent use, but vaguely believed to be of value because historians keep saying they are valuable. The real function of an archivist, however, is that of custodian of legal records of the state, the destruction of which records might seriously inconvenience the administration of state business. Just as you and I keep current business papers in our desks, but lock in our safety deposit boxes our particularly valuable papers such as deeds, so does the state official keep his current business files in his own vaults, but deposits with the archivists for safekeeping his legally or historically important papers.

This belief that archives concern the historian only—the fallacies of which I shall take up in detail in a moment—is due to the fact that historians gave the original impetus to the archives work of this country. . . . European trained historians accustomed to documenting their writings in the large European archives departments, notably the Public Record Office in London and the *Archives Nationales* in Paris, were horrified to discover that the documents they wanted to use here were either destroyed or had been hopelessly misplaced by indifferent officials who knew nothing and cared less about these historical manuscripts. In 1899, therefore, the American Historical Association created its Public Archives Commission, which has probably been the most active single organization working for the creation of archive departments ever since. A few years later the National Association of State Libraries took up the same discussion, feeling that the care of the manuscript

4

resources of the state might well develop from its care of printed documents, just as it had often taken over bill drafting as an adjunct to its legislative reference work. Without in the least belittling the work of the historians' Public Archives Commission, I feel that perhaps the greatest contribution that the Archives Committee of the National Association of State Libraries can make to the cause is to circulate propaganda for proper care of archives as an administrative problem of state government instead of as a mere adjunct to the historical library field. The archivist should be a public official whose first interest is business efficiency, and only secondarily should he be interested in history. If the public records are cared for in a way that preserves their proper provenance, the historian not only of today but also of tomorrow will be as well served as the public official.

That there has been such a reversal of primary and secondary interests resulting in overemphasis upon the historical side of archives work has resulted in certain erroneous conceptions found in actual practice. The first of these is the belief that the more valuable and interesting historical items must be preserved first of all even if we cannot do anything with the rest of the file. People want to see the old colonial charters, the old witchcraft papers, the letters from Washington, the legislative bills presented by Lincoln, and the like, and we all get a thrill from the discovery of new items of this sort in our collection. But all too often we yield to the temptation to remove these interesting items from their proper place in the files and by our indifference to the rest of the file, at the best, break up its proper sequence and, at the worst, encourage its possible destruction as valueless. Officials are interested in their records only as documents subject to legal use, and they are justified in their suspicion of historians or antiquarians who disturb their files. Local historical societies are sometimes insistent upon taking records from the county archives, and these archives perish or are scattered to the four corners of the country when later these societies are disbanded. Recently I made a private inquiry as to why a certain county clerk refused to reply to my letters, and found that a stamp collector had once got into his vaults and had mutilated a number of valuable papers, so he now refuses to let any outsider handle the county records under any pretext.

Another misconception coming from too great emphasis upon history is the current belief that states of the Middle and Far West are too young to have enough official records of historical interest to justify the creation of a separate department. If that is to be the only basis for an archives department that is true. In Illinois, for example, we keep all our records from the governor, secretary of state, and General Assembly dated prior to 1861 in a small vault only about ten feet wide and fifteen feet long. If the physical preservation of those records were our sole *raison d'être*, we might perhaps have better turned the work over to our Illinois State Historical Library.

The greatest handicap to getting adequate support for archives work is the belief that archives work is just another function of the state historical society. Legislators refuse appropriations because they cannot see why another historical department should be created when there is already one historical library; secretaries of historical societies see in archives work an expensive addition to the work of their already overburdened staff and budget; to them genealogical work and the collection of the private papers of famous native sons seem more popular and therefore more important. And all these people are right if the care of historical manuscripts is the main thing we are after. I am not for a moment denying the importance of spending all the time and all the money we can for the preservation of historical documents, but I do maintain that an overemphasis on that type of work and an underemphasis upon the legal functions of an archives department retard both our primary and our secondary objectives. If local circumstances make it seem best to have the archives department under the jurisdiction of the historical society, there should be a distinct separation in administrative detail between the department that takes care of historical manuscripts of a private nature and the department that has charge of official archives. In Illinois we have made an extremely wide separation—the State Historical Library handles only private and printed source materials and is governed by a board appointed by the governor; the Archives Division works exclusively with official records filed with it by other state officials and forms a part of the State Library which is administered by the secretary of state as ex officio state librarian. All publishing even of official papers is carried on by the State Historical Library. In Iowa, on the other hand, the division of public archives is a part of the state historical memorial and art department, but its offices and its staff are administered quite distinctly from the purely historical department.

A few years ago the most popular argument we could give for the creation of an archives department was the need for proper care of official manuscripts of historical value; of late years, however, there have been changes in government that affect the care of records and have shaken the elective state officer out of his old attitude of indifference or even hostility to archival work.

The most striking feature of present-day government is the increasing multiplicity and complexity of its functions. As a corollary to this, official records are being created in appalling quantities by all state departments. Most of these records, because of their legal value, must be preserved more or less indefinitely. The storage of such a mass of material in a manner that will protect it from premature destruction and keep it readily available when needed is becoming increasingly impracticable for most departments. You are probably all familiar with the resultant conditions. Statehouse vaults are inadequate for the storage of records in current use. The offices themselves are cluttered with filing cases, often to such an extent that the floors threaten to give way from the excessive weight. Every nook and cranny in the basements and elsewhere in the state buildings are given over to storerooms, nearly always dark, dirty and unventilated; they are firetraps totally unsuited for the storage of anything, let alone records of great value. Correspondence files only twenty years old recently transferred from one of these statehouse basement storerooms were found to be completely destroyed by mildew and roaches. New records are continually crowding the older and sometimes more valuable records into more and more inaccessible corners. Contrary to public opinion, most state offices are undermanned with efficient workers, and the often long and difficult search for a given paper in this necessarily badly organized material consumes time that should be spent on routine work.

The problem of caring for state archives did not become serious until the 1920s. They were not numerous and locating any given document did not involve a very difficult hunt. For instance, copies of all official letters written by Illinois governors from 1818 to 1831 are to be found in one small volume of 132 pages. Even as late as the first decade of this century it is said that the secretary of state used to be able to read all his morning's mail in the half-mile walk between the post office and his office. Today the statehouse has its own federal post office and nine truckloads of mail are collected and four delivered daily. In rush seasons this number is increased.

When I said that the state official who formerly resented the interference of the archivist now welcomes it, I exaggerated. He does not consciously welcome it. He still asks me bluntly enough, "Hasn't the secretary of state enough to do without interfering in my affairs?" What the state official is clamoring for is more room; more state office buildings with larger workrooms but, above all, more and more space for his filing department. He feels the responsibility for the care of his records and has no thought of delegating it. Unless the archivist can forget more or less temporarily his personal enthusiasm for history and work for the building up of a real archives department functioning as an efficiency proposition in state administration, he is neglecting both his duty as a historian and as a public official. Storage facilities must be provided and soon, and if the archives department does not provide them the various state departments will get what they think they want; more storerooms to clutter up with undigested files (and the trash that storerooms always accumulate), more file clerks, and more and more jealousy against future historical work.

Why should not each state department retain its own files? Why should there be a central filing bureau charged with the care of all records not in everyday use?

The archivist's answer, of course, is that one department can do the work more economically and efficiently than a number of filing departments. His real motive, however, comes from his pessimistic knowledge that the departments left to themselves will continue to make a mess of things as they have in the past, for they will have filing departments and not archives departments. We all know that when an official is confronted with a political appointee who has had no previous business experience and knows neither shorthand nor typing, he usually says, "Put her in the filing department." The average file clerk measures her efficiency by the speed with which she clears her desk, and as a rule she does not care much about whether what she has filed can be found later.

The difference between a file clerk and an archivist is that the archivist has a sense of perspective. He knows that these documents have two phases of use; their present day legalistic use, and their potential historical value. His experience teaches him that some records which seem very unimportant now will be priceless later on, while others much used today will be worthless tomorrow. For instance, we have all the time books for the day laborers, masons, carpenters and other workmen who built our statehouse, preserved because the statehouse commissioners knew they would someday be subjected to a thorough financial investigation. But no one made it his business to preserve a copy of the blue prints from which the building was erected. The time books are moldering on the shelves, but the state architect several years ago had to reproduce the plans of the statehouse at a great cost. Because of his historical background the archivist knows the necessity of rounding out his collection—of making sure, for instance, that reports of commissions, especially when presented in printed form, actually get filed; that memorandums of important verbal decisions are preserved; that the records of defunct bureaus and commissions are not lost; that governors and other persons going out of office do not take with their personal correspondence files records of public interest. For instance, the correspondence of our Civil War governor is missing from the files and is no longer in existence, so far as I have been able to ascertain. We do not know whether Governor Richard Yates took it with him because it contained too much dangerously controversial matter, or whether it was stolen by someone else for his own private reasons.

Another very great reason why there should be a trained archivist is that it is becoming increasingly apparent that we can no longer, as in the past, attempt to preserve all legal records indefinitely. The growth in their bulk is too tremendous to make that either possible or wholly desirable. We are all cognizant of innumerable cases where the wrong records have been destroyed. No one, of course, can be omniscient, but certainly an archivist has a background that must give greater weight in this matter to his opinions than to the hasty and haphazard decisions of busy executives with no such background.

The preservation of records from tampering and theft is much easier when they are in the custody of an archivist than when any member of the department or even an outsider can gain unsupervised access to the files. In the Illinois archives any record is open to public inspection, but only under proper supervision. No record may be removed from the office without a requisition signed by the head of the department of origin to whom a receipt is issued when the document is returned to the files. Under this system the files are as accessible (or more so because more scientifically handled) as when they are in their departmental offices, yet responsibility for what happens to them can be positively fixed. So much is this point appreciated that we are often requested to take current records which are in special need of such precautions—such as pardon papers and confidential correspondence with corporations. A professional and nonpolitical administration of an archives department is essential and much appreciated in times of factional fights such as have recently racked my state.

Again, there should be an archives division rather than merely a series of department files, for as the records grow older more and more inquiries concerning them involve a knowledge of the evolution of state departments that only a specialist can be expected to have. A file clerk, for instance, might assume that the public school system in Illinois dates back only to 1857 when the first superintendent of public instruction set up housekeeping in his own office. But the archivist knows that the first public school law of Illinois was passed in 1825 and that the secretary of state gradually took on the powers and duties of a superintendent of public instruction until that office was separated from his. Likewise, the layman coming to the state files is confused to find that whereas the corporation department is under the secretary of state, the banking and building and loan corporations are supervised by the auditor of public accounts and the insurance corporations by the department of trade and commerce. The state archives correlates such facts as no series of separate file departments can do.

I could go on indefinitely multiplying reasons for having a good archives division in each state. Most of those reasons are well known to you, but those reasons are not known to the average public official. His only reaction to the work "archives" is "history." Right now when he is worrying himself about how to take care of his records, we archivists have to drop our talk about saving historical records and attempt to correlate our work with his. You have noticed that I have talked in terms of a central filing bureau, and have doubtless wondered what basis we use for declaring a record old enough to be sent to the archives. In Illinois we have no set rule for this, each department head transferring records of as recent date as he sees fit. In general our rule is, "Do not send records which you are apt to call for oftener than once in six months." This rule has worked well for over seven years and seems more practicable than to set a given date, such as ten years back, as records vary greatly in the nature of their use. Some records, such as election returns, are filed with us as soon as the state canvassing board has met, other files such as corporation charters from the beginning are retained by the department of origin.

Everything that has been said concerning the importance of proper care for state archives applies with double emphasis to county and other local records because these records come so much closer to the life of the people. Every man and woman has business at the county courthouse. The county archives are a vast and, so far, practically untapped source to the social historian. County officials, handicapped by poverty and with poor and inadequate vaults or no vaults at all and often ignorant of the value of their records, must have the assistance of the state if many of these priceless records of pioneer days are not to be lost through destruction or disintegration. Four years ago a bill was introduced into the Illinois General Assembly which would have permitted any county official to destroy any record in his office over seven years old. Comment is unnecessary. This does show that the record problem of the county official is identical with that of the state official.

The state archivist's relations to the county official, however, are quite different from his relations to the state official, a difference which is not as clearly appreciated by American archivists as it should be. It is simply this: the state archivist is a part of the state administration, and centralization of state records in a state archives department relieves the congestion of other state vaults and so promotes greater efficiency in the various state departments; whereas, so far as the county official is concerned, centralization of records in the state capital does not greatly increase his efficiency since the constant use to which most of his records are subject demands that the bulk of his records remain at the county seat. A substitution of certified photostat copies of county records does not help his filing problem, for photostats usually take up as much or more space as the originals. From the point of view of the state archivist, the cost of providing storage space and of duplicating records by photostat for extensive centralized files seems prohibitive for a state as large as Illinois. The archivist's work with county records must lie chiefly along the line of some sort of state aid in caring for county archives in the county courthouses themselves, probably most effectively through such state agents as Connecticut and New York employ to enforce state laws regarding proper vault equipment and other housing requirements. Such local records as the state can centralize, either by collecting the originals or transcripts, will be largely confined to files of primarily historical interest. Such a centralization might more properly be a function of the state historical society than of the state archivist, or if under the supervision of the state archivist, there should be maintained a distinct division of function—centralized collections of state records being used primarily by the administrator, centralized collections of county records used primarily by the historian.

2 / Scope and Function of a State Archives Department

The addition of new words to a language through slang and new technical processes is a more or less conscious process.[2] Alterations in its vocabulary due to subtle and gradual changes in the meaning of old words tend to go unnoticed. Such a transmutation has been taking place with respect to the word *archive*, which in American usage has come to connote an *historical manuscript*, presumably, but not necessarily, of governmental origin. As a matter of fact, an *archive* may be a vitally important document yet have no historical importance whatsoever; it need not be more than a few moments old; it may not even be a manuscript. So greatly has this incorrect usage of the term *archive* affected both thought and practice that no discussion of the scope and functions of a state archives department should start without a discussion of the fallacy of treating archives merely as historical records and without a redefinition of terms.

First of all, we must disabuse ourselves of the idea that the acquisition by the state historical society of a few historical records—such as, for example, the first state constitution, the territorial legislative journals, some early militia rolls, and a few election poll books—automatically transforms the curator of manuscripts into an archivist. It does not, even though he edits and publishes some of the documents. An archives department is the governmental agency charged with the duty of planning and supervising the preservation of all those records of the business transactions of its government required by law or other legal implication to be preserved indefinitely. The origin of governmental and of private business archives is the same—both are records of business transactions made and preserved because such records might later be required as evidence in lawsuits involving those transactions. It is only because the government touches the lives of relatively more people that its archives tend, as their legal use becomes less frequent, to take on a relatively greater historical significance than do private archives. The state census returns, for example, were taken to form the basis for apportionment of representation to the General Assembly, for apportionment of the school fund, and to ascertain the militia strength of the various communitiès. The census taker was interested in statistics and not in family history, which explains why those records prove so disappointing to the genealogists of today.

The archivist needs to understand the historical and social significance of the records in his custody, of course, but primarily it is his duty to be able to produce a given document when needed to suggest the type of records in which to seek needed data and to protect the records from theft, mutilation, and physical deterioration. If he keeps this official function in mind, he will not be guilty of the all too common practice of abstracting from official files those documents which seem to him historically significant; and, by his indifference to the rest of the file, either break up its proper sequence or encourage others to its possible destruction as valueless. Officials in whose offices the archives originate are interested in their records only as documents subject to legal use, and they are justified in their suspicion of historians or antiquarians who disturb their files.

The origin of this overemphasis upon the historical aspects of archives is easy to see. Until comparatively recently, no one seemed interested in the preservation of archives except the historian. Had it not been for the American Historical Association's propaganda for the establishment of archives departments, there would probably have been no Society of American Archivists.

The popular belief that the archivist's work is largely historical is unnecessarily limiting his financial support. Legislators and other public officials believe that their states are too young to justify the creation of another historical agency in addition to the existing state historical society or commission. Secretaries of historical societies see in archives work an expensive addition to the work of their already overburdened staff. Historical institutions tend, therefore, to confine their archival work to an unsystematic collection of records of purely historical interest.

The most striking feature of present-day government is the

increasing multiplicity and complexity of its functions. As a corollary to this, official records are being created in appalling quantities. There is also a noticeable tightening of demands for adequate documentation of all legal papers. The problem of caring for this mass of material and of keeping it accessible is an overwhelming burden to department heads. The clamor for more room and the belief that storage space for records would be cheaper to build than desk space were probably the determining factors in the passage, with but one dissenting vote, of the bill making the appropriation for erecting the Illinois archives building. The officials do not know that they want or need an archives department. They feel the responsibility for the care of their records and have no thought of delegating it. They think they merely want more storage space. If the archivist can convince his fellow officials that he can render them a service which will in turn add to their own efficiency, he will tap a source of support infinitely greater and more potent than that of historians.

A second fallacy with respect to archives is the belief, especially on the part of other officials, that an archives is merely a central filing department and that the head file clerk's assumption of the imposing title of archivist is an affectation. To the average official, filing does not seem a particularly difficult task, specially since most of the records transferred from his office have already been filed, often in accordance with a system scientifically designed for them by an expensive outside filing expert. Surely the mere keeping of such files after transfer should be no very serious or difficult task. Such officials are surprised to be told that the file clerk plays only a minor role in an archival establishment.

Most modern records come into the archives department fairly adequately filed. Older records generally have to be sorted and filed to correspond as closely as practical to the prevailing system of departmental filing, or some other system must be devised or adopted for them. Some annual transfers have to be filed in with older accessions. Documents removed temporarily from the files must be refiled when returned. The amount of filing required depends upon the condition in which the records are received. The amount of time required may be considerable, yet filing is a comparatively negligible item in archival administration.

It is the duty of the file clerk to preserve all legal records. One of the duties of the archivist is to assist in the destruction of useless papers. Records are piling up in such appalling quantities that it is obvious that considerable weeding must take place. Surveys made for the National Archives indicate that from 1917 to 1930 the federal government accumulated a bulk of records equal to twice the amount for the entire period up to 1917, and that the accumulation between 1930 and 1937 equaled that of the 1917 to 1930 period. The same condition exists with respect to state archives. Microphotographic copies can be made of some records, permitting the destruction of the originals. But even microphotography cannot cope with such a deluge. It is unnecessary to tell archivists what sad mistakes are made when department heads attempt to destroy files as no longer valuable. They are too apt to want to save only those records which relate to their own financial integrity and to throw away records for which there will be a different use, usually historical, after the passage of years. An archivist cannot always foresee what use the scholar of tomorrow will make of the records of today, but at least his knowledge of departmental development and of political science and history should give him a better perspective than that of the generally short-termed official. The archivist should have some veto power over the destruction of records. One of the crying needs is for the archivists, especially the state archivists, to formulate recommendations relating to this subject.

Archives departments are frequently compared to libraries. Although the analogy is superficial, the processes through which archives have to go before the most effective use can be made of them are similar both for archives and for books. The files transferred to the archives from a given department do not consist, as many persons picture them, of just one continuous series but may include perhaps fifty different types of records kept over a period of years. Departments are created, expand, contract, are abolished or absorbed in whole or in part by other departments in the most complex and confusing variety of ways. The classification of these varying sets of records into a system reflecting this organization in relation to the types and contents of records kept at different periods requires expert knowledge of departmental history and functions. Library books increase in value as reference tools in proportion to the completeness with which they are cataloged and indexed and the librarian's personal familiarity with these books and with their significance. The same is even more true of the records in an archives department. To the file clerk, the letter from President Andrew Jackson to Governor John Reynolds about some difficulties between Indians and whites in northern Illinois is just another letter in the "J" folder for October 1831. To the archivist it is a newly discovered bit of source material relating to the Black Hawk War. The absence of a census record requested by an applicant for old age pension calls only for polite regrets on the part of the file clerk. The archivist, remembering that marriage licenses require a statement as to ages, suggests looking in that set of records which proves to yield documentary evidence of age. Other phases of archival work, analogous to library work such as binding and repair, photographic and other copies, and the like, cannot be discussed but only mentioned as being other phases of work not within the scope of a mere filing department.

The misconceptions concerning archives work . . . are fallacies to which state officials, including some state archivists, have been particularly prone.

Having defined in general what an archives department stands for, the next step is to decide how it shall function. Some state archives are administered as independent boards or commissions; some are divisions of state or historical libraries; some are directly under some elective state officer, generally the secretary of state; recently several have been set up as divisions of state university libraries. Since there are examples of both good and poor archival administrations under each of these types, it is unnecessary to comment here upon the relative merits of these basic forms of legislation.

Perhaps there is no other state historical agency and the archives department must add to its work that of a historical library. There are always limitations upon available housing and finance. Building up the confidence of other state officials takes time and patience. In the following description of the scope of a state archives department, however, the assumption is made that adequate financial support is available and that the department can devote its entire time and energy to archives work proper.

After a determination as to the form or organization best suited to local state conditions, consideration must be given to what records shall be considered as coming within the scope of the state archives department.

In all states, the archives group themselves into federal, state, local (that is, county, municipal, and so on), and private archives. State records are naturally the immediate concern of the state archivist, though he will interest himself likewise in the proper preservation of all these other records insofar as other official care is lacking or inadequate. State records fall naturally into three overlapping groups—current, semicurrent and noncurrent records. Current records are those which, because of their frequent use in the department of origin, must of necessity be kept under its immediate jurisdiction, generally in vaults adjoining its office. Semicurrent records are those to which reference by the department of origin is only occasional but over which that department desires to keep immediate jurisdiction. Such records, if transferred to an archival establishment, need to be withdrawn from time to time for departmental use. Noncurrent records are those which, generally because of age, tend to be of relatively greater historical than legal interest. The date at which records pass from one classification to another cannot be determined categorically. This depends upon the nature and frequency of use and the attitude of the head of the department of origin toward that use.

A fourth possible classification would consist of those records still in current use but treated as noncurrent and nonremovable from the archives department because of their special legal value. Among such records are the state constitution, the enrolled laws, deeds and abstracts to state property, leases granted by or to the state, and records of lands sold by the state to individuals. Other materials which might seem to fall in the same category are securities deposited with the state by insurance companies, bonds of state officials, registers of unsold or outstanding state bonds, and the like. These, however, are always kept in the vaults of their pertinent departments and are never deposited in the state archives.

The new Illinois archives building makes provision for the first time in American practice for the housing of archives in accordance with the above use classification. There are two entirely separate series of vaults in this building. Into one section of the building will go those records designated by the respective department heads as noncurrent and not subject to removal from the archives. These archives will be under the absolute control of the archivist. Into a second series of departmental vaults will go those semicurrent records subject to the immediate jurisdiction of the department of origin and removal for temporary departmental use. These departmental vaults will be operated on the principle of safety deposit boxes in banks. The Archives Division will censor what may be filed there to ensure that the vaults are used for record storage only; it will keep general inventories of the records and issue passes to aid department heads in fixing responsibility for what happens in the vaults. The departments themselves will be solely responsible for the arrangement, filing, removal and return of their records. Archives Division clerks will not remove or consult these records.

The considerations which moved us to adopt such a system are set forth in the last biennial report of the division as follows:

It is no solution of the archives problem to empty attic and basement storerooms where dirt, heat, mildew, vermin and insects have destroyed the earlier records filed there, if these same storerooms are promptly refilled with the overflow of departmental vaults. Neither is there a solution from the transfer of this overflow of semi-current material to the Archives Division. That would result in turning the

Archives Division into a central file department, imposing upon its staff an overwhelming burden of duties really belonging to the departments themselves, to the neglect of its purely archival functions. Furthermore, experience shows that such a transfer does not ensure the fulfillment of the primary purpose of an archives establishment, namely, safeguarding against loss of records. Where semi-current records are on file in the archives, it is necessary to permit withdrawal of documents for departmental use. Even though such withdrawals are permitted only upon signed requisitions promising the prompt return of documents to the files, there is no way for the Archives Division to enforce this return. Again, it is difficult for officials to see why they may not withdraw any or all of the files if some can be withdrawn. Several instances could be cited where particularly important historic records deposited by one state official were requisitioned back by his successor and never returned to the archives.[3]

These plans of Illinois for the care of its semicurrent records are dwelt upon in detail not merely because they exemplify a new archival practice, but because they have met with so enthusiastic a response from state officials that one is led to hope that perhaps a consideration of a similar proposal by other states might help in getting sorely needed support for archival work.

With the establishment of the National Archives, the state archives department needs no longer to feel much concern for the preservation of the federal archives within its state. There are, however, federal archives on deposit in many state departments. Several state archivists have rescued the papers of federal courts and post offices threatened by destruction during building or moving operations.

The United States government generally donated the records of its district land offices to the state when those offices were abandoned. These records are only in part duplicates of similar records in the U.S. Land Office at Washington which alone has authority to issue certified copies relating to the land titles involved. Such records are generally found in the office of the state land commissioner or the state auditor. They constitute one of the most valuable single series of historical source materials and belong in the state archives department.

A third type of federal archives is of interest to the state archivist, and that is the record of federal aid projects and joint federal and state boards. These records are for the most part too recent to be coming into state archives departments as yet, but if present tendencies continue the question of whether some of these records shall be considered the property of the federal or the state government may be a nice problem for the archivists to settle. In a similar category are the records resulting from interstate boards and commissions and treaties between states.

The question as to the state's responsibility for the preservation of local archives involves the much controverted discussion as to whether local archives should be centralized at the state capital or retained in local repositories subject to state supervision to enforce the use of durable materials and proper housing. North Carolina, Connecticut, and Virginia have made some progress toward centralization of older county archives; New York, Massachusetts, and Connecticut send out state record inspectors; Indiana and Illinois are making photographic copies of early county records. So far as results are concerned, however, it must be admitted that state regulation as respects local archives is negligible.

What is the state's interest in the proper preservation of local and, particularly, county records? So far, the attention of archivists has been almost exclusively directed toward their preservation as rich and unexploited source materials for the social historian. The historical implications of these records have been pointed out many times and it is unnecessary to repeat them here. Probably from the point of view of historical research the archivist should try to concentrate such records by transcripts if not the originals.

Does the state's interest in local records cease when the demands of the historians are satisfied? Up to a few years ago we could have said and did say, yes. That belief received a rough jolt when old age pension acts flooded archives departments with frantic and generally futile appeals for aid in locating proofs of age.

The demands of Social Security on local records have been sudden and dramatic, yet another increasing interest of the state in local records is unnoticed and little known. That is the fact that the state government is encroaching upon the powers and duties formerly considered as the sole prerogatives of local government, in exactly the same manner as the more publicized federal encroachments on so-called states' rights. Time permits but a bare mention of some of these relatively new state functions: gathering of vital statistics, licensing of professions, public health and sanitation, agricultural pest control, labor relations, conservation, and hundreds of other activities. As state activities tie in directly with the older records of local law enforcement, state officials frequently wish that the law would direct the transfer of pertinent county records along with the county functions.

As an example of the interest which county archives have to state officials, the following is quoted from the manual of the WPA county research project sponsored jointly by the Illinois State Tax Commission and the University of Illinois Agricultural Experiment Station:

The general objective is to provide information which will assist the Tax Commission in (a) surveying, equalizing, and improving assessments, (b) in formulating recommendations to the governor and general assembly relative to policies and procedures affecting financial operations of local and state governments. Specific portions of the project will fulfill this purpose differently, at the same time serving other purposes, as follows:

1. Land transfer data—To be used for determining real estate assessment ratios; trends in land values for particular regions and types of real estate; rates of land turnover; and, in the case of rural lands, the relationship of land values to farm income, soil types, location and other circumstances. The studies relating to rural land values (other than assessment ratios) will be supervised by the Agricultural Experiment Station of the University of Illinois.

2. Revenues and expenditures of local governments, 1926 to 1935 —To be used for determining trends in local government finance, particularly with respect to the adequacy of existing revenue sources for current functional needs. Illinois has no system of central reports covering local finances; this survey may reveal the possibilities and indicate to local officials the potential usefulness of such a system.

3. Indebtedness of local governments, 1926 to 1935—To be used in connection with the data on revenues and expenditures; also to make available information about the overlapping debt of all governments operating within any given area; and to yield data respecting future requirements by years for interest and for maturities.

4. Tax delinquency—To provide the comparative and historical data for studying relative effectiveness of collection procedures in prosperity and depression under varying geographic, economic and social conditions. . . .

5. Taxing district boundaries—To be used in preparing taxing district maps which will assist the Tax Commission in its routine studies of local tax rates and assessments, and will assist local officials in accurately determining the taxes to be levied on particular parcels of real estate.

6. Assessments and tax extensions—To provide a continuous authoritative record of property values and the amounts of property taxes extended in each county or, if possible, each township. These data are essential for comparative and historical studies of tax burdens and governmental debt, and they are important for studies of tax delinquency. . . .

In addition to administrative uses specifically mentioned, the data will serve as a basis for policies relating to the transference of functions between governments, reorganizations of units, state-administered shared revenues and grants-in-aid, limits in tax rates and borrowing powers, uniform accounting systems, and other aspects of financial administration. The land transfer data, for example, will yield real estate assessment ratios which will be in the equalization of real estate assessments, development of scientific assessment procedures, historical and comparative studies of real tax burdens on lands, and (through the Agricultural Experiment Station, University of Illinois) in economic analyses of farm land utilization, productivity and related problems.

Just what the proper relation should be between the state archives department and the local record-making bodies needs careful study and a definite program. It seems likely that that relation will be similar to that of the state library to local public libraries— the recommendation and setting of standards and encouragement toward better care of records, with a limited amount of state aid.

Private archives need no particular discussion here because private archives, except insofar as they comprise semipublic papers of public officials such as governors, belong, so far as the archivist is concerned, in the category of historical manuscripts. They may be cataloged and classified in accordance with archival principles; they may be housed in a state archives establishment; but they are not records of public business and should not be regarded as a part of the archives proper.

On the border line between governmental and historical archives come the transcripts of records relating to the preterritorial period of the state's history. There are many archives in the records of Ohio relating to the government of Illinois as a part of the old Northwest Territory, petitions from Illinois in the Virginia archives, and records in Indiana relating to Illinois as a part of Indiana Territory. Going back even further one finds material in foreign archives, particularly in the archives at Quebec. In some states, transcripts of such material are collected by the state historical agency, as in Illinois; in other states the archives department treats the material as a part of the state archives. Such material, though relating to the government of the state in question, forms a part of the archives of other governmental agencies and are not archives of the state involved. . . .

2

The Purpose and Nature of Archives

1 / Archives and Historical Manuscripts

WHAT PRACTICAL DISTINCTION should be made between archival and historical manuscripts with respect to their collection and preservation, arrangement and cataloging, and administration and use?"

The term "archives" as used here refers to official records of government agencies, excluding the archives of churches, corporations, and individuals. Government archives fall into two chief categories. The first class includes records filed with or by a government agency as proof of private ownership of a commodity or privilege, or which establish citizenship or other rights. Examples of this type of records are deeds, wills, licenses to practice professions, marriage and birth records, naturalization papers, and the like. The second class comprises records of the administration of governmental functions including law enforcement through the courts. Such records show methods, results, and the history of policies affecting the welfare of society. The first distinction between archives and historical manuscripts therefore is that archives

◄§ PART 1 OF THIS CHAPTER, "Archives and Historical Manuscripts," was originally published in *Illinois Libraries* 25 (December 1943): 399–402. Part 2, "Legal Aspects of Archives," was originally published as "Some Legal Aspects of Archives" in *American Archivist* 8 (January 1945): 1–11.

are primarily legal documents and only secondarily of historical value even though archives constitute the most important historical source materials there are. Some of the most valuable records, from the legalistic archival point of view, have very little historical interest.

The official in charge of public records, whether he be the head of the agency in which the records originate or the archivist, is bound by law to protect the integrity of those records in such a manner that their value to the individual and to the government shall not be impaired. Although some of the older archives may seem to have ceased to be of administrative value and to be of further interest only to the historian, that is not recognized by law and does not release the custodian from his legal and moral responsibilities in regard to that maintenance of the authenticity of the records. The fact that a document may not have been consulted for a century does not rule out the possibility of the fact that tomorrow some attorney may attach great significance to it. The longer the experience of the archivist, the more he becomes convinced that there is no such thing as a noncurrent government record and that *all* official records should be arranged according to archival principles.

The curator of a manuscript collection, on the other hand, is restricted legally in his methodology only by such private contracts as may have been agreed upon between his institution and the previous owner of the collection. Right here is the crux of the differences between the collection, arrangement, and servicing of private manuscripts and of public records. Most of the mistakes made by amateur archivists seeking to modernize their procedure stem from a failure to grasp the implications of archives as legal evidence.

The first of the basic principles involved in the care of public records is that under a democratic form of government the people are sovereign. That is, the records of the government belong to the people and the official who creates, files, and services the records is merely acting as custodian for the people. As custodian, he is subject to criminal prosecution if he "shall steal, embezzle, alter, corrupt, withdraw, falsify or avoid [*sic*] any record." Only the people, through their elected representatives in the legislative body which defines the duties of that officer, can authorize the destruction of any of the legal records of his office. This principle is universally recognized although, it must be acknowledged, it is not always obeyed.

The second principle is that the custodian must handle the records in a manner that will not impair their value as evidence should any ever have to be produced in court. The outstanding work on this subject is *A Treatise on the Anglo-American System of Evidence in Trials at Common Law* by the late John Henry Wigmore. Sections 2128-69 deal with "Authentication of Documents."[1]

All written instruments, as distinct from oral testimony, submitted in court are subject to rules for sufficiency for circumstantial evidence. These rules provide for authentication by the tests of age, contents, custody, and official seal or signature. Wigmore states on this point, "When in a government office are kept permanent records under the custody of an officer appointed to that duty, there is commonly little danger in inferring that records found there existing are genuine. It would be difficult as well as criminal to substitute or to insert false records. Moreover, the usual mode of authenticating such documents (as by proving the clerk's or officer's handwriting) would be both highly inconvenient, on account of its repeated necessity, and also often impossible, on account of the change of officials as well as the antiquity of many portions of the records. It seems, therefore, never to have been doubted that the *existence of an official document in the appropriate official custody* is sufficient evidence of its genuineness to go to the jury."[2] The common method of presenting documents to a court is by means of a copy certified under seal, by the head of the department involved, that this is a true copy of a record on file in his office.

When records are transferred by the department in which they originated to the archives department, that removes the records one step from their "natural place of custody." The archivist can only certify that a document in question is a document taken from an official file transferred from the department to which the record appertains. Since the law authorizes the transfer to the archives department, which is also a government agency having a seal which is required to be judicially recognized, the question of authenticity of certified copies made by the archives department does not arise. If the record is merely on deposit in the archives, the department of origin not having yielded legal jurisdiction to the archives department, it is customary for the department to borrow back the document and to certify the copy under its own seal. Since technically it is incorrect to certify any document as a true copy which has been away from the physical custody of the person making the copy, a court might question such a copy though if the point has been raised in this country it has not come to our attention.

In Illinois this dubious practice of a departmental certification to a record in the archives is avoided by the statement in the archivist's receipt to the department depositing records that this transfer is accepted on condition that legal jurisdiction over the records is relinquished by the department.

It is interesting to note in this connection, however, that at least two sets of important Illinois records have not come to the archives because the wording of the laws governing the exercise of function connected with those records would seem to prevent acceptable certification by either the department or the archivist in case of transfer either by deposit or by waiver of jurisdiction.

The necessity for acceptable certification is the basis for the adoption of provenance as the basis for the classification of archives. By provenance, archivists mean that the records of each department and of each of its subdepartments should be kept together and that the main groupings or files of records, generally called series, as set up by these departments of origin shall be retained. Records should never be transposed from one file to another except in the case of an obvious mistake in filing. For instance, it would be improper to transpose an early trademark record originally filed in a miscellaneous file, to the separate trademark file set up by the department a few years later. If this were done, one would run the risk of having some court question the authenticity of that document because it had happened to have been cited in an earlier case as having been produced from the miscellaneous file.

How should the archivist handle archival documents thrown into a subject arrangement which has destroyed their original provenance? How should he deal with records which have been out of official custody but which the archives department acquires through gift, purchase, replevin, or other means? The answers given here are pragmatic and the subject might well be discussed and studied further by American archivists.

When subject collections of archival material have been in existence for some time, especially if citations under the subject form have been made in published material, no attempt should be made to break up the collection to restore the individual documents to their place in the original series. Even if the collection were broken up, the archivist could not certify from his personal knowledge that a given document was actually the original document from a series, even though it apparently fits an existing gap. Rather he should make notes about everything he can discover about the original compilation of the collection and on the presumptive provenance of each document. He can only certify to the fact that a particular document is to be found in this particular collection and that in his personal opinion, based upon his knowledge of the history of the collection and from internal evidence he believes this to be the original document from a certain file.

An Illinois illustration of this point is the so-called Perrin Collection. These are the early French records of Cahokia and of early St. Clair County which the late J. Nick Perrin rescued from the courthouse wastebaskets, attic and cellar, or which he removed from the files with the consent of the county officials. These documents the county board ordered placed in a museum room for greater protection against theft or careless destruction and appointed Mr. Perrin county archivist in charge of the collection. After his death, the local historical society became custodian until its removal to the state archives. There is little danger then in assuming that a given document is the original inventory of an estate, because it fits a gap in a series the main part of which is still in the county archives; and the history of the compilation of the Perrin Collection is known. To be acceptable to the court, the archivist should certify merely that this document found in the Perrin Collection is presumed to be the document missing from the files of the St. Clair probate clerk's records.

If it is desirable to compile a subject collection of material in the archives, it is usually sufficient to do this by means of calendars or bibliographical lists. In extraordinary cases it may be necessary to remove documents from their regular place in the series and to file them elsewhere. This happens when manuscripts are too large or too fragile to be kept in the regular folders, or those to which brittle or pendant seals are affixed, or those which need special protection. For instance, it has seemed advisable for a variety of reasons to keep all Lincoln records in the Illinois archives in the safe. In each case where an original document has been removed a photostatic copy of the original to which a note is attached explaining the location of the original is inserted as a cross reference in the files. A note signed and dated by the archivist is attached to the original indicating the exact place in the file from which it was removed. The archivist can then certify of his own knowledge that he is furnishing a true copy of the original manuscript.

When records which have been out of official custody come into the archives, the archivist cannot properly return them to the original file, because he cannot certify that these are the original documents, free from any taint of having been forged or altered in any respect. He should rather, as in the case of unnatural subject files, record and note in any certificate or copy he may have occasion to make, any information he has as to the history of the documents including the circumstances of their coming into the archives.

Jenkinson cites an interesting bit of Shakespeareana in illustration of this point. "The echo of this legal point in a literary or historical setting may be seen in the case of the well-known volume, part of the Accounts of the Master of the Revels, which was for a considerable time in the possession of the antiquary Peter Cunningham though it has long since been restored to official custody. No certified copy from this document is given by the Record Office without a statement of the above fact in its history, and those interested in Shakespearean chronology are still disputing . . . whether the entries on one page are or are not an interpolation by Cunningham. So great is the value of custody that the constant effort of private forgers in all periods has been to get copies of their forgeries enrolled in some public series, because they knew that the authenticity of the enrolment would never be called in question and hoped that by a confusion of ideas the thing enrolled would pass uncriticized."[3]

Collections of nonarchival manuscript materials which may come into the archives department are of course treated under the ordinary procedures for the care of manuscripts, since they have no legal significance in the archival sense described above.

"Archive quality is dependent upon the possibility of proving an *unblemished line of responsible custodians*."[4] This is the way Jenkinson sums up what we have been trying to explain. It is because of legal requirements and not because of unwillingness to accept modern methods introduced by curators of historical manuscripts that archivists continue, and seem likely to continue, to cling to the old theory of provenance as the correct basis for the arrangement of archives; and which makes them conservative, though it is to be hoped not reactionary, about the adoption of such new methods as the lamination method of repair.

2 / Legal Aspects of Archives

At the annual meeting of the Society of American Archivists in 1943 I participated in a discussion of some of the differences between archives and historical manuscripts as those differences affect methods of care, preservation, and use.[5] Limiting my discussion to official governmental records, I endeavored to make the point that the archivist is limited in his procedures for the care of records entrusted to his custody by a paramount duty to preserve the integrity of their use as acceptable legal evidence. In preparing that discussion, I discovered that although we are spending our lives caring for legal records, practically nothing has been written by American archivists on philosophical aspects of the subject of legal aspects of records. I am aware that this is but one phase of archival work and also that it is not a topic particularly suitable to an audience composed largely of persons chiefly interested in archives as historical manuscripts. Nevertheless, I propose, with your indulgence, to discuss a few phases of this matter as indicative of just one direction in which we need to do more research.

The philosophy of records as affected by our democratic system of government is something we accept without much thought until we try to discuss some of our problems with fellow archivists from foreign countries. Then we discover that our ways are not their ways. An archivist from a country with a highly centralized government cannot understand why the records most important to individuals—title records, marriage registers, probate records, and vital statistics—should be left to the unsupervised custody of what to them appear petty officials of the lowest grade politically and professionally. "Why doesn't the government do something to correct this?" they ask. We try to explain that public records in a democracy belong to the people; that our government is made up of officials merely delegated to do for the people what the people cannot do effectively as individuals; that our officials do not own the records which they create but merely act as custodians of the records on behalf of the people; that the origin of the custom of placing our most important records in the hands of county officials was to be able to watch over them and control them as officials of a remote central bureau could not be watched and controlled.

The second legal aspect of records also grows out of our democratic system of government—that is the theory that government records once created may not legally be destroyed without authorization from the representatives of the people in general assembly—by that body which authorized the creation of the records by direction or by implication. The national government and all state governments have statutes making unauthorized destruction of records a criminal offense, yet these prohibitory laws are constantly flaunted with impunity. The most generally accepted explanation for this is that prosecution for violation of the law must be by fellow officials who hesitate to prosecute because of social or political pressure.

The real reason why records are destroyed with impunity is that the law is impracticable because it fails to give an adequate definition for the term "records." Under a strict and commonplace interpretation of the law, almost any piece of paper with writing upon it which flutters by chance into a government office must be deemed a record. The absurdity of treating as equally sacrosanct a record of a transfer of a piece of real estate and an office memorandum requisitioning a typewriter ribbon is undoubtedly at the bottom of the contempt of the average official toward prohibitory laws in the face of patriotic calls for scrap paper. Most officials fail to take a long-range view of their records and are interested only in preserving those records which would prove their financial honesty in case of an investigation of their department. Some legal control over the creation and disposal of records must be applied.

The best solution to the disposal of valueless records which has been tried so far is through laws creating a commission, board, or other official body which passes upon the advisability of destroying records submitted for consideration. That this is not completely successful is attested by the large number of records which are still being destroyed illegally without consultation with the records commission.

A profitable study for archivists would be a redefinition of the term "record" as used in laws relating to the destruction of records. This redefinition might be in terms of purposes for which records are created, requiring that records which accomplish certain purposes, such as establishing property or citizenship rights, must be preserved permanently; that other records such as those administrative records establishing policies may, subject to the consent of the records commission, be kept in microfilm copies only; that certain records of temporary utility such as records of investigations of complaints may, also subject to review of the records commission, be destroyed after a period of years.

As our record disposal laws are now working we are compiling long lists of records already created which have proved to be of doubtful utility. This is a negative process. It is not contributing toward the creation of a well-rounded archives system. From my own study of the history of state administration, I can faintly see a pattern emerging which might make possible such a record disposal law as I have outlined above. Would that some of the energy spent by graduate students in rehashing the history of the Illinois and Michigan Canal could be diverted to useful and basic studies on the history of governmental functions!

A third legal implication of our democratic system is that all records of public business are public records and as such must be open to any person applying to see them, subject only to reasonable regulations as to hours of access and to necessary safeguards for their physical protection. That theory is embodied in the working of many laws creating records and is implicit in all others except where the law specifically exempts certain records from public inspection as being of a confidential nature. Records may be classed as confidential only where examination by outsiders would be prejudicial to public or to private good—for instance, in the case of certain financial reports made by corporations in connection with franchise or other taxes, and such personal records as pardon papers. Departments transferring records to the archives sometimes do so with the condition that the records may be shown by the archivist only on orders from the department. If this stipulation is so worded that it does not in effect prevent an interested individual from demanding access to the records through the department, this is not construable as a violation of the law. It does save the archivist many headaches in borderline cases which the department can pass judgment upon more wisely than the archivist. The knowledge that information can be obtained only by going through certain formalities also acts as a definite check to sensation mongers.

The substitution of a certified copy to save wear and tear on the original record, an increasingly common practice, is likewise perfectly legal, especially when the original has been preserved as a check against possible error and for use upon those rare occasions when only the original can suffice. Certified copies of these certified

34

copies, particularly when the first copy has been made photographically, are also acceptable to the court.

Opening of records to public inspection implies a duty to supervise that inspection to protect the records against undue wear, theft, mutilation, or deliberate or accidental tampering of any kind. This theory of free access to records has been carried to a dangerous degree in many offices, particularly in the county courthouses. In some of our county recorder's offices the abstract companies have practically taken possession of the records and order the recorder and his deputies about as if they and not the recorder were in charge. In most recorders' offices in Illinois the deed and mortgage record books are on open shelves, among which all comers are welcome to browse without restraint. This custom has become so rooted in tradition that progressive officials who feel some safeguards should be applied find it difficult to interpose the minimum checks. These officials should be encouraged to substitute certified copies of the original for public use wherever possible. The probate clerk of Cook County (Chicago), Illinois, has found this practice the only means of curbing serious abuses particularly in the way of substitutions and thefts of individual documents in his unbound files.

Another legal aspect of archives is the power of replevin. All governments have laws permitting the seizure of public records found in private hands. These laws are useful in the recovery of deliberate thefts from the archives but are practically never successfully invoked in the case of records taken by officials going out of office, which is the most common way by which public records disappear. Letters, for instance, which discuss matters of office policy in one paragraph and political gossip in the next paragraph tend to end in the official's private files. A century or less ago it was not uncommon for a county or township official to keep his office records in the back of the account books of his law office or his store. All sorts of legal complications can and do arise where it becomes necessary to get back official records thus taken away accidentally or deliberately. Once again we feel the need for a more precise definition of the qualities which constitute an official record.

Audits of accounts of financial receipts and expenditures and inventory checks of furniture, filing equipment, typewriters, and pencil sharpeners between outgoing and incoming officials are becoming routine matters, but similar checks on public records so transferred are practically unknown. In Illinois law the county recorder and the probate clerk are the only public officers in the state who are required to sign a receipt to their predecessors for records turned over to them. Less loss of records and better quality of records would result if the laws were amended to require an inventory of records to be compiled, checked, and receipted for in duplicate, one copy to be given by the incoming official to his predecessor and one copy retained as a part of the official records of his office.

Most states have laws making provision for the reconstruction of public records in case of destruction of the originals through fire, flood, or other catastrophe. It has been stated that 80 percent of Illinois counties have lost at least part of their records that way; most states have also had similar losses, some of them of major proportions. In general these laws name commissioners, generally some court, to which private persons and government officials may submit evidence from which the public records may be rebuilt. Illinois, for example, has very detailed laws on these points, necessitated by the destruction of all the Cook County and Chicago municipal records in the fire of 1871.

Much work is being done throughout the country in the microcopying of government records, particularly county records, as insurance against loss of the originals. We find that very little, if any, attention has been given to certifications which would make these copies acceptable to courts as evidence. We find that commercial firms are glibly citing court decisions accepting photographic copies of public records, but we doubt whether the courts will accept photographic or other copies as paramount evidence where proper certificates have been omitted. . . .

This brings us to the matter of records as court evidence. This subject has been largely ignored in American archival literature. It is impossible to discuss it here in any detail. . . .

The first question which the judge asks concerning a document presented in evidence is, "Is this actually the document which it purports to be?" Next he asks, "Are the facts alleged in the document true or false?" Ordinarily the archivist has to reply only to the first question. It is the rule of evidence that "the *existence of an official document in the appropriate official custody* is sufficient evidence of its genuineness to go to the jury."[6] This proof is shown by presenting the document to the court in one of several ways. First, the original document itself may be presented by its legal custodian, who takes oath verbally before the court that this is the document in question. In the case of a public record it is improper for the custodian to remove the record from its legal repository without a subpoena from the court. Because of this impropriety of removing the record, the court is commonly satisfied with a copy certified under the seal and signature of its custodian that this is a true and complete copy of the original. Some of the complications which arise in the presentation of a record or a certified copy thereof as the result of transfer of custody from the department of origin to the archivist, and in certifying records which have been returned to the archives after having been for a time out of official custody were discussed in my paper last year. . . .

In addition, the court may demand proof that the person producing the original or signing the certified copy is indeed the legal custodian of the document. When the court is within the same state and the identity of the custodian is easily ascertainable, it customarily suffices for him to state in his verbal oath or in the certified copy that he is the official whose title he names, and that as such he is the official custodian of the document. Where the court sits under a different jurisdiction and particularly where it is under a foreign government, it is customary to add a certificate under the great seal of state to the effect that the custodian has been legally appointed or elected, as the case may be, to the office, and that he is authorized by law to sign and seal the certified copies.

Occasionally government records are presented as evidence by private persons. Since the taking of an original file from official custody by a private person exceeds all bounds of propriety and safety, the court rejects such testimony in all but the most extraordinary cases, "When a *private person* testifies to a *sworn* or *examined copy* of a *public record, i.e.* a record examined by him for the purpose of making the copy, it is obvious that proving the copy includes not only proof that its contents are a correct transcription of the original, but also that the original was the genuine one it purported to be. . . ."[7]

It would be profitable and interesting, if time permitted, to compare the lawyer's methods of appraising the veracity of the contents of documents with the historian's. One of my friends who is noted for his critical acumen as a historian once told me that he had learned more historical methodology while acting as secretary of a local historical society under the presidency of an able attorney than in all his graduate courses in history. "He not only made me document every sentence I wrote, but he taught me how to evaluate those documents." We archivists cannot assume that the court will tolerate careless handling of records on our part if that handling impairs their legal status in any way.

Time does not permit a discussion of other phases of legal aspects of archives, such as laws which permit the archivist to exercise a salutary supervision over papers, ink, vaults and safes, or various other phases of record making and preservation. What I have tried to show is that there is still much room for study along these lines, not only by our committee on legislation, but by each of us archivists as individuals.

3

The Organization and Operations

of an Archives

1 / ORGANIZING A NEW STATE ARCHIVES

THERE ARE SEVERAL STEPS in the creation of a state archives department: 1. crystallization of sentiment in favor of establishment; 2. determination of the place of the archival agency in the hierarchy of state departments; 3. appointment of the archivist; 4. securing of the enabling legislation; and 5. securing appropriations for operation, housing, and equipment.

A whole article could be written upon the question of how to get government officials and legislators to take action. Most frequently the demand for the creation of an archival establishment comes from the state historical society and persons interested in preserving the historical heritage which will be lost if better care is not taken of the records. An effective procedure used by such groups of persons is the publication of articles based upon the records and articles in newspapers and magazines pointing out the historical significance of specific types of records.

Local and state bar associations are in a peculiarly favorable position to call attention to the necessity for better care of records.

PART 1 OF THIS CHAPTER, "Organizing a New State Archives," was originally published in *Illinois Libraries* 28 (December 1946): 496–503. Part 2, "The Duties of an Archivist," was originally published as "What Does an Archivist Do?" in *Illinois Libraries* 29 (May 1947): 211–20.

Attorneys, more than any other persons, recognize the value of records and know the consequences of improper care or destruction. A large proportion of the members of most legislative bodies are lawyers by profession and it should be comparatively easy to enlist their sympathy.

Pressure for additional storage space and the desire for advice in matters relating to the reduction in the bulk of their records and better documentation practices are the most potent and helpful factors in the campaign for the establishment of an archival agency.

A fire which threatens or destroys important records, particularly those in which veterans' organizations are interested, is the most spectacular propaganda and has often been the factor which brought archives departments or new buildings into being. Naturally no one would advocate so drastic a measure as arson. However, persons who are interested in better protection for government records should not hesitate to draw a moral from the frequent reports of losses sustained by business houses because their records have been destroyed by fire and should point out the obvious fire hazards to which the state records are subject.

The point of departure for this article, however, is the procedure to be followed once it has been decided that an archives department is to be established.

The first matter to be determined is what form of organization will be best for the particular state involved. That organization may take the form of a state department of archives and history; an independent agency under its own governing board; a division under an elective state officer or department as the secretary of state or state department of education; a division under the state library; or a section in the state university history department or library.

Where there is no existing state historical agency, it is likely that a state department of archives and history will be created. Such a department generally comprises a reference library which collects books and pamphlets on national, state, and local history, genealogy, newspapers and private papers; an editorial staff which publishes a periodical, edits the transactions of the state historical society, and issues books, maps, and pamphlets on state history; a museum of history; and the archives department. The director of such a department usually bears the title of state historian and has as his general duties the promotion of interest in the history of the state and the care of historic sites and buildings. Such a department is a recognition of the natural affinity between records and other historical source materials and draws to its support the not inconsiderable body of prominent persons all over the state who are interested in history, also the patriotic societies and veterans' associations which can aid materially in efforts to get appropriations. The chief disadvantages of the state department of archives and history from the point of view of the archivist is that such an affiliation tends to limit his scope to the records which are of recognized historical interest, making it more difficult for him to persuade other state officials that the archives department can aid them in solving their records problems of today. This is especially true if the history department is not located close to the capitol and other state office buildings. Furthermore, the history department is seldom allowed a budget sufficient to give adequate support to the subordinate archives department. Examples of states which give archival service under the combined history and archives department are Alabama, Mississippi, and North Carolina.

Theoretically the ideal archival agency would be one which is independent of all other departments, governed by its own policymaking board and responsible only to the legislature. Where such agencies are created, the governing board may consist of ex officio members; a board appointed by the governor for staggered terms of office; or a board combining ex officio and appointive members. The board should comprise persons who represent, among other qualifications, the interest of the legal profession, the government, and the historian. A justice of the supreme court, the president of the state bar association, the president or secretary of the state historical society, a member of the governor's cabinet, or an elective state officer like the secretary of state or attorney general are frequently named to such a governing board. This archival board or commission should not be merely an honorary body (though the archivist sometimes doubtless might wish it were), but it should have both the prestige and the authority not only to advise the archivist but also to secure the necessary appropriations and to stand back of his decisions. The advantages of a separate and independent archival agency are obvious: good record work requires the entire time and energies of the archivist and his staff; appropriations are generally larger than when they are a part of the budget of some other department. The disadvantages are generally whispered: a separate archival department is apt to be too small and weak to protect itself against political interference and to maintain a professional staff. Delaware and Maryland are examples of independent archival agencies.

The Massachusetts archives is an example of an agency which devotes all its time to record work as a department under an elective state officer. This department, however, services only the records of the secretary of state and the General Court. . . .

Some of the strongest state archival agencies are departments of state libraries. State officials traditionally turn to the state library for efficient reference service and other forms of cooperation and generally respect the need of that institution to be maintained upon a professional basis. The extension of the library's service to the field of record problems is accepted as a natural evolution. While technical procedures in library and archival work are based upon quite different concepts, there is enough similarity to permit considerable integration of administrative and even of professional work. For instance, at Illinois, the administrative office of the State Library takes care of all personnel matters, securing of the budget, ordering of supplies, bookkeeping and similar administrative work, freeing the archival staff for purely professional work. All photographic work for the library is done in the archives laboratory; the art department cooperates with the archives department in setting up exhibits; the shipping department serves both library and archives and the archives fumigation, cleaning and spraying equipment is used by all; the Illinois documents department services requests coming into both the general reference and the archives department; in an emergency an exchange of stenographic, reference, and even cataloging personnel is possible. . . . The danger of having the archives department a part of any state library is that inherent in any form of organization in which the archives department is not independent: appropriations may be relatively too small, and other phases of the work of the library may absorb the physical as well as the financial resources which should be spent upon archives work. Examples of other states in which the archives department is a part of the state library are Indiana, Oregon, Tennessee, Texas, and Virginia.

Occasionally it will be found that the state university is taking the initiative in preserving the archives of the state, particularly by collecting county and older territorial and state records. For instance, the University of Illinois laid the foundations for the present Illinois Archives Department. About forty years ago when it began urging the establishment of such a department, a state historical survey was created, receiving its appropriations through the Illinois State Historical Library but actually administered by the Department of History at the university. This survey collected and published transcripts of documents relating to Illinois, inventoried state and county records, and secured legislation permitting local officials to transfer noncurrent records to the university library. The publication functions of the survey have in recent years been transferred to the Springfield office of the Historical Library, while the archival functions of course have long since been taken over by the present Archives Department. A present-day example of the same sort of work is to be found in Louisiana. In one important respect the situation there is different from that at Illinois, in that the Louisiana State University is located in the same city as the capitol, whereas in Illinois the two are separated. It may well be that the Louisiana archives will continue to be affiliated with the university.

In summary, the selection of the particular type of organization for any state archives will depend upon governmental trends in the state in question. Constitutional provisions or legal practices in the state may have an influence upon the departmental setup of the archives department. For instance, the fact that the secretary of state is the state librarian largely determined the creation of the Illinois Archives Department as a section of the Illinois State Library. In Illinois the secretary of state not only has important records in his own department but is also the custodian of the records of the General Assembly, of the constitution, and of the constitutional conventions, and is the official recorder for the governor. Putting the Archives Department under the secretary of state, therefore, immediately put under its jurisdiction a very large bulk of the most important records of the state. More than one state archival agency has had a discouraging slow start because it took so long to get other state officials into the mood for transferring records to it. No question of conflicts of jurisdiction required amendments to the laws as might have been the case if the Archives Department had been put under some other elective state officer. Successful examples of each kind of archival agency are found; on the other hand, poor examples of each kind exist in the same proportion. In general, it would seem that in states where there is a tendency toward consolidations of departments into large administrative units, as is the case of Illinois, the archives department should preferably become a division in an established and strong department. In a state which operates under a number of separate boards, commissions, and departments, so that another small department would not find itself being "pushed around" politically, it is better for the archives department to be a separate and independent department.

It will be noted that we have listed the appointment of an archivist as coming before the passage of enabling legislation. The state archivist of Oregon, David Duniway, remarked at a meeting of archivists, "You will understand that the Oregon archives department as yet has no legal existence—I, the archivist, am only an appropriation item in the state library budget." This is entirely proper. Instead of having to start in with a new building and an appropriation calling for the immediate organization of a large staff, as happened at the National Archives, Mr. Duniway was given time to study local conditions to find out what is needed before he goes to his general assembly for legislation and appropriations.

The matter of selecting a state archivist will be touched upon only lightly here because archivists themselves are not agreed as to the desirable qualifications and training for archivists. It is generally considered that the state archivist should hold the doctorate in one of the social sciences, or at least be thoroughly grounded in research techniques. Until recently there was no formal training for archivists offered in this country. American University at Washington offers courses for records administrators both on the graduate and undergraduate level, also a summer course for archivists in service in cooperation with the National Archives and the Maryland Hall of Records. Most archivists of today were recruited from the ranks of the National Archives, from the executive staff of the late Historical Records Survey, from historical libraries, or from among history teachers. It should go without saying that the archivist, as a professional man, should be recruited through civil service and should be protected from political interference. The archivist should hold himself strictly aloof from politics, not because he considers himself above it, but because he cannot win the confidence—and the records—of the department heads if they fear the use or withholding of records for partisan purposes. On the other hand, the archivist must not seek an ivory tower to which to retire to write history. The archivist must be primarily an administrator and as such he will find himself turning over to other historians the source materials he knows he never will find the time to exploit himself. Above all, the archivist must be a realist who will not let himself become unduly disturbed over the petty jealousies and ruthless struggles for power inherent in our governmental system, even when those things seem to be blocking the progress of his department. Administrative ability, facility to speak and write well, patience to do routine tasks thoroughly yet imagination to plan constructively—these and all the other intangible qualities sought for in an executive—are necessary to the archivist. For obvious reasons, it is desirable for the archivist to be a native or resident of the state, though the primary basis of selection should be his qualifications to do a satisfactory job, and the best candidate should be picked regardless of the locality from which he comes.

As soon as the archivist has been appointed, work should begin on drafting legislation creating the archives department. The committee on legislation appointed by the Society of American Archivists drafted two model acts which will be helpful. The first of these was a bill to create a state department of archives and history.[1] The second was a bill for an independent agency to be governed by a board of trustees.[2] Attention is also called to an address by A. R. Newsome, "Uniform State Archival Legislation"—a discussion of records legislation in force in the various states.[3] It should be realized that these two model bills are not intended to create uniform legislation (despite the unfortunate title to the 1940 bill). Rather, they are intended to suggest subjects to be included in bills, couched in precise legal terminology. Before introducing these bills into any legislature, they should be carefully examined to determine whether they are applicable to the needs of the state and also submitted to the state bill drafting agency for coordination with existing records legislation.

The most common fault to be found with most proposed archival legislation is the attempt to include too much in the act creating the archives department. Such an act should be limited to clauses creating the department, giving it a legal name, defining its powers and duties, and authorizing other officials to transfer records to it. In general the bill should state what the department is to do but not be explicit about how it is to perform its duties. The shorter and more concise the act the better. There are two reasons for that. The first is a psychological one. When the archivist approaches an official to discuss possible transfer of records, that person will properly demand to know by what right the solicitation is made. If the archivist has to present a copy of an act ten or twelve pages long, the inevitable reaction will be an impatient, "That is too complicated—I don't understand it and I haven't time to figure it out. Now, in a nutshell, just what can you do and what can I do?" The other reason for keeping the act simple is that a bill burdened with elaborate definitions and descriptions of procedure invariably calls for interpretation and too often rules out the possibility of a commonsense modification to fit a peculiar situation. This may even result in the act being thrown out as unconstitutional. In any event, the attorney general will have to be asked for opinions. One of the most useful bits of advice the writer received as a new archivist was, "Avoid asking the attorney general for opinions. Nine times out of ten he will say 'No' and it will be almost impossible to get that 'No' exchanged for a 'Yes.' . . ."

We raise this point as to how little the archivist can get along with in the matter of an archival law, because it is not always possible to get a more specific and elaborate law. Our law looks quite innocuous, and it is likely that a similar law could be put through any legislature which was not definitely hostile to the creation of any archival establishment.

The matter of record laws is not, of course, settled when you have created an archival agency. Whether or not the state has an archives department, certain general acts concerning records should be and generally are already on the statute books. Among these laws should be provisions prohibiting destruction, mutilation, theft, and tampering with the records; compelling outgoing officials to turn over records to their successors; providing for replevin of records taken out of proper custody; providing for public access to records not specifically named as confidential; providing for certification of records and fees therefore; permitting use of photography, under proper restrictions, for copy work, recording, and reduction of records; procedures for disposition of records, including both destruction and transfer to the archives; setting up standards for paper, ink, and photographic materials; restoration of lost, missing, or destroyed archives; copying of fading or damaged records; disposition of archives of defunct or transferred offices or agencies; requiring the keeping of records in fireproof vaults. In our estimation it is a mistake to try to include such subjects in the act relating to the archives department unless that department has specific duties in relation to the enforcement of the provisions. Even then we feel that it is better to pass a series of separate laws on each subject, including the powers of the archivist in the respective acts. Two things are accomplished by that procedure: the laws are kept short so that it is easy to hand out the specific act as the subject of the act is discussed; and second, since these subjects frequently need

revision you do not each time open your satisfactory law governing the archival department to the danger of an unapproved
amendment.

The newly appointed archivist has several immediate tasks
before him. He must find out as quickly as possible as much as he
can concerning the records of the state and the departments which
create them, and he must win the support of the officials from
whom he hopes to secure transfers of the records. Two things are
necessary on the first point. He needs to study the statutes to learn
the history of administration in his state, and he needs an inventory
of extant records.

The quickest source of information on state departments is
the statistical and encyclopedic publication such as is issued by
most states and the reports of the departments themselves. Histories
of departments are particularly to be expected on tenth, twenty-
fifth, fiftieth, or other anniversaries of their founding—either in the
form of articles published somewhere or as the special feature of
their biennial reports. Constitutional conventions or proposed major reorganizations of state government call forth special bulletins
on the history of governmental functions.

After assembling all such available information the archivist
should endeavor to familiarize himself with present-day departmental organization, especially as it results in the making of records,
by running down all references to all state departments to be found
in the index to the latest edition of the revised statutes.

Next the archivist should start to compile the history of the
various departments through a detailed study of the session laws,
beginning with those for the territorial period. Perhaps the easiest
way to do this is to write index slips for all laws relating to or im-
pinging upon the past or present duties of state departments, giving
bibliographical citations both to the original law and to subsequent
amendments and codifications, and the names of the state departments concerned. It is better to work forward rather than backward
in doing this work, because amendments frequently fail to mention
the departments concerned and too many points would be omitted.
After the laws for one constitutional period have been thus indexed,

the slips can be sorted by names of departments and notes made on the development of functions for each. The process is repeated for each constitutional period or other reorganizations of the governmental structure.

The compilation of complete notes on the history of the various state departments will prove the work of years, but after a few months the archivist will get a working knowledge of the structure of his government useful not only in classifying the records transferred but also in helping to make other state officials realize that he knows what he is talking about. Occasionally some graduate student can be found who will do part of this work as a thesis, but the archivist need not feel too sorry for himself if he has to do this research himself, for the very act of digging out the facts will impress themselves upon his memory.

His history of state departments will give the archivist a fairly good idea of what types of records he should find in each state department, but before making plans for the care of such records as may come into his custody at some future date, he must secure inventories of the state records together with their location. Some states were fortunate enough to have had inventories of state records compiled . . . by the Historical Records Survey. In only a few states were such inventories compiled and edited, but the original work sheets for what was done can generally be located and will give a start. Occasionally a state department has employed a commercial filing analyst and will have an inventory of its records. For the most part, however, the archivist and his assistants can expect to have to spend many months in old clothes, climbing ladders, lifting heavy boxes, and burrowing under heaps of dust and unmentionable filth. Discoveries of invaluable material in the most unlikely places will provide enough thrills to compensate for the disagreeableness of the task.

For the making of inventories the best textbook is the manual prepared for the untrained labor of the Historical Records Survey. Although this manual was never released for universal circulation, copies can occasionally be picked up. If the manual itself is not available, it is fairly easy to find a copy of a worksheet which lists the information to be noted in making an inventory.[4] Actually, however, the archivist will not be able to take the time for such detailed inventories. He can generally get along with one line entries giving the title of the series, the inclusive dates and the number and size of the volumes and containers, arranged in the order found in the vault. The name of the department and the designation and location of the vault or storeroom will of course be noted at the top of each page. Where the title of the series as shown by the labels is not sufficiently explicit, he can add a brief explanatory description. On the basis of these preliminary inventories, the archivist and the department head can discuss what records are to be transferred to the archives department within the immediate and the foreseeable future, and the archivist can plan for suitable equipment and housing accordingly.

The archivist will need a very small staff in the beginning. As a minimum he should have a stenographer and at least one husky assistant to help with the heavier part of inventory taking. If he can obtain the right kind of persons for taking inventories for him, he will be fortunate. The number will depend upon circumstances. Those taking the inventory might well be persons in training for key assistants in the archives department later. The new archivist is warned against optimism on that score, however. He should also be warned not to overload his staff at the start with permanent employees, for he will find that the kind of help he needs in the first couple of years will be quite different from what he will need later. At the beginning he will need more people with strong right arms and more clerks for routine sorting and unfolding. These employees may prove entirely inadequate for the more professional aspects of later work. In the early years the archivist can quite well use the untrained employees whom the politicians are always trying to place. The danger is that when the archives department starts out with that type of personnel it will be hard to convince his superiors later that professional civil service assistants are needed. In selecting the first staff it is desirable that at least the stenographer should be a veteran employee of the state who knows the departments and the accepted routines and practices of the government.

Such a person can often save embarrassment by preventing what would seem to fellow officials mere stupidity in the use of the standard forms.

The success or failure of the archivist will be determined in his first contacts with other state officials. Two rules of conduct, if observed, will go far toward achieving success. The first of these is: asking advice is the greatest form of flattery. The second of these is: never criticize.

The archivist will do well to select some well-established division chief who seems friendly and make him guide and mentor. Of course such a person should not be bothered during his rush season, but ordinarily he will be deeply touched by the archivist's dependence upon him. The writer will never forget the kindly old gentleman who used to say, "Now boys, the little lady knows what she is talking about—you listen to her"; or his drawling voice saying, "No, I don't think I would approach the matter from that angle. Why don't you go to Mr. B instead of to Mr. A—he's the man who has the real say-so"; or his, "Now don't worry about Mr. C's refusal to talk to you—let me get those records for you." Do not approach a man with the attitude that you have come to help him—rather, ask him what he can do to help you with your problems.

Perhaps one has to break the speed laws to get to the city dump to rescue a territorial legislative journal which some official has insisted must be thrown out as "junk." It is a temptation to tell the newspapers that "New archivist rescues priceless volume from destruction; cites that as reason why archives department is needed." Be more subtle in the approach. Take the volume to the official with a nice little publicity story already written, crediting him with the discovery of a long-lost document, the significance of which is explained in the article; stating that the official made the discovery while he was making a survey of his records preliminary to transferring records to the new state archives. The official will come to believe that he found the document himself, the archives department will be mentioned, and those who know how publicity originates will realize that the credit probably belongs to the archivist.

From this point on, the archivist's problems cannot be said

to become simple. Quite early he will be called upon to define the
limits of his collecting activity: shall he accept only official records
and if so within what time limits? What shall he do about caring
for semicurrent records for which the departments wish the pro-
tective care of the archives department, but which they must occasionally withdraw for their own office use? Will he accept private
papers and if so to what extent shall he compete with other institutions collecting in the same general field? Is he going to try to centralize county records or will he promote better local care for them?
How much of a reference library will he have and particularly what
is his policy with respect to newspapers and genealogy? How much
space and effort will be devoted to exhibitions? How much will he
do in the matter of publication? Will he have duties in relation to
registration of veterans' graves, historical highway markers, or other
historical duties?

The archivist will have recurring worries connected with housing and equipment for the records and securing appropriations for
administration. Once he has gained an overall picture of his government and its records and has persuaded the first official to entrust
records to his custody, he should be on more or less familiar ground
and should be able to cope with situations as they arise. The archivist who has organized an archival agency is apt to agree with
the ex-doughboy: "I would not go through that experience again
for anything on this earth—but I would not have missed it for anything, either."

2 / THE DUTIES OF AN ARCHIVIST

"What does an archivist do, anyhow?" That question is nearly
always asked an archivist by a new acquaintance. Webster defines
an archivist as "keeper of archives or records," and archives as "public records or documents preserved as evidence of facts; as, national
or family archives."

The term archives has two common connotations: that they
are historical records (and as such are chiefly valuable for promot-

ing patriotism and for genealogical reference), or that they are diplomatic and military documents containing secrets to be acquired at any cost by enemy agents (a romantic notion fostered by novelists and writers of movie scenarios). Although certain records do have such attributes, most of them are of a more prosaic nature, being fundamentally records of business transactions. The term archives is equally applicable to the business records of an individual, of an institution, of a commercial firm and of a government, though it is from the point of view of government records that the subject will be discussed here.

The objective of a government archivist is to work toward a well-rounded program for all departments. He is interested not only in those records already in or about to be transferred to his custody, but also in the creation of records. As defined by Theodore R. Schellenberg[5] before a National Archives staff conference, "archival concern with the management of current records has two objectives, namely, (1) to obtain a full and adequate documentation of functions and activities; and (2) to obtain efficient management of records in order to facilitate (a) orderly segregation and elimination of useless records as they become noncurrent and (b) ease of reference service both before and after the records are transferred to the archives."[6] Putting the same thoughts into different words, we may say that the work of an archivist includes the physical care of records entrusted to him; helping departments to eliminate from their holdings those records which have no further legal or historical value and documents having no record qualities; helping them to reduce to workable proportions the bulk of records which must be preserved for a while longer; and to advise them in the creation of new records so that future record accumulations shall be adequate in scope, compact in form and scheduled for planned destruction after an appropriate period of time. As custodian of records of enduring value, the archivist must not only furnish suitable housing facilities for such records as other departments are willing to relinquish to his custody, but he must also be vigilant to forestall destruction of other records of permanent or historical value. The records entrusted to his care must be put into good physical condition and arranged, inventoried, and otherwise described in a manner which will permit efficient and quick production for service; and he must be prepared to supply copies either with or without certification.

Among the types of governmental records generally deposited in the archives department are the following:

1. Records relating to obsolete functions of a department, or records which for other reasons are so seldom consulted for office purposes that the department is willing to release them to the jurisdiction of the archives department, as, for instance, colonial or territorial records. Such records are generally chiefly of historical interest.

2. Records of discontinued boards, bureaus, commissions, and departments whose functions have not been continued by some other department. Illinois has comparatively few records of that type, but the archives of the State Council of Defense (World War I) and of the War Council (World War II) are examples.

3. Records in active but not current use. By that is meant that the records in question are no longer used by the department in connection with its own business but are called for frequently by outsiders. Revolutionary and Civil War service records, for instance, formerly used chiefly for establishing pension claims, are now consulted almost exclusively for genealogical purposes.

4. Records requiring special security, as colonial charters, the constitution, enrolled laws, and records relating to government-owned real estate. Such records normally are not loaned to other departments but must be consulted in the archives building under the immediate supervision of the archives staff.

5. Older county records, particularly those for the colonial period. Some of the smaller states, notably Delaware and Maryland, are trying to concentrate all colonial records in the state archives. Other younger states or those of relatively large area (especially New York) are encouraging the creation of county archival agencies or otherwise promoting better care of the records by local officials.

6. Records used only occasionally for government business, usually referred to as "semicurrent records." Such records are gen-

erally permanent and of especial importance, needing the physical and moral protection of the archives building, but used in a manner which requires that the departments retain immediate jurisdiction over them. An example of this category of records is the file of case records on professional licenses. Records of that type are either deposited in the archives with the stipulation that they are to be loaned back to the department as needed, or else the department may be assigned a vault in the archives building to which it has exclusive access.

Traditionally, the American archivist has concentrated upon the care of records of historical value. That this has been an important service no one can deny, since government records form the primary and often the only source material for early American history. Because of this emphasis upon historic aspects of archives, this care of historical documents has come to be regarded as the principal duty of an archivist, and most state archivists are required to act also as state historians. As such, they have to spread their time and resources over a broad field which has little relationship to the science of archives as records of government. The state historical department has as its primary duty the promotion of the study of state and local history. This objective is reached through the accumulation of a historical library (including manuscripts as well as books); through publications of books, articles, and often historical periodicals; through speeches, exhibits, radio programs, projects for visual aid for schools, maintenance of historic sites, erection of road markers, and conducting pilgrimages. The state historian's interest, so far as records go, is chiefly in selected individual documents of historical or biographical interest. His impulse would be, to use an Illinois example, to remove the Black Hawk War items found in various filing units in the archives of the governor, the secretary of state, and the General Assembly, and to reassemble them into a "Black Hawk War Collection." He might be almost wholly neglectful of other records in those series because they relate to routine government business and may not seem to have much historical interest.

The archivist, on the other hand, while far from indifferent to the historical value of those individual documents, would think first of the manner in which they would be used for the legal purposes for which they were created and handle them as an organic part of the records of the government agency to which they appertain. The archivist may find it desirable to segregate certain exceptionally valuable items, as we have done in Illinois in the case of the Lincoln documents, but he will do this in a manner which will preserve the legal identity of each document. He will punctiliously place in the folder from which each was removed, a photographic copy of the original together with a memorandum to the effect that the document has been removed for safekeeping to a specific file. Accompanying each original, there will be another memorandum explaining exactly where the document belongs in the file from which it was removed.

In other words, the historian is interested in archives primarily from the subject side, whereas the archivist never loses sight of the fact that archives fundamentally are legal records, records which were created to facilitate government business. Government records are used to justify an official action, to record proceedings, to explain and record policy decisions, and to establish rights under the law for citizens and the government, either separately or in relation to each other. No matter how much historicity may accrue to a document, the archivist must be able to attest to its authenticity, citing its specific source and place in the records of the agency which created it. In fact, the longer the experience of the archivist, the more convinced he becomes that a record must be very old indeed that will never again be used for legal purposes.

Not only the arrangement of the documents but the type of finding mediums are based upon different principles in the case of historical manuscript collections and archival documents. Fortunately, the proper type of guide for archives is equally useful to the historian and to the government official, the principal difference between guides for the older and for the more modern records being that the older records may call for somewhat fuller descriptions.

In saying that a state historian is not *per se* an archivist, we do not mean to imply that a state historian is incapable of applying archival principles and that many state historians who are combining both types of work are not also competent archivists. We do maintain, however, that because of the differences in point of view and in methods of preparing and servicing materials, it is advisable to separate the offices of state historian and state archivist. The archivist who is limited to working with older records, which is almost always the case where the two functions are handled by one staff, is not performing all of the services which other state officials have a right to demand from him.

If the first duty of the archivist is to act as custodian of records; his second equally important (some say paramount) duty is to work for a well-rounded and adequate records system for his government. This implies three things:

1. The archivist must be the specialist in government who can see the picture as a whole, permitting him to judge the comparative value of records.

2. He must relieve the present critical storage problem of government departments by showing them how to select noncurrent permanent records for transfer to the archives and how to reduce the bulk of other records by substitution of microfilm copies where practicable, and authorize them to destroy records which have no further legal or other value. Left to themselves, departments may preserve records which duplicate material to be found in more usable form elsewhere, or they may destroy records under the mistaken idea that some other department is preserving a record which that department in turn has destroyed because it believes the first department is preserving the record. Departments are generally competent to judge whether they will have further legal use for their records, but they often seek to destroy records which have taken on unthought-of research value. The archivist as a specialist in governmental administration and in history and the one official who has an experienced overall view of his government's records is more competent to judge these values than the department alone, though he will of course be guided by advice from the responsible records officials of the departments.

3. He must help departments to create future records more scientifically. He will show departments how to "schedule" their records to predetermine how long various categories of records are to be preserved, and how to set up files so that the process of weeding is automatic. Even more important, the archivist will help departments to provide adequate documentation. The inability of persons to prove their age and citizenship status from official records which resulted in so much hardship during the war years called attention dramatically to the fact that a failure to create necessary records is at least as grave an error as that promiscuous and unauthorized destruction of records against which American archivists have fulminated for half a century.

This newly evolving science of "record control" is a recent development. The National Archives was the first archival agency in this country to tackle the problem on a large scale, but in recent years most states have amended their record laws to the extent of setting up better procedures for destruction of records which have outlived their usefulness. During and after World War II, several federal departments and scattered departments in a few of the larger states have been experimenting with methods of achieving adequate and compact records. Those who are working in this field are generally called "records administrators" or "records coordinators," and the terms apply both to records persons working within a department and also to archivists who are specializing in the care of modern records. There is some tendency to limit the use of the word "archivist" to those working especially with the older and more historic records. Technically, however, the term "archivist" refers to the custodian of records transferred to the archival agency.

The above discussion of the duties of an archivist still does not answer the question as to how he proceeds to carry out his functions. The custodial duties of an archival agency are the most numerous and varied. In some phases they are very similar to the work of any manuscript curator, though based upon different principles.

Receipt of records. At the time of deposit the archivist must make arrangements with the several departments for safe transportation. At Illinois the archivist does not assume responsibility for the records until they have reached the archives building, but practice in this respect varies from one archival agency to another. Since the Illinois archives building is connected to the capitol and adjacent Centennial Building, most records from those buildings are trucked in by hand; records from other state offices are generally brought in commercial trucks or departmental cars. Records from out of town are usually brought in moving vans with a state police escort.

As soon as records are brought into an archives building, they must be fumigated to kill all insect life and to prevent infestation of other records in the building. As much dirt as possible is removed before the records are taken to the vaults. This is generally done in a special apparatus that employs a combination of compressed air and vacuum.

Next the records are taken to a vault, either to a place especially prepared for them or to a temporary place of deposit pending preliminary preparatory work. As soon as possible after the records come to the Archives Department, a working inventory and a receipt to the department of origin are prepared.

Physical preparation of records. After the most suitable type of container has been fixed upon, bound volumes are shelved and unbound records unfolded (if necessary), placed in folders and containers, and suitable guides and labels prepared. This process is called "packing."

Many records, particularly older ones, come to the archives in such fragile condition that they must be rehabilitated before being handled by patrons. Bound records must be repaired and leather bindings lubricated. Individual sheets of paper must be cleaned and repaired.

There are two principal materials in common use for repairing paper. Crepelin is a silk chiffon pasted on both sides of the document and dried slowly under pressure. This process is still preferred by many archivists because it does not alter the physical appearance of the paper and can easily be soaked off if necessary. The other material is cellulose acetate, a very thin plastic foil applied to both sides of the paper under heat and great pressure, in effect making an indissoluble bond between paper and the repair material. The crepelin process requires only simple and inexpensive apparatus but requires a skilled operator, is slow, and the material is expensive. . . . On the other hand, the cellulose acetate process requires expensive machinery but the material itself is very cheap, the process is easy to learn and is relatively fast. Accelerated aging tests conducted by the National Bureau of Standards indicate that cellulose acetate is a permanent material, but time alone will tell how successful the process will be. A knowledge of paper chemistry and manufacturing processes, also practical binding methods, is essential to the archivist.

Most people look upon an archivist as a sort of "glorified file clerk" and are surprised to hear that filing occupies a comparatively minor amount of staff time. Most modern records come to the archives already filed by a tried method, often initiated upon the advice of commercial filing analysts. Older records often are received in utmost confusion, and in that case a suitable filing procedure must be applied. Occasionally it will be found that the reason why a record unit is seldom consulted is because of an improper or inadequate arrangement which the archives department proceeds to correct by refiling. Certain types of records transferred periodically must be interfiled with other documents of a record unit already in the archives. To illustrate this latter point, the annual reports of corporations filed with the Illinois secretary of state are, because of the nature of the reference to them, kept in one alphabet, all reports of each corporation filed together. Adding sixty thousand new reports each year to a million earlier reports takes the full time of one file clerk several months each year but is worthwhile because under this system we can and do answer a large proportion of questions involving those records over the telephone.

Descriptions of records. The time-consuming function of an archives department is the preparation of descriptions which afford quick and efficient access to any record in the archives, whether the search relates to a general subject or a specific document is sought. The basic finding tools for an archivist, besides the filing systems employed, are inventories, guides, and various types of indexes.

These finding mediums will be used from varying points of view. The archivist uses them to answer the questions, "What records do you have?" and "Do you have a specific record?" also to permit his staff to give prompt service to persons applying to use the records. The patron, on the other hand, may also want to know whether or not a specific record is in the archives, but quite likely he is going to want to know, "Does the archives contain sufficient information about my field of interest to warrant a visit?" or "What help can the archives give me in collecting material on a given topic?" The archivist, in compiling his finding mediums, should think clearly about what purpose each should fulfill lest he shall miss his objective.

The inventory is comparable to a librarian's shelflist in that it lists all record units in the order in which they are placed within the vaults. Generally this inventory takes a condensed form. At the head of each page is given the vault number, then the name of the department by which the records were created, then arranged in the order in which they are found (with specific locations noted), a brief title entry for each archival unit, the inclusive dates and the quantity and size of the container or volume as the case may be. With a subject and functions index, this inventory is used by the reference staff to locate a given file or to answer the question as to whether a file of a certain date is in the archives. Such an inventory is of little utility to the public because it gives no description of the contents of a record unit beyond what is implied by the title and is arranged usually, not in accordance to the classification, but according to convenience in vault arrangement.

The National Archives publishes what it calls checklists. These are intended for the use of the public and serve as a preliminary to the more detailed guides described below. These checklist inventories list the records deposited in the archives by department, arranging the items according to the preliminary classification scheme, give some idea as to dates covered and material, but do not attempt to give a full description. . . .

For public use, a "guide" or series of "guides" is necessary. A guide is a description, department by department, of each set of records in the archives. A brief history of the department with a statement as to its organization and principal functions, particularly as they result in records, serves as an introduction to the description of the records in each department. Then follows a classified annotated list of the different record series, giving for each the title, exclusive dates and quantities as in the inventory, plus a statement as to the nature of the contents. Sometimes this guide includes notes about other records still retained by the department and reference to analagous records to be found in some other repository. The guide should have a subject index.

These guides to the records are frequently compiled in notebook form. In Illinois, however, we have found it advantageous to copy this information onto cards, and to add subject, functional, and analytical entries, with cross-references, arranged in the dictionary form to which patrons are accustomed in library catalogs. The principles of description, however, are in accordance with archival and not library practice.

Such guidance may be further elaborated upon in a number of ways. One of the most useful types is a subject guide that cuts across departmental lines and describes the record groups in which all material on a given topic is to be found in the archives.

As a preliminary to the making of detailed guides, the archivist spends months and perhaps years in research on the history of administration in his government. The Archives Department at Illinois, for instance, has a nine-volume "History of State Departments," elaborately cross-referenced, which gives a comprehensive summary of information about every department, board, bureau, and commission which has ever functioned at state government level, beginning with territorial origins. In addition there is an elaborate bibliography of Illinois laws upon every function which has ever been under state jurisdiction which permits the user to find out what other agencies, state or local, have ever enforced regulations relating to those subjects.

In addition to the three preliminary types of finding mediums, that is, guides to the records of a government agency, subject guides, and histories of state administration, the archivist makes other elaborations on descriptive lists. Indexes of various types are perennial work projects. These indexes may take the form of indexes to one volume or set of volumes, to each drawer or to all the records in one archival series. Generally there is also a consolidated name index covering all records for a given period of time, and there may also be place or date indexes. Many indexes have already been prepared by the departments for their own use, and these indexes must be integrated with indexes made by the archives staff. Where the department wishes to retain its indexes in its own office, the archives department generally obtains permission to make a photographic copy for its use.

Frequently it is desirable to make false entries or other analyticals to bring out the location of records on a given subject or to be found in part of a miscellaneous file. For instance, no one would be likely to look for information about the silver service presented to the U.S.S. *Illinois* in the records of the Illinois War Council, yet that is the department which preserved the record. Again, the trademarks registered with the secretary of state in the early 1890s were filed with the miscellaneous records of his office, known as the "executive file." What adds to the confusion is that even after the numbered trademark file was started, certain types of trademark records continued to be filed in the "executive file." To remove these records to the trademark file would run the risk of having some court repudiate the records because when last certified to the court they were listed as a part of the "executive file." Such items can be pulled into proper perspective through entries in a consolidated guide. This can most easily be handled through a consolidated card file which we call, not a catalog, but "the reference file."

Sometimes it is desirable to compile a list of contents for each folder in a set. Occasionally bulky records are tabulated for quick reference, as in the case of election returns.

Normally the archivist has occasion to make calendars only

for older records of a miscellaneous nature, principally correspondence files, which will be consulted chiefly for historical purposes. This is in contrast to the manuscripts curator whose interest in individual documents leads him to use the calendar as his catalog. Archival finding mediums are compiled from the point of view of the record group as a unit, not as a description of individual documents.

Servicing the records. The justification for the existence of an archival agency is that records no longer in current departmental use can be produced more efficiently by an archivist who specializes in administrative history and who makes it his business to familiarize himself with outmoded files. Records required for legal use will generally be called for as individual items, those wanted by historians by subject, while genealogical inquiries demand name indexes. Unless the archivist has planned and carried out a proper program of prepared finding mediums, his capacity to give adequate service will break down at some point.

Under American law and practice, any record produced in the course of government business must be open to consultation by anyone, provided the law creating the record does not specify that the information in a given record shall be deemed confidential. Government records are designated as confidential only when the use of the information contained in them would be harmful to an individual, as would happen if, for example, income tax information were divulged; or if national security would be jeopardized by opening military or defense records. When anyone asks for any information from any unrestricted record, for any purpose whatsoever (unless with obvious criminal or libelous intent), it is the duty of the archivist to produce that record for inspection. It is not for him to question the value of the use to which the record is to be put. Many archivists object to genealogical work as requiring a disproportionate amount of time. Insofar as the genealogical inquiries he receives relate to the use of official records rather than to the building up of an admittedly expensive library of genealogical literature, the archivist should be able and willing to give that service also. It is the lack of adequate indexes which slows down his ability to give quick service on genealogy, and it is the archivist's duty to compile those indexes (which will be used for other purposes also) as soon as his resources permit.

Publications. The fact that archives are unique documents and cannot be loaned puts the burden upon the archivist of supplying copies as needed. Photocopy and microcopy are the accepted forms of copies. The copies required may be simple copies supplied to the patron free or at small cost or they may be certified copies for which a fee is specified by law. To permit issuance of certified copies, the archivist is usually provided with a seal which the law specifies shall be judicially recognized.

Historical records in the archives are often edited and printed, either by a full transcription or by a calendar. Sometimes this publication is done by the archives department but where there is an established historical library or commission with an editorial staff, as in the case of our own Illinois State Historical Library, the Archives Department generally does not do the actual publishing though it may cooperate with the editing.

One of the most important divisions in an archival agency is the photographic laboratory. Among the applications of photocopy and microphotography are the following:

1. Supplying copies of records deposited by the various departments for their own use. This work is generally done gratis. The knowledge that they can have copies whenever needed is often an inducement to department heads to relinquish the originals.

2. To obtain copies of records which for one reason or another ire not being transferred to the archives. Copying of departmental indexes, mentioned above, is a frequent application.

3. Making copies for patrons, in order to supply them with facsimiles or to cut note-taking time. The Archives Department generally requires an agreement that these copies shall not be reproduced by print or otherwise without permission. Patrons are occasionally authorized to bring their own cameras to make copies under supervision.

4. Microfilm copies of records made as insurance against complete loss in case of destruction of the originals. Copies of county archives are frequently so deposited in the state archives. In the case of insurance microfilm, the original negative is deemed a master copy and is used only for making contact prints for other use.

5. Substitution of certified photographic copies for public use where the originals are in fragile condition or when there is danger of tampering. The probate clerk of Cook County, for example, microfilms all records as they are received and no paper is deemed legally filed if such a microfilm copy has not been made.

6. Recording by photography. Many types of records do not take effect until they have been registered with and recorded by some governmental agency, most frequently a county official. The saving of the manual labor involved in copying a document and the unimpeachable evidence of a facsimile are making record officials turn more and more to photography for such purposes. Normally the archivist, being a custodian rather than a maker of records, does not do photographic recording. Occasionally, by special arrangement, the photographic laboratory of the Archives Department may be called upon to take the pictures, but acceptance of the photographs as records by affixing a file mark or other means is the responsibility of the department for which the copies are made.

7. Reduction of the bulk of records by substituting microfilm copies for originals. This work is not normally done by the archival agency. Such copy work involves not only handling large quantities of records, but preparing for the work by checking the records for completeness and accurate filing, attaching proper certificates of authenticity and checking the completed films for retakes and omissions. That work is properly the responsibility of the department of origin. Bringing the records to the archives to be filmed involves handling the records twice and calls for special temporary housing facilities. Usually the work is most conveniently done *in situ,* whence the copied records are removed and destroyed immediately. The archivist should hold himself in readiness to render technical advice and may be called upon to approve the quality of

the work. Certain types of records may be microfilmed for office use and the original records placed in the archives for safekeeping. The adjutant general of Illinois made that disposal of World War I soldiers' bonus records.

8. Infrared and violet ray photography is employed to bring out faded, deleted, charred, or otherwise disfigured writing, and for the detection of forgeries.

Advisory services. The above described work of the archivist stems from the duties as custodian of records. His duties in relation to record control are chiefly advisory. Because advice is largely intangible it is not possible to go into much detail as to specific ways of accomplishing his objectives.

The archivist offers to assist other officials of his government on all matters relating to better record making. That may take the form of demonstrations, group conferences, or seminars or planned programs for the reduction of records. Largely, however, the archivist exerts his influence through personal contacts, either casual or through encouraging officials to bring their record problems to him. He helps them analyze their needs, suggests criteria for scheduling records for retention or destruction, helps them design more compact forms, advises them on setting up files, serves as a bureau of information on government functions, and in many other ways tries to make himself useful.

In some states the archivist is required to set standards for papers, ink, typewriter ribbons, and other record material to be used by both state and local officials. State archivists generally have no authority over county and other local officials except that the latter are permitted to transfer older and historical records to the state archives if they see fit. At least one state, Delaware, requires that records prior to a certain date be deposited and many states, notably Connecticut, Maryland, and North Carolina, have been successful in garnering their colonial records. Illinois has a law which prohibits the destruction of county records prior to 1870 and directs that they be deposited with the state archives if the counties cannot care for them. New York has a regular inspection service and can compel local governments to keep their records in approved vaults. The federal government has no jurisdiction over state or local vaults.

The supervisory powers possessed by archivists over the other departments in their own government varies from state to state. The National Archives has the strongest archives law. "All archives or records belonging to the Government of the United States (legislative, executive, judicial, and other) shall be under the charge and superintendence of the Archivist to this extent: He shall have full power to inspect personally or by deputy the records of any agency of the United States Government whatsoever and wheresoever located, and shall have the full cooperation of any and all persons in charge of such records in such inspections, and to requisition for transfer to the National Archives Establishment such archives, or records as the National Archives Council . . . shall approve for such transfer, and he shall have authority to make regulations for the arrangement, custody, use, and withdrawal of material deposited in the National Archives Building: *Provided,* That any head of an executive department, independent office, or other agency of the Government may, for limited periods, not exceeding in duration his tenure of that office, exempt from examination and consultation by officials, private individuals, or any other persons such confidential matter transferred from his department or office, as he may deem wise."[7] This act has been supplemented by acts giving the archivist of the United States broad powers in the matter of approving the destruction of obsolete records and by presidential directives that have strengthened his control over federal records.

No state archives has as great a power over the records of other government officials as does the archivist of the United States. Most of the older archival establishments in this country, including Illinois, have permissive laws which authorize the transfer of noncurrent records if the departments of origin see fit. More recent archival laws generally give archivists certain rights of inspection, and at least require that records of defunct governmental organizations be transferred. Most general records destruction laws recognize the archivist as having a participating interest in the destruction of useless records, though the majority of states have old laws which permit individual departments to destroy specific records after a period of years without the intervention of the archivist. Most destruction laws require submission of lists of records proposed for destruction to the legislative body of the government. Usually such laws permit scheduling of certain categories of records for destruction so that once legislative authorization for a specific classification has been obtained the archives department may authorize future destruction of later records in that class without again going to the legislature.

4

Services and Resources of an Archives

1 / Services of an Archives Department

PROBABLY MOST OF US when we think of archives have a mental picture of an old monk bending over a beautiful illuminated manuscript in the scriptorium of a monastery. Of course we know that state records are not illuminated manuscripts, and those who have followed our exhibits in the state archives are aware that very few of our records are sufficiently photogenic to make an interesting display without much collateral illustrative material. Very few government workers, however, realize to what extent record-making has been revolutionized since the beginning of the last quarter of the nineteenth century, or, what is more important, that until very recently Illinois officials have been handicapped in record making and disposal by obsolete records laws which antedate that revolution.

In the early days of Illinois government, no state office had many employees and the quantity of records produced was very

PART 1 OF THIS CHAPTER, "Services of an Archives Department," was originally published as "The Place of Archives in Government" in *Illinois Libraries* 34 (April 1952): 153–60. Part 2, "Services of an Archives to Business," was originally published as "What the State Archives Can Do for the Business Man" in *Chicago Filing Association Official Bulletin* 9 (November 1940): 17–21.

small. Our slang phrase "Keep that under your hat" refers to the habit of Lincoln and many of his contemporaries of carrying their papers in their "stovepipe" hats much as present-day lawyers and businessmen carry briefcases. There is one amusing instance in Illinois history of a legislative clerk reporting that a gust of wind had blown away both his hat and the enrolled bill which he was carrying in it on his way back from taking the bill to the governor for the latter's signature. The members of the General Assembly were not quite sure how to handle this situation but finally passed a joint resolution explaining what had happened, nullifying the original document, and ordering a reengrossing and resigning of the bill.

Paper and parchment were scarce and expensive. Records were not set down in writing unless they were important. Such records might be called, for want of a better term, "record records." These consist of: first, official documents given as an expression of some legal right, such as deeds and patents for real estate, contracts, bonds, and like instruments; second, registers of facts kept by the government to protect the rights of individuals or of the government, or to record official acts. Examples are registers of wills, marriages, official registers of duly commissioned civil and military personnel, proceedings of official boards and the file of documents presented to those boards for action.

The invention of cheap sulfide paper, of the typewriter, of the mimeograph, and more recently, of punch card tabulators and microfilm have revolutionized record-making facilities. The first nonrag paper appears in Illinois state records shortly before 1840, the first typewritten document found in the archives is dated 1876.

Parallel to these new facilities for making records, there developed increasing complexity in governmental organization. The number of functions to be performed and the rapidly growing number of employees made it increasingly difficult for executives to keep track of what was going on in their offices. Just as manufacturers hit upon the idea of the assembly line as a means of dividing mechanical processes to the point where more people could do more work with less supervision, so administrators turned increasingly to the use of forms and multiple copies of documents as a means of dividing and at the same time controlling the work of their subordinates.

The period of rapid expansion in the creation of records began in the last quarter of the nineteenth century. The National Archives surveys showed that federal records for the period 1917 to 1930 equaled the bulk of all such records from 1776 to 1917, and that the records for the period from 1930 to 1940 equaled the quantity for those two periods together, while World War II piled up records in astronomical proportions. The same story could be told for the state archives of Illinois.

The creation of records was, until quite recently, a matter of expediency. Each new executive demonstrated what a bright young man he was by the number of new forms he devised and the new filing system he installed. Emphasis was all upon how to accomplish today's work most expeditiously, but no thought was given as to how the resultant records could be used in the future. No attempt was made to segregate the ephemeral from the permanent material —everything was filed together.

The inevitable happened—no agency could afford the amount of storage space required to keep everything. Only the executive was capable of sorting the wheat from the chaff, and he had neither time nor inclination to do so. Increasingly, department heads and division chiefs were irritated by the inability of file clerks to produce older records needed for purposes of consultation.

The archives, originally in most states looked upon as a luxury —a place to preserve "historical" documents, was inundated with records in which the departments could not locate needed documents, but which, by some sort of magic, the archivist was supposed to be able to service quickly and efficiently. Soon even the archival system threatened to break down. Many department heads simply closed their eyes to periodical cleaning out of storerooms, despite the section of the criminal code which sets a penalty of from one to seven years in the penitentiary if "any person whatsoever, shall steal, embezzle, alter, corrupt, withdraw, falsify, or avoid [sic] any record. . . ."[1]

This section of the criminal code has come down to us, unaltered, from 1845, written thirty years before the typewriter and its train of record multiplying facilities. If this law were interpreted narrowly, any slip of paper that fluttered into an office would constitute a record. The obvious absurdity of a law which makes no distinction between a clerk's requisition for a pencil and the enrolled constitution of the state, naturally bred contempt toward its observance. We know of no instance where a state official has ever been prosecuted under this act for destruction of records except where he was accused of doing away with a record to cover up an otherwise criminal procedure. However, many an executive has been embarrassed and handicapped by his inability to produce documents which had been inadvertently lost or destroyed.

More precise definitions of the terms "records" and "nonrecord materials" were attempted in the 1951 revision of the State Records Commission. The commission was also authorized by this law to give further interpretations to the term "nonrecord materials."[2]

State officials are now aware of the connection between efficiency in their records system and in their office organization. A new profession, called records management, is emerging. Because this work is so new there are as yet few practitioners. In 1950, Congress passed a law requiring each federal department to employ a full-time records management officer whose duty is to coordinate all records systems in the department and to engineer the records created to the precise needs of the agency. Thus, instead of the old-time sorting out of permanent from obsolete records after the records have accumulated, the records management program will indicate, at the time the records come into existence, which records shall be deemed of permanent value and how long each category of records needs to be retained for administrative purposes. Furthermore, records management sees to it that there are no gaps in the information which should be filed.

We in Illinois are working toward planned records systems, each designed for the needs of the department and implemented by retention schedules which will permit departments to make appropriate disposal of their records as soon as each category of records ceases to have further value for administrative purposes of the department of origin. Such disposal will include transfer of noncurrent records to the state archives, substitution of microfilm copies for originals, and destruction of completely obsolete records. Several departments had secured legislation prior to 1951 which permitted retention schedules for some of their records. It is difficult, however, to define categories of records in sufficient precision for such legislation. Some of these laws were too narrow in scope; some gave dangerously broad powers of decision to administrators who in ordering destruction of records might not take into consideration potential values of records for other than current administrative use.

The Schaefer Commission to Study State Government recommended that the State Records Commission should be enlarged by the addition of representatives of the legal and financial departments of the state, and that this commission review and approve all proposals relating to records destruction.[3] The Sixty-Seventh General Assembly revised the 1943 state records act accordingly. The ex officio members were abolished, the archivist and the state historian are chairman and secretary, respectively, the state librarian was continued as a member and two new members were added, namely, the attorney general and the director of finance. A section was added which reads, "Regardless of other authorization to the contrary, no record shall be disposed of by any agency of the State unless approval of the State Records Commission is first obtained."[4]

Many are familiar with the operation of the Archives Department so that it is unnecessary to elaborate here upon the various functions of that institution. The principal functions of your Illinois archives are 1. the housing of permanent state records in two types of vaults, archival and departmental; 2. advisory services to state and local officials and to other interested parties; and 3. the photographic laboratory which does work not only for the Archives Division but also for all departments of the state library and for the secretary of state's office.

In general, records, which are housed in the archives proper must be consulted at the archives building under the supervision of the archives staff. Records in departmental vaults are subject to the immediate jurisdiction of the departments to which they belong, the departments alone have access to those records, and documents may be removed from the files for departmental office use at the discretion of the department. Many states are confused as to the types of records suitable for transfer to the archives and those which they should place in departmental vaults.

Housing of permanent state records and security microfilm copies of state and county records in the archives vaults (that is, of records placed under the legal custody of the archivist) includes physical care of the records and servicing reference calls for their use. Physical care involves placement in proper filing equipment, keeping the records free from deterioration caused by dirt and deleterious atmospheric conditions and repair where necessary. Reference calls require the making of inventories, guides, indexes, and other finding tools to facilitate rapid service; also a knowledge of the history of the development of the functions of state departments is needed to enable us to understand the objectives and contents of noncurrent records. This specialized acquaintance with older departmental organizations and records, which it is the business of the Archives Department to have, permits more adequate service than can be given by clerks who can only be expected to know present-day procedures.

The advisory services offered by the Archives Department take the form of advice on problems relating to records management and participation in the work of the State Records Commission by the state librarian and the archivist. Advice on records management concerns disposal of records, planning of records, planning of records systems to keep down the bulk, and advice on proposed microfilming projects (what and where applicable, and equipment). Properly speaking, the creation of records is the function of the department and not of the archivist whose principal duty it is to take care of the permanent records entrusted to her. However, until the various departments are able to set up their own records managment programs, the Archives Department is probably in the best position of any to be helpful in such matters. These advisory serv-ives on records to state officials are also available, on request, to county and other local officials. . . .

The microfilm section of the photographic laboratory is equipped with both a portable and a large size machine, the latter taking copies of extra large and bound volumes. Owning our own processing machine and enlargers, we are able to give quick service to patrons desiring copies of archival records. The camera is also used for copying documents for the library where we can only bor-row a copy, also in making copies of rare items for interlibrary loans. We are not equipped to do microfilming for large-scale proj-ects. The making of records on film is, as stated above, the responsi-bility of the department involved, a process of creation, in contradistinction to the process of preservation, the latter function only being that of an archival agency. The microfilming needs of the various departments call for individual study and selection of type of equipment needed to do the particular work contemplated.

Since the records officers of the various departments show some degree of confusion over what types of records are suitable for transfer to the archives building—which types should go to the archives vaults and which types are suitable for transfer to their own departmental vaults—it may be helpful to discuss some of our recommendations in this respect.

First of all, the archives building is not a warehouse. The ex-pensive construction used, fireproofing and other safety devices, air-conditioning and the finest of equipment, limited the size of building which could be erected under available appropriations. We often call the archives building the "safety-deposit box" for state records. To ensure that the more important records shall not be crowded out by trivia, it is necessary to be selective and to limit the records acceptable for housing in the building to permanent, original records.

What types of records are acceptable? The initiative as to whether a certain category of records shall be deposited in the ar-chives vaults (that is, with legal jurisdiction relinquished to the Archives Department), is left to the department to which the records appertain. Legal and use limitations to deposit in the state archives are best understood by the state official concerned. By and large, the following categories of records are considered suitable for transfer to the jurisdiction of the Archives Department. Some of the examples cited might, of course, be listed in more than one of the classifications below.

1. Historical treasures. Examples of such records now in the state archives are the first state constitution (1818), the earliest Cahokia notary record (1737–68), the territorial executive register (1809), the journals of the territorial General Assembly (1812–18), the first census (1818), records of Lincoln's service in the General Assembly, and the enrolled laws starting with 1812 and containing many interesting documents such as the first free school law and early charters of towns, cities, schools, railroads, and businesses. In saying that records of historical importance are suitable for transfer to the archives, it should be noted that the practice of abstracting individual documents from files to put them in the archives is frowned upon, since integrity of files is a basic principle in archival administration. The whole file for the periods covered should be transferred.

2. Records deposited for safekeeping because of their extreme value. Among such records now in the Illinois archives are the constitution of 1870 and the records of the constitutional convention which wrote it; the deeds and abstracts to the real estate which the state owns; the enrolled laws; interstate compacts; corporation reports; and insurance microfilm copies. Some of these records are current records which for obvious or security reasons are in need of special protection. Departments depositing current records may impose reasonable restrictions on use of the records, such as requiring that the department be called upon to secure and issue information from the records.

3. Records still in active use, but for purposes other than administration of the department in which they originated. For instance, the service records of Illinois soldiers in the Civil War are referred to heavily by persons writing family histories, seeking admission into hereditary societies, marking graves, and by other

states completing their GAR records. There is no reason why these records, which have no relation to the civil defense activities which are the main duties of the adjutant general, should be serviced by his staff. To the information found in these records, the Archives Department is often able to add helpful collateral data, saving the patron the necessity of writing to two departments.

The Illinois and Michigan Canal records include among other items, records of sales of canal lands and original field survey notes. These land records are in frequent use by abstract companies and lawyers in clearing titles and dovetail with collateral records from the executive department of the secretary of state's office. The original field notes, often merely penciled notations, are proving invaluable in establishing the state's right-of-way for the new superhighway into Chicago which is to supersede the old canal.

The census records, originally taken to form the basis for apportionment of representation in the General Assembly and the Congress, are now used entirely for genealogical purposes. How we now wish that those who planned the forms had thought of a few additional items which could so easily have been included and which would provide so many missing links in family histories!

When the state architect restored the old Vandalia state house a few years ago, he depended quite largely upon legislative inventories, contracts and allusions in the journals of the General Assembly. The early election records might also be cited as one of many records used now chiefly for historical purposes—and for settling election bets.

4. A fourth type of records suitable for the archives are records having no further administrative use, but with present or potential research value. An excellent example is the series of agricultural statistics taken jointly by the state and federal agricultural departments. These show for each farm in the state the varieties of crops and livestock produced, in what quantity, the sales prices, profits and losses, number of acres, whether the land is owned or rented by the farmer, and other matters. These are of slight interest at present, but we suspect that the economic historian of fifty years hence will be thrilled by this detailed information about the revolu-

tion from corn as the principal Illinois crop to the more diversified farming of today and be able to study the effect of mechanization and other social factors on sizes and ownership of farms.

5. Where microfilm has been substituted for original records for official use, it is sometimes desirable or necessary to preserve the original records, and in that case the archives is the proper place in which to preserve them. Two instances come to mind. The World War I bonus records were badly charred and partially destroyed in the state arsenal fire of 1934. The adjutant general has microfilmed these documents for office use and deposited the originals in the state archives.

The Department of Registration and Education has kept its application files on professional licenses in its department vault in the archives building. Efficient administration demands such frequent consultation of the records that the department is now microfilming the file for office use and depositing the permanent original records in the archives.

6. Inactive records which can be serviced adequately without removal from the archives building. Example of such records are minutes and other records of superseded boards and commissions (such as, minutes of the old Board of Administration) deposited by the Department of Public Welfare; and superseded registers of the predecessors of the Department of Mines and Minerals. The Insurance Department, for instance, has deposited its older, very bulky reports by insurance companies.

It may be of interest to note how the records in the state archives are used. Seventy-six percent of our reference calls relate to state business, 16 percent to family history, 6 percent to history, and 2 percent to advisory services. Under the classification "family history" we include service on military service records from the adjutant general's office, which we have through the Spanish American War. Some of these calls still include pension and civil service status claims, requests from other states for completing their records on Illinois veterans who later lived in those states, and for information useful in marking graves, all of which might properly be added to the list of references for state business. The relatively low percentage of calls for genealogy and history is accounted for by the fact that the Illinois State Historical Library performs many functions ordinarily assumed by the state archival agency.

What sort of records should be deposited in the departmental vaults? As stated above, the records in the departmental vaults are those permanent records still in semicurrent administrative use, over which the department retains immediate jurisdiction. The Archives Department through its chargeout system for the keys issued to authorized clerks, keeps track, for the convenience of the department head, of the goings and comings to these vaults, but the archivist and her staff have no access to these vaults. Records may be removed for office use without any checking with or interference by the archival staff. Some of the many more important state records which the departments have felt need the physical and moral protection of the archives building are the following:

1. Supreme court. Case records, 1818–

2. Civil Service Commission. Case records on state civil service employees.

3. State treasurer. Record of warrants issued; bond registers.

4. Auditor of public accounts. Record of warrants cashed and canceled; the basic land records of the state; the surveys and sales records of the U.S. Land Offices in Illinois; sales of state owned lands.

5. Department of Mines and Minerals. Mine maps (being originals of those used by the Mine Rescue Stations).

6. Division of Architecture and Engineering, Department of Public Works and Buildings. Original plans, specifications, and contracts for state buildings.

7. Department of Insurance. The "official file" on authorizations of insurance companies doing business in Illinois.

8. Teachers' Retirement System. Case records on teachers paying into or receiving benefits under the system.

9. Division of Vital Statistics, Department of Public Health. Original birth and death certificates.

10. Secretary of state as recording officer for the governor. Applications for pardon and commutation of sentence.

11. Adjutant general. Service records for the Illinois National Guard.

2 / Services of an Archives to Business

Both the filing expert and the archivist are primarily interested in documentation—in our ability to produce a given record quickly when it is needed. This implies not merely being able to find a given document in the files, but of being sure that such a record got into the files in the first place.

Before attempting to describe the services of an archives department, it is necessary to be sure that we are all thinking of the same thing when we use the term archives. The relationship between the filing expert and the archivist will next be taken up, particularly from the point of view of what the filing expert can do to add to the effectiveness of records as archives.

First of all it is necessary to emphasize the point that archives are not historical documents—they are not diaries of Civil War heroes, or militia rolls which will prove one's eligibility to membership in a patriotic society, nor are they autographs of the presidents. Archives are business records of a government, a business firm, an ecclesiastical body, or even of an individual, preserved as a memorandum of business transactions, and particularly because they are potential evidence for any court or other legal proceedings which involve matters recorded in such memoranda. These documents may or may not be of interest to the historian. Certainly the majority of the records in the Illinois archives are of no particular interest to present day historians, though of immense legal value.

Government records affect the interests of all citizens as contrasted with the relatively smaller number of persons concerned with the records of a private business corporation. Naturally, therefore, government records tend as they grow older to take on an increasing historical interest. Naturally, also, it is the old records seldom referred to in ordinary official business transactions which come into the archives department in greatest numbers. This means that the use of state records for historical purposes has so overshadowed the conception of archives as legal records that most people forget that the real purpose of the state archives department is to ensure the preservation of those records which involve property and citizenship rights. No government record, at least so far as the Middle West is concerned, is so old that only the historian is interested. The Illinois archives has frequent requests for certified copies, for court use, of documents going back to our earliest territorial period.

Accepting the premise that archives are records of business transactions, it is easy to see how important the filing expert is to the archivist. More and more government officials are turning to these experts for analysis of their record-making functions. This results in better forms as well as more scientific filing systems. The making of such analyses requires a technique of its own, and the wise archivist encourages the employment of such persons instead of attempting to give this service himself.

The two most serious problems of present-day record-keeping are the appalling increase in the bulk of modern records presented for preservation and, conversely, the failure to make records of word of mouth transactions. In the solution of both problems, the filing expert can play a major role. The typewriter and carbon paper have made it easy to duplicate records so that it is not unusual to find copies of the same record in four or five files. It is easier to file everything—routine requests for pamphlets, for instance—than to select for preservation only the most important. One state department cut the bulk of its major series of records in half by a simple redesign of its annual report questionnaire to go into four instead of eight pages. Another state department is combining four forms into one, with a proportionate reduction of its record space requirements. Suggestions for reorganization of routines to permit such reductions of bulk come with better grace from outside efficiency engineers than from the archivist.

A very large part of present-day business is transacted over the telephone or by personal interviews, which means that important matters of policy are frequently decided upon without necessarily being recorded. Executives need simple and positive methods for keeping memoranda of such conversations. Another loss of records results from officials removing official papers with their personal files when they retire from office. Keeping of official files separate from private files through duplicate copies is a simple matter but is seldom practiced. All these matters can be, and usually are, arranged for in the course of the office management expert's surveys.

Illinois completed an archives building in 1938 which now makes it possible to ensure the preservation of the records of the state's business transactions with its citizens. When one considers the nature of those business transactions, the importance of a department which devotes its entire energies to that preservation is manifest.

Under the law, any state or local official may deposit any non-current permanent records in the Archives Department. The State Library encourages local communities to improve facilities for the preservation of their own records. Where records are in danger of destruction because of the inability of local officials to care for them properly, or where local archives contain records of statewide historical interest, deposits of local archives are accepted.

So far as state records are concerned, it is our policy to urge the transfer to the archives building of all state records of a permanent nature which are not in active files. Records turned over to the Archives Department pass into the immediate legal jurisdiction of the archivist and must be consulted in the archives, not subject to withdrawal for departmental use. Naturally, a very large proportion of the semicurrent records must remain under the jurisdiction of the departments which have to remove documents for office use. These semicurrent records are of extreme legal importance, however, and need the physical and moral protection of the archives building. These semicurrent records are housed in a separate series of departmental vaults. The Archives Department exercises a censorship over the categories of records authorized for transfer to the departmental vaults but the individual departments service their own records, being allowed to withdraw and refile documents at will under regulations similar to those used in safety deposit vaults of banks.

Everyone complains of increases in tax bills, but few persons have any conception of the number of services they expect their government to render them. Records are a by-product of government. An attempt to justify their creation and preservation would be an attempt to explain and justify our whole governmental setup, which is obviously not within the scope of this paper. Perhaps, however, a description of a few types of records kept in the Illinois state archives will help to explain why Illinois officials consider such a place so indispensable, and why we cannot, as often suggested, "throw away all those records when they are five years old."

Social Security and Old Age Assistance legislation suddenly made it necessary for many thousands of needy persons to prove their age and citizenship. In Illinois, the first birth registration law went into force in 1878, and this law was only enforced strictly from about 1916 when the State Department of Public Health took over from the counties the function of keeping vital statistics. Candidates for Old Age Assistance have to establish their birth dates from other available records, and the frantic appeals for documentation which could not be supplied were heartbreaking. At least one old man who had been regarded as a model citizen for forty years had to turn to his pardon papers to prove his age. He wrote, "When you read my record, you will know how desperate is my present need, that I must reveal my past to my neighbors." He had been in prison for murder. Perhaps murderers do not deserve our sympathy, but Illinois feels that its citizens should in the future be able to prove their citizenship status through properly kept vital statistics records.

Most people carry some form of insurance. They know in a vague sort of way that the state regulates insurance companies. The state maintains elaborate machinery to protect policyholders, even to the extent of requiring the deposit of securities which could be sold for the benefit of the insured. These securities themselves are not in the archives, but all records pertaining to these deposits are in the Insurance Department vault, along with every document relating to the authorizations of insurance companies to do business in Illinois. Included in the collection are charters, copies of bylaws, amendments to charters and bylaws, sworn reports by companies, and all official correspondence between the companies and the state.

No corporation may do business in the state without the supervision of the Corporation Department of the secretary of state. No stock or bonds of any nature may be sold without approval following investigation by the secretary of state. More than one corporation lawyer has been disappointed to find that the state keeps its correspondence and can refute his statements about what his corporation was allowed to do in certain matters. All these records for the protection of investors and other corporation records are in the archives.

One of the most important departments in the state government is the Department of Registration and Education, which examines and licenses the practitioners of the principal trades and professions. A man's professional life depends upon the completeness and accuracy of the records relating to his qualifications. The Department of Registration and Education takes no chances against their being destroyed or tampered with. These records are in the archives building vaults.

The basis upon which present-day law and order rests is the constitution, the enrolled laws, and the interpretations of them made by the supreme court. The state preserves these records in the archives.

One could go on indefinitely pointing out records produced by state departments which are important to its citizens. . . . The measure of service to the individual businessman depends upon his relations with his government. The state archives building gives assurance that the state can document its side of its business transactions. The ideal toward which the Archives Department is striving is that in the future neither citizen nor state shall ever be called upon to suffer loss because important state records had been lost or destroyed.

5

The Comparison of Archival and

Library Techniques

1 / Archives and Libraries

W_{HAT ARE ARCHIVES} and what is the relationship between archives and libraries?" This is a question frequently asked. . . . There are radical differences between archival and library techniques and also there are overlapping techniques. . . . This . . . series of articles will attempt to explain the difference between archival establishments and libraries and to evaluate the contribution which each can make to the other.

A library is obviously a collection of books, pamphlets, and the like, generally printed, though manuscripts may also be included. The books have been written by numerous authors and the classification interest is generally a subject one. Theoretically, at least,

 ❦ Part 1 of this chapter, "Archives and Libraries," was originally published in *Illinois Libraries* 21 (March 1939): 11–13. Part 2, "Classification and Cataloging," was originally published as "Archives and Libraries: Classification and Cataloging" in *Illinois Libraries* 21 (April 1939): 2–4. Part 3, "Inventories, Calendars, Indexes," was originally published as "Archives and Libraries: Inventories, Calendars, Indexes, etc." in *Illinois Libraries* 21 (May 1939): 9–11. Part 4, "Public Documents," was originally published as "Archives and Libraries: Public Documents" in *Illinois Libraries* 21 (June 1939): 12–14. Part 5, "Reference Work," was originally published as "Archives and Libraries: Reference Work" in *Illinois Libraries* 21 (August 1939): 26–28.

many copies of the books are in existence so that the contents of one library can be, and frequently are, duplicated in whole or in part by other libraries.

An archive is a collection of records and memoranda relating to an individual, a corporation (such as a business house, a church, a fraternal organization), or a governmental agency. The archive comprises chiefly, though not necessarily exclusively, manuscript material, and it relates primarily to the business affairs of the individual, corporation, or governmental body which keeps the records for its own use. The account books, receipts, canceled checks, correspondence file, and the contents of his safety deposit box (stocks, bonds, deeds) comprise the archive of an individual. The documents which record its business transactions comprise the archive of a corporation or a government.

For instance, the archive of the secretary of state's Corporation Department contains the following categories of records:

1. Records of applications and other preliminaries to granting of charters.

2. Records of charters granted to Illinois corporations or permits to outside corporations to do business in the state.

3. Records relating to any proposed and approved changes in corporate status, such as change of name, dissolution, merger, increase or decrease of capital stock, and change in bylaws.

4. Sworn reports filed annually, giving names and addresses of officers and directors and pertinent data for tax assessments.

5. Corporate tax and fee records.

6. Correspondence with or about each corporation.

In its turn the corporation presumably keeps a similar record of its transactions with the state, which comprise a portion of its own archive.

The quality which distinguishes an archive from a library is its uniqueness. In the case of a lawsuit only the original record of the plaintiff or defendant, as the case may be, is valid as primary evidence. Copies unless certified as authentic and exact copies of the original are not acceptable in court. The value of the original, even, is impaired if it has been out of the custody of its own archival agent and therefore might have been tampered with or without his knowledge. Copies, in the absence of the original, if accepted at all are treated as circumstantial evidence.

The fact that archives are primarily business records, kept because of their legal value and potential importance as evidence in a lawsuit, should always be kept in mind in discussing archives. The term "archive" has come to have untrue connotations in popular parlance. To most persons an archive is a collection of historical manuscripts which have been selected from governmental files. It has already been shown that archives are not limited to governmental agencies, though it is with governmental archives only that the Illinois State Library is concerned, and primarily from that point of view that these articles are written.

It is true, of course, that many old governmental records contain material of great historical interest and are seldom consulted in official business. The archivist, however, though he is aware of and exploits the historical aspects of such records, is primarily concerned with their preservation as legal evidence. He knows that a record may not have been needed in official business for fifty years, yet tomorrow it may settle a dispute involving millions of dollars.

The term archive is also frequently used to designate the noncurrent records which are transferred to the archives department. This is a correct use of the word, also, since there is no other generally accepted term for the governmental agency which specializes in the care and preservation of such records. In Illinois we avoid confusion by referring to current records, semicurrent records, and archives; by archives meaning those records transferred by the various state departments to the legal custodianship of the Archives Division.

Having accepted the thesis that an archive is a unique collection of the legal records of one individual, corporation, or governmental agency, and that archives are generally speaking, collections of the noncurrent portions of the various agencies, it is simple to explain the relationship between archives and libraries. The scope and purpose of the archival establishment and the library are different. The attempt to organize the National Archives into a library pattern broke down and was abandoned. Certain fundamental techniques are quite different. The archivist means one thing when he speaks of cataloging and classification, the librarian something entirely different. The unfortunate employment of the same terms to different techniques causes constant misunderstandings between archivists and librarians. The techniques used differ, though there is more overlapping than some archivists admit.

The public served, though it may differ somewhat in personnel, makes little distinction between archives and libraries when it comes to use. If the research worker can find the information he wishes from printed books, well and good. If that information can be found only in a manuscript, or if he needs a manuscript to verify or illuminate a passage in a book, he will turn to the manuscript collection, be it called historical manuscripts or archives. In other words, the average user of the archives thinks of the institution primarily as a reference library and, without personal interest in the techniques used in achieving the results, he wishes to be able to use the library and the archives interchangeably. . . .

2 / CLASSIFICATION AND CATALOGING

Large collections of books or of archives, to be used efficiently, must be grouped together in such a way as to bring together on the shelves or in the filing cabinets those materials which are closely related. They must also be listed in a way which will indicate the exact holdings of the institution and indicate location of any portion of those holdings. This grouping of related materials is called classification and this list of holdings is called the catalog.

At this point the analogy between classification and cataloging in libraries and archives ends. Both librarians and archivists use the terms "classification" and "cataloging," but the basic principles of each technique are radically different.

The library unit is the individual book which may comprise

one or more volumes. Classification of library books is based upon authorship of the book. Books grouped together by the publisher into a unified collection are called "series." Chapters or portions of a book or library series may be cataloged separately, such catalog entries being called "analyticals."

The archival unit is called a "series." Dr. Roscoe R. Hill[1] of the National Archives coined the word "archimon" as a more expressive term for this unit, but this new word has not yet come into common use by archivists. A "series" or "archimon" is a group of materials representing the same functional use, filed as a physical unit. The archival series may consist of one document only, or it may be a file filling many drawers. The state constitution is an example of a one document series; a correspondence file is an example of a series comprising thousands of individual documents.

The classification of archives is based upon the principle of provenance. This is, all items relating to the business of the agency (individual, corporation, or governmental agency, hereafter designated as "department") which made the archives a part of its records are grouped together under one classification. Within departments there is a subclassification by governmental function represented, not by subjects.

The main archival catalog entry is always the official name of the department. The name of the department in which the documents were filed as a part of its recorded business, not the source from which the individual documents originated, is used for the main entry. Thus, an original letter from the governor to the secretary of state would be classified and the main catalog entry made as a part of the archive of the secretary of state and not under the governor as author. The catalog entry would read (in part):

    Secretary of State
       Correspondence

If this document were deemed of sufficient importance to be given a separate catalog entry, it would be cataloged as an analytical to the series:

Governor
> Letter to Secretary of State [etc.]
> (In Secretary of State. Correspondence [etc.])

Archival classification must precede cataloging since the classifier gives the form of the main entry to the cataloger. Archival classification is much more difficult than library classification.

The librarian has only to fit the books he is classifying into a preconceived scheme, but the archivist has to construct his classification scheme anew to fit the different types of records kept by each department. The fact that governmental organization changes frequently and the types of records varies with such fluctuations makes the task of the classifier exceedingly difficult.

Some of the more frequent problems encountered by the classifier are as follows:

1. The department may be abolished and its functions discontinued.

2. The department may be abolished in part or in whole; its functions may be divided among several departments. The work may be continued by an existing or a newly created department.

3. The name or location of a department or institution may be changed with or without a reorganization of its functions.

4. A private institution may be taken over as a governmental organization or vice versa.

5. A department may be shifted from one major agency to another.

6. The functions of a department may decline in importance or may disappear, with or without a repeal of enabling legislation; new functions may be taken on with or without legal sanction.

7. The functions of a department may be taken over in whole or in part by a higher or lower government.

8. The same series may persist through any or all of the above changes in departmental organizations.

9. Most series start as miscellaneous files of all records of a department, later being broken up into a number of separate series.

10. A series may be combined with a later series, or it may be

discontinued or the contents may be thrown back into a general series, as functions decrease and decline in importance.

Classification should not be confused with filing. Most series come to the archives already filed. True, it is sometimes necessary to do considerable refiling, but that is the file clerk's job. By classification is meant the relating of series to each other. One department may have from a dozen to a hundred or more series.

Perhaps in no other division of work are divergences in technique and backgrounds greater than in archival and library classification departments. The archival classifier must primarily be a specialist in governmental administration. Training in the history and philosophy of library classification may be helpful in stimulating his imagination, but a knowledge of library classification from the point of view of its application has little practical value to him.

Archivists are still experimenting with cataloging methods. European archivists usually content themselves with a descriptive inventory or guide to their holdings. This may vary from the briefest summary list to a full calendar digesting the information contained in all individual documents in the collection. American archivists, dealing with more recent and bulky materials, find the European type of guide inadequate and the calendar too detailed and expensive. They have to make frequent insertions to account for new accessions, especially in the case of series kept currently by the various departments, portions of which are transferred to the archives department at appropriate intervals.

American archivists are adopting the principles of the library card catalog for archival cataloging. The archival unit of entry is the series rather than the book, and the main entry is under department of origin rather than author. Despite these differences, they feel that the archival catalog should, so far as possible, follow a pattern similar to that of a library catalog.

Persons accustomed to library practices can then use the archivist's bibliographical tools with the minimum of confusion. The Illinois State Library catalog rules for archives published in mimeographed form in 1938 was submitted to the Society of American

Archivists by its Committee on Cataloging and Classification as a tentatively approved code.[2]

The Illinois State Library rules are based upon library cataloging codes and symbols so far as possible. The items on an archival catalog card vary from those given on a library card because of differences in the nature of the materials. In form, however, the card is so similar to a library card that the average user is scarcely conscious of the difference. The most noticeable variations are:

1. The substitution of a departmental entry using the name of the department in which the documents were filed, instead of the author entry.

2. Insertion between the main and title entries of classification words indicative of function and subject.

3. The substitution of a date and quantity note for the imprint and collation.

4. The difference in detail and contents of the bibliographical notes.

Individual documents or allied groups of records in a general series are cataloged as analyticals. Filing in the catalog is as follows: 1. departmental entry; 2. functional entry; 3. date.

Subject and other secondary entries and cross-references in general follow library practice. The H. W. Wilson subject headings are generally found to be more applicable to archival cataloging than the Library of Congress list.

The subject of archival cataloging is so new to American archivists that it is still too early to evaluate the contributions which archival and library catalogers can make to each other. Few archivists have had a background of library training, the historians having to date, probably quite properly, preempted the field of archives. Further experimentation will be necessary before one can say how closely the two techniques will parallel each other in the future. It is significant that the two archival institutions in this country which have made the most study of archival cataloging—the National Archives and the Illinois State Library—both have catalog departments headed by library trained catalogers.

3 / INVENTORIES, CALENDARS, INDEXES

An interpretation of the work of an archival establishment to librarians implies a description of other mechanical aids besides the catalog required for reference use.

The archivist must be informed not only as to the records already in his custody, but also he must know what supplemental records are or should be in existence. He must know what records have been required by law to be kept at various periods by the various governmental agencies. He must know the legal disposal of the archives of discontinued departments. If the archives are incomplete he should, if possible, know whether they are in private or public repositories. If destruction of records has occurred he wishes to know, if possible, under what circumstances the destruction took place. He should know whether and where copies of any records exist, either in printed or photographic form. His classification scheme, like that of the librarian, must be broad enough in scope to accommodate new accessions, without drastic revision. Such a classification he can make only if he knows all the ramifications of the various laws requiring the keeping of records.

For the above information the archivist relies upon two basic tools: the history of the administrative functions of his government and the inventory. His knowledge of administrative history he gains partly by experience but largely from an intensive study of session laws, court decisions, and departmental reports. The Illinois archivist has been working for several years on a digest of session laws relating to the history of state administration. A complete bibliography has been compiled for every state department and of the various laws which each was required to enforce, including the regulation of functions antecedent to their enforcement by the particular department being studied. For instance, pure food and drug laws enforced by courts on individual complaint later were enforced as a part of the functions of the present Department of Agriculture. A digest of pertinent laws through 1848 has been compiled. This historical digest will be brought up to date and cross-indexed, giving notes as to court decisions, government reports, and the like, affecting administration of the laws. This compilation will form a veritable encyclopedia of Illinois administration. The Constitutional Convention Bulletins issued by the Illinois Legislative Reference Bureau for the use of the Constitutional Convention of 1920–22; the report of the Illinois Committee on Efficiency and Economy for 1915; and articles in certain departmental reports are also useful in this respect.

The Historical Records Survey of WPA published brief summaries of county administration as it related to the keeping of records in the introductions to its county inventories series. From such studies the archivist is able to construct a theoretical classification scheme which will provide a place for every type of record required by law. The value of these digests for miscellaneous reference use is also manifest.

The inventory is the first step taken by the archivist in preparation for the accession of archives. Librarians are familiar with the inventories of county archives now being published in all states by the Historical Records Survey. These inventories list all records found, with locations and full descriptions of quantity, dates, contents, and so on. The survey is also inventorying state archives, but few of these have as yet been published. A similar WPA survey of federal archives outside of Washington was directed by the National Archives, which also took an inventory of the records in Washington itself.

With a summary of the inventory before him, the archivist checks the items which in his judgment would be suitable for transfer to the archives. The department head likewise checks his inventory and the final decision as to transfers is decided upon between them in a series of interviews. Some states authorize or even require the transfer of all records more than ten years old; others, as Illinois, leave the date to the discretion of the parties to the transfer, who decide upon the basis of frequence and nature of use to which the records are subjected.

From this checked inventory, a shelflist is compiled showing exactly where each item to be transferred is located in the vaults of the department of origin. This list is sent first to the classification department which fits the series into its classification scheme and makes a tentative allocation of space for each series in the archives vaults. Copies of this list then go to the department transferring records, to the clerk in charge of the archives receiving room, and to the classification department.

This preliminary list is then checked with the records actually received, and a receipt is issued in triplicate—one copy going to the director of the department, one to the head of the division making the transfer, and the third retained by the archivist. Subsequent corrections found necessary are issued in triplicate and distributed the same way, with the request that they be affixed to the original receipt. The file of receipts constitutes the accession list.

A shelflist inventory cross-indexed shows the exact holdings of the Archives Department. In the Illinois archives three copies of this perpetual inventory are kept up to date by the classification department. One copy is kept in the reference room, one in the classification department, and one in the archivist's office.

Small archival establishments use this shelflist inventory as a substitute for the card catalog. Except for the use of analyticals and the more detailed subject references of the card catalog, and in fact, for most routine reference work, this shelflist inventory is sufficient even in the Illinois archives. . . .

Anyone who has attempted to find information in unindexed county histories of the seventies and eighties, which are replete with invaluable information almost impossible to locate, will appreciate the problem of the archivist. All archival material is like a library of unindexed books. No matter how detailed his catalog or how accurate and elaborate the filing systems used, the full contents of the series must be brought out further by indexes.

There are two types of indexing in general use in archival establishments—the calendar and the index. The calendar is a full description of each document in the series. It is most frequently employed for the older and more historical material, especially correspondence files. A calendar card shows the date of the documents, by whom written and where, to whom addressed, and it gives a summary of the contents or a list of topics discussed, the number of pages, and uses symbols such as A.L.S., D.S., and so on, to indicate whether the entire document or merely the signature is in the handwriting of the author, whether it is a copy, and the like. Such calendars are usually arranged by date, with an index to names and subjects. These calendars may be on cards or in book form.

The purpose is to help the user to locate a specific document without reading through the entire file. Most older archival establishments, especially those dealing with the relatively few documents prior to 1800, use the calendar as a substitute for a catalog. Calendars are standard in all manuscript (in a nonarchival sense) collections. The Library of Congress Manuscript Division and the Minnesota Historical Society have issued manuals of instruction for making calendars and catalogs for private papers.

Indexes may take the form of separate indexes to each series or allied groups of series, either in volume or card form. Such indexes are essential for proper reference to the records and are genrally compiled by the department to which the records appertain and are sent to the archives along with the records themselves. If no such indexes exist the archives department has to compile them.

There are also general indexes which the archivist compiles to facilitate reference from a broader point of view, generally historical. For instance, the Illinois archives has a consolidated name index which has a card for every allusion to each name found in the records prior to 1850. This card gives a digest of the biographical information found in the document with, of course, a correct citation.

These cards, filed by the soundex system, a code which brings together names pronounced alike despite errors in spelling, furnish a surprising amount of information, despite the fact that state records unlike county records are supposed to yield little biographical and almost no genealogical information. Indexes to place names, subjects, and dates are also of value.

Such are the chief records of holdings kept by the archivist.

4 / PUBLIC DOCUMENTS

In no other field do archival and library interest more overlap than in that of public documents. By public documents here is meant any literature published at the expense of the government. . . . This publication may take the form of printed matter, planographing or other form of "near print," multigraphing or mimeographing, anything which may imply a number of copies. Printed blank forms for office use are not included, nor are carbon copies.

Public documents in a library ordinarily are treated more or less like other reference books, cataloged and classified by subject. The archivist, however, regards public documents from other points of view, based, as in the case of his manuscript archives, upon the method and reason for the production of these publications.

From the archivist's point of view, public documents published by his government fall into the following categories:

1. Archives transcribed and published in their entirety by the government contemporaneously, as in the case of legislative journals or sessions laws. Such a document generally bears a printed facsimile of an attestation from the secretary of state that it is a true and correct copy, and this printed copy is generally acceptable by the courts as primary evidence. Errors creep into the best edited of volumes and certified copies from the originals are sometimes demanded in addition. Printed documents of this type are used for general reference work in the archives department to save wear and tear on the original copy. Such volumes are cataloged and classified along with and beside the original.

2. Archives transcribed and published later by the archives department, the state historical agency, or perhaps privately printed. Such printed copies do not have the legal force of originals, and are used in archival reference because of the greater convenience of the printed page and to save wear and tear on originals. Editorial notes and indexes also add to their value to the user. Such printed materials, which may or may not be public documents, are likewise cataloged and classified with the originals. Examples of such

publications are the governor's letter books, the constitutions, the census records, and such, printed in the Illinois Historical Library's "Collections"; many of the letters from the letter books of Ninian Edwards, territorial governor, printed in N. W. Edwards's "History of Illinois"; the secretary of state's 1898 reprint of territorial session laws; and the printing of the early Canal Commissioners' reports in the 1900 report of the trustees of the Illinois and Michigan Canal.

3. Records filed as archives in printed form: (a) These records may be unique copies, as in the case of the proposed constitution of 1922 printed on parchment. Had this constitution not been rejected by vote of the people, this copy would have been official constitution of the state. (b) One copy of a more or less extended edition is filed as the official report, and this, properly though not necessarily stamped with the official file mark, becomes an archival document. Legislative commissions generally make their reports in printed form and the printed reports may or may not be accompanied by supplemental manuscript proceedings of hearings, exhibits, and so on. In all such cases, such a printed document, whether unique or a selected copy, is classified, cataloged, and filed as a manuscript archive, and may be certified to as other archives.

4. Office manuals, rules and regulations, and instruction sheets relating the departmental procedure whether in printed or the more customary mimeographed form, should be included in the archive of the department in which it originated. In case these regulations are included in the minutes of a board which adopted them, certifications would be properly made from the minute book itself. Frequently, however, the mere publication of the regulations marks the putting of them into force. In such cases, one copy is filed as the official copy for purposes of certification. This copy is likewise classified and cataloged as an archive. The rules and regulations for the classified service published by the civil service commission is an example of this type of document-archive.

5. Bulletins and popular treatises issued as a part of a department's publicity. Examples of this type of document are bulletins on the care of infants and children and popular articles on health issued by the Department of Public Health; books and leaflets de-

scriptive of state parks and highway maps issued by the Department of Public Works and Buildings; bulletins on home economics, poultry raising, native Illinois trees, and a host of other publications, popular and scientific, issued by the various state departments. In one sense such publications may not be archives since they do not relate to specific items of business which might call for certifications. However, the publicity division of each department is an increasingly important link in the departmental machinery and the publications issued properly form part of the archive of its publicity division.

6. Reports. Each elective and administrative officer of the state government is required by law to file a biennial report with the governor for transmission to the General Assembly. These biennial reports may be supplemented by special reports made at the request of the governor or the General Assembly. Reports of legislative commissions have also been discussed under (3). Such reports form a part of the archives of the General Assembly with which they are filed. Most archivists do not regard a biennial report made by a department as a part of the archive of the department which printed it, since the report is based upon the archive or business records of a department and is not, except in the case of occasional exerpts, a transcription of the original documents themselves. In reference work, however, the printed reports are used with the original documents. The summaries and tabulations given in the printed reports not only allow saving of wear and tear on originals, but being in condensed form are a great saving in time in reference use. In one recent reference problem an attorney called for records which would involve handling one thousand volumes of bound manuscript reports; forty volumes of printed reports in which much of the information sought had been tabulated reduced the number of original record volumes consulted to less than two hundred.

The fact that public documents are used from a somewhat different point of view when referred to as archives, than when used in ordinary library reference work, has been taken into consideration in the Archives Division of the Illinois State Library.

Where public documents form a portion of the archive of a given department, the official copy is filed with and treated as a part of the archive of the department for classification and cataloging purposes.

A second copy is placed in what is known as the document archive, for which an attempt is being made to procure one copy of every publication ever issued by Illinois. Where only one copy is to be had, that unique copy (unless specifically earmarked by a file mark as a part of a departmental archive) goes into the document archive. The document archive is classified and cataloged by department of issuance.

The catalog cards are similar to library cards, except that a type word (such as "journal") is inserted before the first word of the title to bring similar material together. Under type words the cards are filed by date, serial cards preceding cards for individual documents. Such a filing and cataloging scheme might well be substituted by general libraries for the usual cumbersome alphabetical-by-title system.

For quick reference use, the Archives Division reference library has another file of session laws, legislative journals, and biennial reports shelved and cataloged as serials, in contradistinction to the broken sets scattered through the archives classification. . . .

5 / REFERENCE WORK

Reference work in various archival establishments varies as much as that in various types of libraries. Some archival agencies are primarily historical libraries with a relatively few archival items treated like private historical manuscripts. Some archival agencies have custody of the older records only which are used largely in historical research. Others . . . service the records of one department only. Still others, like Illinois, have relatively recent records which are used most frequently for legal and departmental purposes. All have three distinct types of reference work, varying in quantity with the relative amount of records servicing each class. These primary uses are departmental (that is by governmental officials), legal (by attorneys and other governmental patrons), and historical.

Library reference experience is of small assistance to the archivist. To be sure, he needs to know the standard general reference library tools, such as catalogs, encyclopedias, dictionaries, statistical and other yearbooks, atlases, also the standard works on history and the social sciences. There are no "Wilson guides" or similar analytical indexes for archives, nor can there be for the contents of one archival depository are not duplicated elsewhere. The archivist must know the history of his country, state, or province in detail, and especially the history of administration in his government. He makes indexes and then more indexes, but in addition he must have that intimate knowledge of the contents of his archives to be gained only from having handled them personally and repeatedly.

It is obviously impossible for any one person to be a specialist on every group of documents in the archives. Therefore it is desirable to build up a group of specialists within the archival organization which is done by making one person responsible for each major group of records. That person handles his special group of archives from the making of preliminary inventories, checking in of records, classification and final arrangement, to catalog notes and indexes. For instance, in the Illinois archives one clerk specializes on corporation and executive department archives, another on election and general assembly archives, and so on. Routine calls pertaining to such records are handled by the assistant on duty in the reference room, but out-of-the-ordinary calls are referred to the person in charge of the records of the appropriate department.

The most common form of reference calls . . . come from the departments in which the records originated. These calls relate to checkbacks on documents required in current work. All routine matters coming through the mail are referred back to the appropriate department for a reply, even though the Archives Division supplies the data. So far as practicable, visitors to the archives building requesting such information are referred to the department which obtains the replies for them. This is not only a courtesy to the department but relieves the Archives Division of the onus of giving out improper or possibly erroneous information. Inquiries coming through the departments generally involve calls for specific documents by clerks requiring little or no assistance in using the material. Records in the Illinois archives proper are not allowed to be taken from the building, but records in the departmental vaults are serviced exclusively by the appropriate departmental clerks. Some departments keep clerks in the archives building to service their records, others send clerks as needed. Ordinarily records taken from the departmental vaults are taken back to the departmental office for use though the archives reference room may be used for their consultation under the supervision of a departmental clerk.

Attorneys and other nongovernmental persons make frequent use of archives as legal documents. Sometimes the inquirer asks to see a specific document. More frequently he states his problem and asks for assistance in documenting his point. Here a detailed knowledge of governmental organization, past and present, is essential. The average person does not know, for instance, that the Tax Commission which was created in 1919 was preceded by the State Board of Equalization, and that the records of that board must be sought not among those of the Tax Commission but of the auditor of public accounts who was secretary of the board. Besides this intimate knowledge of governmental organization the reference archivist must have a certain facility in the use of legal terminology and be able to interpret the meaning behind legal verbiage. Theoretically a lawyer would make a good archivist, though there is only one state archivist at present who is an attorney.

The most frequent and delicate legal questions brought to the archives department involve the interpretation of the wording of the law, or as the constitution puts it, "the obvious intent of the law." The archivist can be helpful here, but he must avoid assuming the prerogatives of the attorney general or of the courts by putting his own interpretation upon the law. He must limit himself to producing all possible documents relating to the passage of the law—petitions, resolutions, the original and amended bill, committee proceedings and reports, transcripts of hearings, debates, legislative journals, veto messages, enrolled laws, and the like. The Illinois archives is greatly handicapped in this sort of reference work by the fact that unlike Congress, the Illinois General Assembly seldom transcribes committee hearings or files committee proceedings.

The third major type of archival reference work is for historical purposes. The quality and quantity of such use is of course dependent upon the historical importance of the archives in the institution. Some archival agencies do historical work almost exclusively. Illinois has a strong historical library, and the Illinois archives are, for the most part, of too recent date to be of much present-day historical interest. Genealogical and general historical inquiries not involving the use of primary source material are, therefore, referred to the Illinois State Historical Library. The historical importance of the collection will soon be enriched by photographic copies of early county records, a project which in all probability will get under way this autumn. Students of social trends are of course finding the state archives of increasing importance as more and more functions of social import are being undertaken by the state.

The technique required for historical reference work calls for a scholar thoroughly trained in the social sciences and historical methods. American archivists have relatively little need for the paleography and diplomatics required for the use of ancient European records, nor for colloquial and dialectical foreign language documents. Illinois, for instance, has only a few documents in eighteenth-century French and nineteenth-century German, all other documents being in English. As soon as the archivist begins gathering transcripts of archives predating the beginning of his state and territorial government, however, he needs to be able to handle these auxiliary sciences. He may not have to date a document by the style of handwriting but he must be as alert to detect forgeries and anachronisms and to fix dates from paper, inks, and styles of penmanship as the mediaevalist. Certainly he needs the critical and analytical methodology of the professional historical writer.

Just how much assistance the archivist should be expected to give the historical student in his researches is, of course, a delicate question for the librarian also. Certainly the archivist with his specialist's knowledge of the contents of his records should be expected to direct the student to all available types of source material, to give him the necessary background for its interpretation, and to render him occasional assistance in the deciphering of obscure words and phrases. He should be also equipped to furnish necessary photographic copies. The archivist should not, though he often finds it necessary to do so, have to suggest methodology nor should he be expected to make detailed translations of foreign languages or obsolete terms. Increasingly, scholars in the social science field are turning to archival source materials, yet very few graduate schools seem to be giving even elemental training in the techniques of the use of manuscript materials. This fundamental training the reference archivist must be able to supply unobstrusively, yet soundly, where it is lacking.

The use of archival material for casual historical reference is similar to the use of libraries for the same type of library inquiry. Ordinarily the inquirer is satisfied with or prefers a printed account. So-called amateur historians who do wish to use original documents are frequently surprisingly thorough in their search and familiar with the sources, if occasionally unsound in the conclusions they draw from their studies. The reference archivist is amply repaid for the little effort he expends upon such persons by the enrichment of his own historical knowledge which he gains from them.

The genealogist is generally the most frequent visitor to the archives department and frequently its most articulate friend. As with the librarian, however, the archivist must adopt a firm policy with respect to the relative amount of staff time which may be devoted to genealogical research. The Illinois State Library has at present only state archives in its collection, and state archives, though yielding a certain amount of biographical material, contain almost no genealogical data. A descriptive list of all names appearing in the Illinois state records to 1850 is being made, and, in general, staff reference work in genealogy is restricted to information to be found on these name cards. . . . Most archival departments have corresponding restrictions on the amount of genealogical work which they can do.

6

The Classification and Description

of Archives

1 / Arrangement and Classification of Archives

The Illinois State Library, of which the state archives is a department, has for its province the care of official records only —the archives of the state and local governments. Private papers, such as church, business, and family records are collected by the Illinois State Historical Library, an entirely separate institution. Space requirements limit the present discussion to the classification of the state archives only.

Archival classification is based upon departmental organization, not upon subject relationships as in the case of library classification. This principle is variously called *provenance* or *le respect pour les fonds*. Briefly, this means that the documents kept by each department as its record of its business activities are kept together,

⤳ Part 1 of this chapter, "Arrangement and Classification of Archives," was originally published as "Classification in the Archives of Illinois" in A. F. Kuhlman, ed., *Archives and Libraries: Papers Presented at the 1940 Conference of the American Library Association Representing the Joint Program of the Committee on Archives and Libraries of the A.L.A., the Conference on Historical Societies, the Midwest Members of the Society of American Archivists, the Historical Records Survey, and the Committee on Bibliography of the A.L.A.* (Chicago: American Library Association, 1940), pp. 78–92. Part 2, "Name Indexes," was originally published in *Illinois Libraries* 28 (April 1946): 217–25.

apart from those of all other departments, and grouped in a manner to reflect the administrative use of those documents. For example, the original of a letter from the governor to the secretary of state will be found in the correspondence file of the secretary of state, the recipient, because that letter is his legal justification for anything he may do in relation to instructions contained in the letter. The letterpress or carbon copy, on the other hand, forms a part of the governor's archives as his record of the transaction. The letter (or copy) should be found in the correspondence, not in a general subject file.

A further exposition of this rule will be found in *Manual for the Arrangement and Description of Archives* by the Dutch archivists S. Muller, J. A. Feith, and R. Fruin. The first English translation, by Arthur H. Leavitt of the National Archives, has been published.[1] The results of a violation of the principle of provenance in the Canadian archives are graphically portrayed in an article by David W. Parker in the 1922 report of the American Historical Association.[2]

Just as the book is the library unit which must be put into classification relationship with other books, so the series is the archival unit which must be related to other archival series in the classification. A series is a grouping of allied documents, arranged as an administrative entity by the department. Although it is difficult to state a satisfactory definition for the term "series," in practice it is rather simple to recognize a series as such. Series generally have descriptive titles, such as the "executive file" or the "brokers file." A series may take the form of bound volumes, unbound documents, cards, plats, or other form of records, or it may be made up of a mixture of several forms. It may comprise one document only, the constitution for example, or it may contain thousands of documents, as in the case of a correspondence file. The main characteristic of the series is that it represents a grouping based upon administrative convenience rather than upon a functional grouping. To avoid confusion between the library term "series" which means something quite different from an archival "series," Dr.

Roscoe R. Hill of the National Archives has coined the word "archimon." Since this term has not yet been accepted by archivists, the old term "series" is used throughout this study.

The archivist who understands the principle of *le respect pour les fonds* would no more consider breaking up a series to throw all records into a purely subject or functional classification than a librarian would think of cutting up a unique copy of a book in order to add certain sections to a subject file.

There are several factors in the classification of archives: (a) relationships between archives of different governments (as between those of the state and of the county, for instance); (b) relationships between the major departments, and in turn between departments and subdepartments; (c) relationships between the various series which make up the archives of each department; (d) the arrangement of individual documents within the series—the filing system; and (e) the finding symbol or call number. With the first of these factors, the relations between governments, we are not concerned here, since this discussion is limited to state archives.

Before the archivist can construct his classification scheme he must have an intimate knowledge of the structure of his government—of its history, present organization, and likely future trends. This he learns partly through handling the records and from reports and other memoranda compiled by the departments themselves. Fundamentally, however, this knowledge is gained from an intensive study of the session laws. He should have at hand a historical digest of the laws and supreme court decisions relating to each department. This digest will outline tersely, with citations for each department, the following information:

1. The legal name of the elective officer, board, commission, department, or institution, and the legal name of the governing board for each department or institution.

2. The date and nature of its creation (whether by the constitution, resolution, act, executive decree, and the like).

3. The name of its immediate predecessor.

4. All variations in names, with dates of change.

5. The composition of the administering body, the number

of members, how they are appointed or elected, their qualifications, tenure of office, and dates of any changes in organization.

6. A list of incumbents, with dates of office.

7. The major duties, rights, and powers, especially such as result in records, with dates of major changes, particularly of code revisions.

8. The specific record-making duties. The exercise of all powers result in records, but the laws frequently specify that certain records be kept or reports filed by or with the department; these should be enumerated.

9. The date of abolition, absorption into some other department, or other reorganization.

10. The name of the successor.

11. The disposition of records on the abolition or reorganization into other departments.

This historical digest, most conveniently arranged in alphabetical form, lists all state governmental agencies, but does not reveal the relationships between them, which is the next step in the construction of the classification scheme.

The introductions to the inventories published by the Historical Records Survey give this information for county departments.

The librarian who has struggled with the subject of corporate entry for printed government documents has some conception of the problem of the archivist who must base his classification upon the shifting sands of governmental organization. If changes in governmental organization resulted in corresponding breaks in series, the classification of archives would offer few problems. The records of each department would be kept together, and the departments arranged alphabetically or grouped to show departments performing related functions. Since records are by-products of administration and since the administration of the laws are not as a rule interrupted by changes in governmental organization, the same series may persist through a number of departmental changes. For instance, the principal series of the present Insurance Department was started in 1851 and has been continued as a single unbroken series under the successive administrations of the auditor of public accounts, superintendent of insurance, Department of Trade and Commerce, and Insurance Department.

In compiling a classification scheme, no distinction is made between those records already transferred to the archives repository and those which remain in the custody of the department. Some of the records may never come to the archives; if they do, a place has been provided for them in the classification; even if they are never transferred, their relationship to allied records is made clear.

We have started with the present organization of the state government as the basis for the classification by departments. The first division is by legislative, judicial and administrative departments. The administrative departments are headed by the elective state officers: the governor, lieutenant governor, secretary of state, auditor of public accounts, state treasurer, superintendent of public instruction, and attorney general. Each of these officials, except the lieutenant governor who is not, as such, a producer of records, has under him a number of administrative departments. The governor, as supreme executive officer of the state, naturally has the most elaborate organization of subordinate departments. These fall into two main categories: the "code offices" and independent boards and commissions. The code offices are major departments each under a cabinet officer with the title of director. The major departments in turn have subdepartments: divisions; fact-finding boards; scientific surveys; and state educational, charitable, and penal institutions. The independent boards and commissions include such permanent bodies as the Civil Service Commission and Illinois Commerce Commission, and temporary commissions such as the Illinois Emergency Relief Commission. *Ad hoc* commissions to make fact-finding inquiries or to draft legislative codes for the General Assembly are classified under the General Assembly.

It is a rule in government that records follow functions. That is to say, when a department is abolished, merged into another department, or otherwise reorganized, its functions are generally transferred to another department, which of course must have the old records at hand to carry on the old functions. When both the department and its functions are abolished, it is customary for the law to direct that the records of the old department be deposited in some existing department. For that reason, the present administrative organization forms the proper basis for the classification.

A genealogical chart for each present department is helpful in understanding how certain records have got into the archives of the various departments. It will also show the archivist what records should be found in each department and help him to classify correctly any records which belong elsewhere but by chance have been deposited in the archive of some other department. For instance, a recent inventory of the vaults of the auditor of public accounts included several volumes of military records of a type never required to be made by the auditor. The genealogy showed that the adjutant general has been required to keep such a record and a check of his inventory showed these volumes filled a gap in one of his series. The archive of the defunct Board of Public Works was directed by law to be deposited with the state treasurer. At some time during the final checking of accounts, all these records had been taken to the auditor's vaults, where they have been left. When and if these records are transferred to the Archives Department, they will be classified as annexes to the state treasurer's archive, in whose custody the law places them, despite one hundred years of adverse possession and a receipt to the auditor of public accounts.

The second rule with respect to the classification by department is that records shall be considered as being a part of the archive of the last department which exercised the function. In other words, a discontinued series relating to the administration of insurance would be classified as a record of the present-day Insurance Department even through no additions has been made to the series since the auditor was superintendent of insurance. Any action involving the content of that series which might arise today would be referred to the present Insurance Department, not the auditor. The auditor's relationship to the series would be brought out in the *catalog* not the *classification*.

On the other hand, many series legally found in the archives of the various departments are there in a purely custodial relationship. The archive of the Board of Public Works referred to above is a clear-cut example. It would properly be classified under the general classification of state treasurer, but as an annexed subdepartment. The question as to when a discontinued series shall be classified as a part of the archive of a present day department sometimes involves subtle distinctions. If the general function has descended to the present department, the series is classified as a part of the archive of the present department. If the function has disappeared so far as the present department is concerned, we classify the series in the archive of the last department which had that function and treat the department as an annexed department under the present department. For instance, the auditor of public accounts was clerk of the Commission of Claims from 1877 to 1903, at which time the Court of Claims was created with the secretary of state as an ex officio clerk. Since the findings of the old commission had been acted upon by the General Assembly of 1903, it was unnecessary for the records to be transferred to the new court and they remained in the custody of the auditor. The records of the Commission of Claims obviously would be classified under the commission as an annex to the auditor's archive. The same classification would be made if this commission had happened to be a mere discontinued administrative division under the auditor.

So far, we have on paper a classification scheme into which all existing records can be neatly pigeonholed. But what will happen to the classification scheme when and if parts of the government are again reorganized? This has happened since 1917 and it will surely happen again. The Department of Conservation was created in 1925 as successor of the Division of Game and Fish of the Department of Agriculture; recently there has been some agitation for its return to division status. That same year the Department of Purchases and Construction was created to take over some of the functions of the Department of Public Works and Buildings; in 1933 it was abolished and part of its divisions were returned to their old department while others were added to the Department of Finance. The present Department of Insurance was a division under the Department of Trade and Commerce from 1917 to 1933, when the latter department was abolished and succeeded by the Insurance Department. Some of the Trade and Commerce Department divisions followed the Insurance Division into the new department, while some were transferred to the Departments of Agriculture and Finance, respectively.

A study of the nature of departmental reorganizations reveals the fact that the basis for changes was always a shifting of functions, and that for the most part those functions are fairly well expressed by division or subdepartment headings. Therefore, a classification which will keep as a collection unit the records of these subdepartments will permit shifts between code or other major departments without ruining the classification system. Therefore, though we are classifying together the records of the minor departments under their appropriate major departments, we are expressing that superclassification as a paper classification only and not using symbols to express it in call numbers or on folders. We talk today about the archive of the auditor of public accounts when discussing the archive of his banking division, but we shall not have to make radical readjustments in anything but speech if tomorrow we have to talk about the newer accessions from the Banking Department. Some archivists have a rule to classify an archival deposit as to the department when the first records come into the archives. That would embalm the records of the present Insurance Department as a part of the archive of the Department of Trade and Commerce, as it was when we received the first deposits. In a few years the existence of the Department of Trade and Commerce will be forgotten, hence our paper and verbal shifting to the new departmental name is both sensible and practical.

After determining what series belong to each department, the next step in archival classification is to relate the various series to each other. Another genealogical chart, this one showing what functions each department has, when it was given each, and who administered them previously will prove helpful. This chart will indicate what types of records will be found in each archive, but it will not tell in what manner or form they will be kept. It will indicate, for example, that the secretary of state keeps the records of the governor relating to appointments, commissions, resignations, land patents, pardons, extraditions, election returns, trade mark registrations. It will not reveal, except in the few cases where the law is specific as to the manner of recording, whether these records are kept in a miscellaneous series of unbound series or in volume form, or where the unbound series are indexed and recorded also in. bound volumes.

The chart will not show that the territorial secretary of state decided as early as 1810 that the notary public bonds and petitions would be so bulky that he would file them in two separate series. It would not show that the secretary continued to record those bonds and petitions in the general executive register until 1858 when he started a new series of registers of notary public commissions. The chart would tell the archivist, however, why he finds no notary public petitions after 1935, that being the year the law requiring petitions was repealed. The chart will tell him, in other words, whether any series or parts of series are missing from the archive of a department and whether there is a legal reason for the apparent gaps. The chart also will fail to indicate certain general records incidental to the administration of the various functions such as correspondence and financial records.

In drawing up a classification for series the first essential is an inventory of *all* series kept by each department, whether or not these series are in the archives repository or apt to come to it. Not infrequently the most important series never reaches that non-current stage which allows the department to release it for archives. For instance, the main series in the Corporation Department is the charter series, inappropriately referred to as the "corporation shucks," which contains all the records relating to charters, amendments to charters and bylaws, and records of dissolution or merger. The Corporation Department classifies this as a current series, which will probably always have to remain in its own office vaults. In building a classification scheme for the Corporation Department archive, however, it is necessary to assign a definite place in the scheme for the charter series because other series already in the archives repository, the annual reports, for instance, are really subseries to the charter series. If at some future date the charter series should be superseded and brought to the archives, it would slip into its proper place in the classification without causing any confusion.

The main thing to remember when dealing with series is that, illogical though they may be and apparently are, they are the creation of the department, based upon some administrative need; they are not the creation of the archivist, and the archivist may not break them up into new series more to his liking. Conceivably the value of any document as legal evidence might depend upon the way it was handled in administration and by whom, as shown by its presence or absence from a given series.

It is not always easy to determine the physical limits of a series. One of the questions which frequently arises is, "How widely may a given record vary from one of similar type previously maintained and still remain the series?" This subject has been so thoroughly and practically explained by Luther H. Evans and Edythe Weiner that it is unnecessary to discuss it further here.[3]

Next it is necessary to decide what the basis of classification of series shall be, since the production of series does not seem to correspond to a strictly functional division. Paul Lewinson of the National Archives has suggested that the recurrence of certain identical types of records in the archives of most government departments may permit the construction of a scheme for classification of series which can be universally applied.[4] It is true that each department produces correspondence series, fiscal records, indexes, but the construction of such a classification as Dr. Lewinson suggests will require lengthy research based upon all or most of the federal, state, and county inventories proposed to be published by the Historical Records Survey. It is quite possible that the results of this investigation may show the coincidence of form to be too superficial to make a universal classification code practicable. Certainly, however, it would yield universal symbols for call numbers which could indicate that the series was, for instance, a separate card or a separate volume index, or a letter book or an unbound correspondence file.

We try so far as possible to group together series of similar functions. General series which do not fit into such a functional division we group at the beginning as general administrative series. The way this is done can be most easily demonstrated by giving the classification headings with some illustrations, used by a typical department, that of the Executive Department under the secretary of state:

I. General administrative records
   A. Correspondence
      1. Letter books
      2. Unbound correspondence
   B. "Executive records"
      1. "Executive register"
      2. "Executive file" (a series of miscellaneous unbound documents recorded in the register)
   C. Fiscal records
      1. Fee books
      2. Contracts
      3. Semiannual reports by departments
II. Bank records (pertaining to former state banks only)
III. Criminal records
   A. Convict registers
   B. Extraditions
      1. Requisitions on other states
      2. Requisitions to other states
      3. Record of requisitions refused
      4. Warrants and sheriffs' quietus
   C. Pardon and parole records
      1. Applications
      2. Pardons
   D. Commutations of sentence
   E. Restorations to citizenship

IV. Internal improvement records
  A. Illinois and Michigan Canal
  B. Railroads
  C. Funding operations
V. Land records (disposal of lands granted to state; supplemental to land records in the archive of the auditor.)
  A. Certificates of purchase
  B. Indexes to patents
    (N.B., the patents are recorded in the general "Executive Record"; the two sets of indexes by tracts are separate.)
  C. Records relating to certain types of land grants
    1. Salines
    2. Seminary lands
    3. Swamp lands
VI. Records of commissions to state and county officers
  A. Certificates of qualification
  B. Bonds
  C. Commissions
VII. Records of towns and cities under Act of 1872
VIII. Registration of trademarks and labels

The arrangement of individual documents within the series—the method of filing—has for its only purpose the speeding up of production of the documents for reference. No legal significance attaches to the fact that the contents of one series may be filed alphabetically, a second numerically, a third chronologically, and a fourth geographically. Strictly speaking, filing is not a part of archival classification. Most series come to the archives already filed, frequently in the case of comparatively recent records by expert filing bureaus who make it their business to analyze the use of documents and to install suitable systems.

When series come without any apparent system of filing or in disorder it is, of course, necessary for the archivist to arrange the documents according to what, upon study of the ways in which they will be called for, seems the most efficient method. It is legally permissible for the archivist to change the basis for the filing system—for example, to rearrange a chronological file into an alphabetical sequence, but the archivist should hesitate a long time before making such a change, for ninety-nine times out of one hundred the original arrangement will prove the most practicable one because it is based upon actual reference requirements.

One caution should be observed in any refiling which is undertaken, and that is to be sure that documents which really belong together do not get redistributed. For instance, enclosures in a letter should be filed with the letter to which they relate, not distributed where they might seem to belong if they were separate documents.

Groups relating to a subject "assembled and combined in a packet at the time when the archival collection was still living" are technically called "dossiers," but usually spoken of as "case records." Examples are the supreme court docket cases, which are the records of individual lawsuits; the Insurance Department's "official file," which contains charters and other documents relating to the power of insurance companies to do business in Illinois; and the Executive Department "pardon cases" which contain applications for pardon and other documents pertinent thereto. Such records are treated in filing as though each dossier constituted a single document. Dossiers are generally arranged numerically or alphabetically by subject.

Because of the determination of questions of provenance arising from enclosures and dossiers, the preliminary sorting should be done by the archivist. Once a dossier has been broken up it is difficult and often impossible to reassemble it, and great damage may result.

The archivist, like the librarian, finds it convenient to use a finding symbol or call number for quick reference to the series. We are still experimenting on this point. At present we are using the crude but workable device of a subject index to our shelf inventory. The completion of our departmental history cards now permits us to look at the classification as a whole before committing us to symbols which would later prove unworkable. We expect to build our call numbers around the following elements:

1st line: Capital initial or abbreviation for major department, followed by a dash (—) and the subdivision initial or abbreviation.

2d line: Function-subject represented by a code initial, followed by a number to represent the series number in the classification system.

3d line: A code letter or symbol to signal whether the series is filed with the bound or unbound records, and if unbound, whether in cap, letter, card, or map drawer. This refers to a purely local arrangement of records within a vault.

Those who have expected to find here a tailor-made classification which could be adapted with slight modifications to the archive of another state will be disappointed. Tables have been deliberately omitted lest someone try to do this, which would prove unsatisfactory since no two states have the same governmental organization. Neither has it been possible to give detailed rules for classification, because space limitations would forbid examples without which such rules would have little meaning. This fairly detailed discussion of some of the broader aspects may be useful in affording American examples to illuminate the Muller, Feith, and Fruin manual which is the great authority on the subject.

2 / NAME INDEXES

No finding tool is more useful than an index to personal names found in manuscript and archival collections. The compilation of calendars requires a high degree of professional skill and historical knowledge, and the process is a slow one. For the miscellaneous documents which comprise the average manuscript collection in historical and other libraries, the calendar is an almost necessary guide to subjects. Most archivists, on the other hand, have comparatively little need for detailing the contents of individual documents except in the case of correspondence and an occasional miscellaneous file. For the subject approach, archivists depend largely upon guides which list the various series and give descriptions of the general nature of their contents. Most reference to archival materials, both for official and for historical purposes, however, requires detailed name indexing.

Curiously, little has been written upon the technique of making name indexes, presumably because the process is relatively simple. Years of experience in revising index slips shows that all beginners are bothered by the same problems. It may be helpful, therefore, to give a detailed description of a typical name index, namely the one in the Illinois archives.

First of all, the person who starts out to make a name index must reconcile himself to the fact that the task is both monotonous and tedious. Fortunately, the nature of the work is such that interruptions do not seriously break the chain of thought, which means that indexing is ideal pickup work for nonrush hours at the reference desk.

The indexing of some types of records is a mechanical piece of work which can be done by anyone having a gift for accuracy. Other indexing is as difficult and as technical as calendaring. All types of name indexing call for mental alertness and imagination to decipher vague scrawls and phonetic spelling. The indexer has many a smile when he figures out an unintelligible phrase which proves to be merely some clerk's attempt to use "big" legal terms which he cannot spell and the meaning of which is, to him, equally vague. A knowledge of foreign languages, especially French and German, is helpful. Otherwise one might not recognize Dan McCann and Frank Perry when their names were spelled by their French neighbors as Daneuil Mequenne and Francois Pairais, respectively; nor realize that Teunberger, Chonberger, and Shinbarger are variations of the German name Schoenberger. Familiarity with legal terminology is also useful, or lacking that knowledge, assiduous thumbing of a good law dictionary.

All names found in documents in the Illinois archives prior to and including the year 1850 are being indexed. There are close to one million cards in the Illinois file at present. A card is made for every name found in every document indexed, though there be only a mere allusion to the surname.

At Illinois we use three-by-five-inch white catalog cards of 100 percent rag stock, medium weight, die cut, punched for the guide rod, with a guide card for about each hundred cards.

On the top line of each card is typed the name, inverted, in all capital letters. Titles (usually abbreviated) as Mrs., Capt., Governor, and the like, also such abbreviations as "Sr." and "Jr.," have only the initial letter capitalized. When only initials are given and the full name is not known, six typewriter spaces are allowed between the initials. On the second line is typed the name of the county, and if stated in the document, the town or township in which the individual resided at the date of the document. One line is then skipped. Beginning with line four, all biographical information given in the document is digested, together with date or dates. On the line following the biographical data the customary symbols for authorship and signing (A.L.S., D.S., and the like) are given, if appropriate. Lastly, the bibliographical citation is stated, skipping a line between the symbols and the citation if there is room on the card. We do not type on the call numbers for the documents, because the major part of the indexing here was completed before the main series were cataloged. However, we leave a left-hand margin of about three-quarters of an inch in case it becomes desirable to add the number later.

All items on the card are usually typed at the same indention, relying upon the blocking to differentiate between the name, place, the biographical data, and the bibliographical citation. Occasionally, when several biographical facts are included on one card, these are set apart by starting each item on a separate line or by a two-space indentation. When the same or analogous biographical information appears in two or more documents we combine this on one card. For instance, we would not make a separate card for each time John Jones's name appeared as county clerk, but would use one card for all dates, signatures, and bibliographical citations alluding to him in that official capacity.

So far as possible, all information found in one document is typed on one card. Where additional cards are necessary the words "See next card" are stamped in the lower right-hand corner of the first card with the words "Card 2," or whatever the number may be, typed at the upper right-hand corner of the added card. The name and county are repeated on the first two lines, one line is then skipped, and the biographical information continued on the fourth line. A bibliographical citation standing alone on the second card should be avoided. The wording should be so spaced that the cards can be matched from their context in case they should become separated. Some archivists tie the first and second cards together, library cataloger style.

When a volume or series with current information, such as marriage, census, or land records, is to be indexed, forms mimeographed on the card save the indexer's time and ensure complete coverage of data.

Except where mimeographed forms are used, no typing is done until the entire volume or series has been indexed on bond paper slips, three by five inches, written preferably in ink. All personal and place names should be printed, and in case of questioned spellings possible alternative readings indicated in parenthesis with a question mark. Square brackets [ ] are always used to indicate letters or information supplied by the indexer, question marks in square brackets [?] to indicate a dubious interpretation of a word or phrase. In writing slips, corrections should be made by crossing out the incorrect word or figure and rewriting it correctly, never by writing letters or figures over those already set down.

The slips are kept in the exact order in which they were written until they have been checked by the reviser, those for each page or document being held together by clips or a rubber band. After checking for omissions and other corrections, the cards are alphabetized. The reviser then decides upon the spelling of the name for filing purposes, writes cross-reference slips for various spellings of names, combines slips where possible, and otherwise edits them.

The slips are then sent to the typist. The surname as spelled for filing purposes is typed first in all capitals followed in parenthesis by the variations of spelling found in the particular document being indexed, capitalizing only the initial letter; then a comma; then the Christian name or names. Example: [SCHOENBERGER]

(Tcunberger, Choenberger), LAURENT. The rest of the card is then copied from the revised slip. After the index cards have been typed and proofread, they are counted for statistical purposes, then sent to the file clerk.

All cards are filed in one alphabet so that a person consulting the name index can find in one place and without having to consult the original records all information available about persons whose names are to be found in the records on file. . . .

Item 1: Names

All names mentioned on the handwritten index slip should be spelled on the preliminary slip, exactly as in the document indexed. The typed entry uses the spelling under which the name is to be filed, followed by variations found in the document. In the biographical section of the card all names are spelled exactly as they appear in the document.

Cross-references are made for each variation of the spelling of surnames, referring back to the spelling used for filing. Minor variations in the spelling of christian names are ignored in filing. If, however, the variation would throw the christian name into another letter of the alphabet, a cross-reference card should be made. For instance, a cross-reference would be made from Baptiste Clermont to Jean Baptiste Clermont, and from Zusanne Clermont to Susanne Clermont. No cross-references would be made if the names were spelled Jean Baptist or Suzanne.

Titles commonly used in connection with names, such as Sir, General, Governor, and the like, are given in abbreviated form, capitalizing only the first letter, and inserted between the surname and the given name. Less frequently used titles, such as commandant, prothonotary, and such, are best incorporated into the biographical section. Senior (written Sr.), Junior (written Jr.), and II or III (or written 2d or 3d) are appended to the name when appropriate. The courtesy titles Mr. and Miss are customarily omitted. "Mrs." is used in connection with the husband's name, as SMITH,

Mrs. JOHN, but the name would not be written SMITH, Mrs. CATHERINE unless to distinguish between two women of the same name, when it would be written, preferably, SMITH, CATHERINE (Mrs. John). The word esquire (written Esq.) may be appended to the name, as Perrey, Jean Francois, Esq. Titles indicating occupation or social status are preferably embodied in the biographical section of the index card.

Slaves and other persons having no surnames are entered and filed under their christian names. Immediately following, in parentheses, type (slave of . . .).

In deciding which spelling of a name to adopt for filing purposes one often has to be arbitrary. If an autograph is found in the collection that is generally the spelling to use. Sometimes, however, it is found that men changed the spelling of their signature from time to time. For instance, Jean Baptiste Dubuque, a prominent trader out of old Cahokia, Illinois, signed his name Dubuc until 1781. In default of autographs, the next best guide is present-day spelling of names by known descendants. County histories and the oldest directories for the community are frequently helpful. It should be noted, however, that descendants do not always spell their names the way their grandfathers did. For instance, one branch of the family of Samuel McClintoc (commissioner for the Illinois-Indiana boundary survey of 1821) spells the name as he did, McClintoc, while another branch spells it McClintock. Families of foreign descent frequently Anglicize the original spelling.

Never use a form of name not found in at least one of the documents even though different from the modern spelling, unless very certain from reliable sources that the name has been misspelled in the documents. For instance, it would not do to correct a spelling of the name written Barbee, to Barber, on the guess that that is really the name, because it so happens there were Barbee families in Illinois. Even though there may be a John Christian it is not safe to assume, without proof, that Jacques Chrestien is of the same family. We suspect that the old Illinois French name Cesirre (also spelled Cecire, Cecirre) is a phonetic spelling of St. Cyr (or vice versa), but in lieu of proof to the contrary we are using both names, making "see also" cross-reference cards for both names.

Besides county histories and dictionaries, the D.A.R. *Lineage Books*,[5] and, for New England names, the *New England Historical and Genealogical Register*,[6] will prove helpful. The U.S. War Department in 1920 published a *Guide to Similar Surnames: For Use in The Adjutant General's Office, War Department*.[7] Perhaps the most useful reference book for eighteenth and nineteenth century names is "General Table 111" in the U.S. Census Bureau's *Century of Population Growth, 1790–1900*, entitled "Nomenclature, Dealing with Names Represented by at Least 100 White Persons, by States and Territories, at the First Census: 1790."[8]

. . . .

We do not attempt to give dates of birth and death or other data not found in the manuscripts indexed, though when found we make separate cards for biographical information given in printed books other than standard state histories or biographical encyclopedias.

Name index filing follows Cutter rules so far as possible, filing first a surname which stands alone, then by initials and christian names.[9] Where a name which appears both with and without the designations Sr. and Jr., 2d, 3d, and the like, the rule is to file first the name as it stands alone, then Sr., then Jr., then by numbers, 2d, 3d, and so on. Mrs. John Smith would be filed immediately behind the cards for John Smith. Military and other titles are generally ignored in filing. The cards under each name should be filed by dates. Distinguish between contemporaries of the same name by filing by the county in which each lived.

Item 2: Place of Residence

The name of the county in which a person resided is important not only to distinguish the identity of persons of the same name, but is very helpful to genealogists as a clue to where to apply for further information to be found in county histories and county archives.

It is fairly safe to assume that a person whose name appears in documents originating in a certain county probably resided in that county unless the documents themselves or other knowledge indicate otherwise. The indexer should not jump to the conclusion that ownership of real estate in a certain town or township implies residence therein. Unless the document itself uses the phraseology, "at his home in Prairie du Pont" or something similar, the residence should be given merely as the county. Even though the indexer may know from other sources that the person was residing at Prairie du Pont at the date of the document he does not add that to the card. This index is an index only to the information found in the document.

The name of the county should be given, of course, as it was at the date of the document, not according to the present day division of county lines. . . .

Item 3: Biographical Data

Anything, no matter how trivial, that throws light upon the biography of the person whose name is indexed should be brought out on the card. The only card in the whole file about James Ratcliffe may merely mention that he was excused from jury service on a certain date because of illness. That bit of information may tie up with other information to establish the approximate date of his death; it may mean nothing more than the slight glow someone will feel from finding that grandfather has not been completely forgotten. Remembering the fine-tooth combing of the records by Lincoln scholars, the Illinois archives staff has a saying, "When you index consider everyone a Lincoln."

This detailed indexing gives everyone searching the records all the information he could find by seeing the original records. Looking at name indexes in other institutions which are sometimes little more than lists of call numbers, we have wondered (but not out loud) how many patrons and archival clerks have had the time or patience to look at a hundred documents to glean the meager information that James Jones served on the grand jury a few times, signed a couple of road petitions, once sued one of his neighbors for payment on a $10 I.O.U., and purchased a featherbed at the auction of another neighbor. Occasionally a document will contain an extensive biography, too much to be included on the card. In that case the searcher would want to see that original document anyhow. By and large, however, the information to be gleaned from an archival collection, is "here a little and there a little."

It is most important for the indexer to cultivate concise and precise ways of digesting biographical information. The revision of index slips written by a second person astounds one as to the ambiguity of the English language. "Asked for a writ"—does that mean "he asked the court to issue a writ," or "the court instructed him to prepare (or perhaps, to serve process on) a writ?" "His name under a road petition" upon checking proved to mean that a copy of a road petition signed by the person had been transcribed into the county commissioners' proceedings. The proper entry would be "Signed a petition for a road from Wood River to Cahokia. Copy of D.S." "Gave his consent to be wedded to Susie Brown," the formal wording on the minister's certificate, does not imply a shotgun wedding; simply write "Married Susie Brown." Do not say, "Member of the grand jury, Dec. term 1806: ditto Jan. 1807; ditto Oct. 1808," but rather "Member of grand jury, Dec. term 1806; Jan., Oct. terms 1808." "Signed a note with James White" implies that he was a party to the obligation. "Witnessed the signature of a note given by James White to John Brown," would have been the more accurate description.

Use the precise term for the information given—do not use the words "asked" or "requested," for instance, when the correct word would be "petitioned," "ordered," "decreed," or "instructed," as the case might be. Use such words as "elected" or "appointed," rather than "chosen," and so on. Watch for the subtle distinction between "recorded his livestock marks and brands"—the register merely showing that he did so—and "Record of his livestock marks and brands"—indicating that if one were to turn to the reference cited he would find a facsimile of those marks.

In digesting legal documents use precise legal terminology, such as affidavit; testimony (before court); administrator of the estate of _____, deceased; executor of the will of the late _____; record of; registered; judge's docket of the circuit court; writ of attachment for _____ livres; court decreed. On the other hand, avoid the use of technical legal phrases that no one but a lawyer would understand. Do not use such terms as "Cepi corpus," "write of error coram nobis," "writ of capias ad satisfaction" or "writ of fiere facias," even though those words may have been used in the document. Instead of saying "Court issued writ of ad quod damnum re dam," explain that the "Court ordered a jury to assess the probable damage to be caused by erection of the proposed dam."

Be particularly careful in the use of pronouns, repeating names if possible to avoid ambiguity. For instance, one index slip read "Langlois: Member of committee appointing G. Blin guardian for his sister-in-law Mary Alary _____" was Langlois or Blin the brother-in-law? Actually, as the rechecking of the document proved, it was Blin. Such errors would never be made in formal composition, but they are apt to be very common when a person is writing a great many slips as fast as possible.

Conciseness is something that one tends to ignore in setting down facts in the order in which they come to light in reading the document. The reviser will catch this, but the indexer, if his mind wanders, will come up with something like this: "He had a son named George. George was born in Kaskaskia, by Marie Laperche, James' wife. He was a blacksmith. He married Catherine Dubois who was born in Cahokia. Her father was Charles Dubois; her mother was Angelique Laroche. They were married at her father's house in Cahokia, on December 31, 1791. His father and mother were dead by the time of the wedding." It would have been better to have reduced this sort of information to a standard form for marriages, and to write, "George Brown, blacksmith, a native of Kaskaskia, son of the late James Brown and Marie Laperche; married Catherine Dubois, daughter of Charles Dubois and the late Angelique Laroche, at Dubois home, Cahokia, Dec. 31, 1791."

Quote phrases of biographical import the meaning of which is not clear or which are flavorful. Examples: "Beaupere" (father-in-law? or stepfather?). "Judge LaCroix forbade sale or gift of intoxicating liquors on holidays and Sundays except for 'an emergency or indispensable necessity.' " "The court instructed Girardin to address himself 'to the government which is to come,' 1786." "Baptiste Wiser, apprenticed to 'the Trade and Mystery of a Farmer.' " "Married according to the rites of the Church of England."

Save space by using figures instead of spelling out the numerals. Use abbreviations for names of months and for English and American (but not for French or Spanish moneys); for the U.S., for names of the states and for such other easily recognizable words as Ft. (fort), St. and Ste. (saint), sess. (session), and co. (county or company, according to the context). To the clerk writing fifteen thousand index slips for court records, the abbreviation C.C.C.P will always mean County Court of Common Pleas, but it will have no meaning to the patron or the archival clerk of ten years hence.

In combining index slips keep like matters together. Do not, for instance, in indexing court proceedings put together on one card the fact that a man was witness, juror, and two of his lawsuits were in process at a given term of court. It is more useful to keep all index items on each lawsuit together, despite the fact that the suit may be pending for several years; his services as juror at various terms can be combined on one card. In other words, it is of less interest to know what a man was doing day by day than to know what inclusive dates were covered by one type of activity, as his tenure of office as a judge or county clerk, for instance. In writing slips it is wise to remember this principle. It will save the reviser's time if each biographical item is given a separate slip, even though that may seem to be a waste of time. The purpose of the primary slips is to get down the biographical facts, not to edit or combine them. In this connection also, the indexer should be encouraged to write notes that will not be used on the typed card but which may help the reviser when he comes to editing the card. For instance, "No further information in this document" to explain an inconclusive statement; or "the words look like _____; "illegible," and so on.

The indexer must reconcile himself to monotony which he should not attempt to vary by changing phraseology. The same wording for the same type of information should be used throughout the series.

Perhaps the best general rule is that given by the Historical Records Survey for calendar entries. Each card should indicate "who did what, where, when, and why?"

Item 4: The Date

The date of the action described on the index card should always be given, also the date the document was written, if different. If there is no date on the document, approximate the date if possible, as "prior to July 20, 1819 (date of Smith's death)"; or [between 1800 and 1810?]. If no date can be given, use the phraseology [n.d.] (no date, in brackets). On an index card it is not necessary to explain where one got the date, as "Endorsed January 9, 1800," as one would do in the case of a calendar entry. If the document is a copy of a much earlier document, however, it is well to point that fact out, thus (June 15, 1753; 1786 copy).

Item 5: Signatures

The standardized designations for autographs are used: D.S.—documents signed; A.D.S.—autograph document signed; L.S.—letter signed; A.L.S.—autograph letter signed; D.S. (by mark) or D.S. (M)—document signed by mark; Copy of D.S. (or of A.D.S., etc.).

"Unable to write" (or whatever phraseology is used in a document which is not a transcript of an original document).

If the date of the signature is different from the date given as the date for the document, as, for instance, a later endorsement, the date of the signature should follow the signature designation, as "D.S. (endorsement). Jan. 16, 1801."

Item 6: Bibliographical Citations

Citation should be given to the document indexed precisely as in the case of any footnote or other bibliographical reference; that is, with sufficient detail to make it possible to locate the document readily. It is assumed that unless otherwise stated the document belongs to the institution in whose index it appears.

7

Making and Control of Administrative

Records

1 / RECORD MAKING

THE RECORDS SYSTEMS of most government offices, like Topsy, "just growed." Records have come into existence as a by-product of government activity rather than as planned entities. In the days when all documents were written by hand, records were not made unless they were important. It was, therefore, both necessary and possible to preserve them all. Today typewriters, carbon paper, the mimeograph, cheap printed forms, and governmental questionnaires, together with an increasing complexity of governmental functions undreamed of a generation ago, are piling up files in astronomical proportions.

Record laws, aimed at preventing inconvenience or loss to the state or to individuals, prohibit the destruction of any records without specific permission. Under a literal interpretation of the law, almost any piece of paper with writing upon it which flutters by chance into a government office must be deemed to be a record which may not be destroyed. This restraining law plus the fact that it is easier for an executive to order all records to the files for storage than to select the more important ones for preservation has brought

⌐ؤ PART 1 OF THIS CHAPTER, "Record Making," was originally published in *Illinois Libraries* 27 (February 1945): 127–33. Part 2, "Controlling Administrative Records," was originally published as "Control of Administrative Records" in *Illinois Libraries* 27 (March 1945): 182–89.

a chaotic situation in most state offices. Filing systems break down because they become too cumbersome. Current records which must be kept close at hand push less frequently used, but legally important, records to storerooms where at best they are jammed together in inextricable confusion and where at worst they are destroyed by vermin, insects, heat, dampness, and dirt. The absurdity of treating as equally sacrosanct a deed to real estate and a written requisition for a box of pencils creates a lack of respect for all records. When war stops the building of equipment and storage space, and patriotism calls for wastepaper, it is inevitable that valuable historical and legal records will be sent to the pulp mill along with the worthless papers. A destroyed record, no matter how badly needed, can no more be restored to life than a dead man.

Even departments which have meticulously preserved all their files frequently are embarrassed because certain records now needed were not made in the first place. Personal interviews and telephone conversations are important factors in policy making, yet they are seldom recorded. For instance, all time sheets for day laborers on the capitol are in the state archives but no one made it his business to preserve a copy of the plans and specifications needed every time repairs or alterations have to be made.

When the records of the World War I Council of Defense were studied for suggestions and precedents for the organization of civilian defense at the beginning of World War II, we found a list of Liberty bond purchases by individuals—surely a matter between the conscience of the individual and the U.S. Treasury rather than a proper state record. No usable description of the organization or operation of the old Council of Defense could be found in these files. Shortly after Pearl Harbor, the U.S. Census Bureau announced that probably at least sixty million Americans cannot prove their citizenship through acceptable legal records.

Somehow departments must get control over the records of state government which cannot function effectively without them. We must replace "files" with "records"!

Illinois is attacking its record problems from three angles: 1. through selection of useless records for legalized destruction; 2.

through reduction of the bulk of the records by substitution of microfilm copies for the originals (the 1943 General Assembly created the State Records Commission to accomplish these two procedures);[1] 3. to create records more scientifically by a study of what records are essential to efficient administration, by providing for systematic and automatic reduction of records as they cease to have further value, and by transfer of noncurrent records of permanent historical or legal value to the state archives. . . .

The word "record" has been defined as "an artificial memory." In seeking to obtain control of records, the first point to decide is what forms of artificial memory are needed for efficient administration.

So much has been said about records as historical source materials that some conscientious officials fear to recommend the destruction of any record lest some precious fragment illuminating the biography of a now unrecognized Lincoln might be destroyed. Government records are the principal and sometimes only historical source materials for the pioneer period. For example, no effective social history of the United States could ignore the rich vein of information to be found only in the archives of the county courthouses. The historian of the future who writes about life in America today, however, will not have to depend wholly or even largely, upon government records. He will also find as source materials newspapers, periodicals, books, photographs, newsreels, and sound recordings.

The head of a state department, therefore, need not concern himself with consciously created history. Rather, it is his duty to determine what records—"artificial memory," if you will—are necessary for the most efficient administration of his office and for the information of his successors.

In this connection one should be mindful of the implications of democracy as that affects records. In a monarchy or totalitarian system of government the people are creatures of the state, and the records of government belong to the rulers not to the people. In a democracy, on the other hand, the people delegate the functions of government to their officials who do not own the records which result from their activities but merely act as custodians of the records on behalf of the people. Since government functions for the benefit of the public, the people have a right to demand that their citizenship and property rights as individuals and their communal property rights as administered by the government shall be protected by the creation and preservation of proper records. Only the duly elected representatives of the people, the General Assembly, may authorize the destruction of government records.

A further implication of democracy is that the records of the government are public records, open to inspection by anyone who applies to see them subject only to reasonable restrictions as to hours of access and protection against theft, alterations, or other physical hazards. Use of government records may be restricted as confidential only when public inspection would obviously be injurious to the public or to private good—as in the case of certain confidential corporate statements of earnings used as a basis for taxation or pardon papers. The power to withhold such categories of records as confidential must be specifically granted by law.

Before attempting to make concrete suggestions for record organization, it may be helpful to discuss the principal purposes for which records are made as expressed in the forms they take. No state department makes all the following types of records, but all make some of them.

1. *Charters*, such as the various state constitutions, which of course must be preserved in their original form.

2. *Registers* of documents which do not take effect until those documents have been *"entered as of record"* in a specific public office. The oldest record in the Illinois state archives, probably one of the oldest if not the oldest extant civil record west of the Alleghenies, is the register of contracts, property settlements, donations, and so on, kept by the successive notaries at Cahokia from 1734 to 1763. A large proportion of the records kept by certain county officials fell into this category. Deeds and mortgages, for instance, are recorded by making full copies of the originals in bound volumes after which the originals are given a dated and numbered file mark and returned to the owner of the instrument. An unrecorded deed

has no legal effect, but loss of the original deed does not invalidate ownership because the legal record is the copy in the county recorder's office. Laws governing the manner of recording and indexing of such records are rigid and detailed. In the case of some records, such as wills, both the original instrument and the official record copy are preserved in official files. Occasionally, as in cases where printed forms are involved, the law permits filing the original in the archives of the department and merely registering the fact of filing as opposed to copying *in extenso*. There can be no doubt that these are true records which should never be considered for destruction and which should be given the best possible physical care.

These official copies of recorded instruments are increasingly being made by photographic processes, the most popular being photocopy. Such copies, since they are facsimiles, have been made legally acceptable as evidence in court. The Corporation Department in the office of the secretary of state, for instance, records documents relating to incorporations, amendments to charters, and other documents affecting corporate powers by photocopy. Some space economies can be effected through photocopying on both sides of the sheet and reducing the size of the original slightly. Making such records on microfilm only is frowned upon because of inconvenience for quick consultation and the danger of mutilation of the record by scratches on the film. In general, we must plan space for the permanent preservation of such records in the form in which they are made. Microfilm copies of the official copies or of the original records, however, kept in some other repository, are a desirable and cheap form of insurance in case of loss of the original files through fire, flood, or other catastrophe.

3. *Black's Law Dictionary* defines a register as, "A book containing a record of facts as they occur, kept by public authority; [e.g.] a register of births, marriages, and burials."[2] Registers of one kind or another are made by most government offices. There are the simple diary forms of which the most conspicuous example is the executive register kept by the secretary of state, "a fair register

of all the official acts of the governor," as the law puts it. This record, started in 1809, is being kept today. Generally the more important of these registers are preserved in their original form. Sometimes, however, where the registers are not referred to frequently, the register can properly be made on microfilm. An example is the record of warrants issued by the state treasurer, made on 16-mm film. It should be noted, however, that in this case parallel records—the warrant records—are kept by the auditor of public accounts in ledger form.

The most frequent form taken by registers of official acts is the official list of licenses granted. Such registers range in importance from hunting and fishing licenses and tavern permits to civil service registers, licenses to practice professions, and records of incorporations. Generally speaking, registers of licenses should be considered permanent records at least so far as their contents go. Applications and other documents which accompany these license registers may or may not be treated as permanent records. Documents relating to corporate rights should be preserved indefinitely; those protecting individuals in personal rights and privileges should be preserved at least for the lifetime of the individual. Documents other than registers relating to licenses which are primarily a form of taxation, as for instance motor vehicle licenses, can generally be destroyed after an appropriate term of years.

A third type of registration is the registration of acts of other governing bodies, matters which do not take effect until registered with a designated official or body. For instance, a corporation chartered or licensed to do business in the state by the secretary of state may not do business until that authorization has been recorded by the recorder of the county where its home office is located. The official register of names of cities, towns, and villages are recorded by the secretary of state. Local bond issues are sometimes required to be registered with the auditor of public accounts.

A fourth and very important type of register is the statistical record of sociological importance which, in the words of Black's definition are, "a record of facts as they occur, kept by public authority." The most conspicuous examples are the vital statistics collected under the supervision of the Department of Public Health and the census records by the federal government. The physical type forms in which such records are kept is not so important as the fact that the contents of these records must be preserved at all costs.

4. *Minutes, proceedings, and debates* of boards, commissions, and other official bodies acting as a group made up of individual members. Registers record the decisions reached; minutes, proceedings, and debates record the manner in which the decisions are reached. Minutes, frequently but incorrectly used as a synonym for proceedings, are technically the rough notes taken during a meeting by the clerk used as a basis for writing the formal proceedings. Proceedings record the form and manner of conducting the business of the board, commission, and the like. Proceedings are properly required to be legalized by the signed approval of the president, after giving the members an opportunity to make corrections. The minutes from which the journals are made up, therefore, are not considered records and are generally not preserved. The most conspicuous example of proceedings are the journals of the House and Senate. Proceedings should be preserved as permanent records, though the originals of relatively unimportant bodies could be preserved in the form of certified microfilm copies. Proceedings merely note that speeches were made by certain persons. Debates record the text of the speeches. The *Congressional Record* is an example of debates. The Illinois General Assembly does not record its debates for which it is necessary to rely upon newspaper accounts.

The documents presented to the board for its consideration, often called "docket files," should be preserved as long as the record of proceedings which they illuminate. From a historical point of view these docket files are often of greater value than the proceedings.

5. *Judicial records* are similar in nature to the records of boards, commissions, and the like, described above. The terminology and methods of preservation are different, however. Judicial records in-

clude not only such obvious records as those of a court like the supreme court, but also of the judicial functions involved in enforcing laws through investigations of complaints. Some state departments like the Illinois Commerce Commission function primarily as though they were courts, and the administrative divisions of the department can be conceived of as fact finding or research bodies attached to the court.

Other departments, like the Department of Labor, have a separate judicial body (in that case, the Industrial Commission) which acts as an adjunct to administration. The Department of Labor administers the workmen's compensation act, basing the administering of awards upon fact finding in relation to the merits of each individual case by the Industrial Commission.

Judicial bodies keep as records dockets, records of decisions, and "case records." "Case records" comprise petitions, complaints, transcripts of evidence presented, reports to the court, and so on, and are called "case records" because all documents bearing upon each case are filed together as a unit. Once more the importance of the governing body and the nature of the cases determine the length of time such records need to be kept. Ordinarily dockets and records of decisions are considered permanent records. Case records of courts are also kept indefinitely. Judicial procedures relative to enforcement of acts through investigations of complaints and similar procedures generally result in case records which can be destroyed periodically.

6. *Administrative records* comprise, first, those "housekeeping records" common to all business—bookkeeping records concerning receipts and expenditures, personnel records, and the like; second, correspondence; and third, those administrative records peculiar to the respective departments which enable them to carry on their governmental functions effectively.

Insofar as administrative records include the first four categories of records described above, the amount of control over the creation and limitation of the bulk of records by the department is limited. It is the miscellaneous records lumped together here under the general heading "administrative records" which create most of the problems of control. . . .

7. *Reports*, including reports made to the department by other agencies, public and private, reports made by the department to other agencies, and intradepartmental reports. Both printed and manuscript reports may be considered archival material. It is impossible to generalize concerning a retention policy for reports since they vary greatly in purpose and importance.

8. *Research data* used as the basis for a government report are not considered record material. Because that data may be useful in connection with studies of allied subjects, it is sometimes desirable to deposit them in the state archives or some university.

9. *Nonrecord material.* The following is quoted from the excellent manual, *Disposition of Official Records*, issued by the U.S. Department of Agriculture:

Library and museum material preserved solely for reference or exhibition purposes and stocks of publications and processed documents are not considered "records." There are many types of nonrecord materials that should never be allowed to accumulate in the files. It is difficult to enumerate with any degree of certainty the specific types of material that could be considered of nonrecord character, because some types of documents would have record character and some would not, depending upon their use. If it is intended to keep them for future information or action they assume record character. The following, however, are a few examples of the kind of material that ordinarily would not be construed as "records," and therefore may be disposed of without the required authority:

1. Extra copies of papers used solely for convenience of reference. This may include so-called "reader file" copies, "tickler" or "follow-up" copies, if their use is essentially temporary.

2. Informational memoranda and transmittal letters that do not serve as bases for official actions.

3. Preliminary drafts or work sheets that do not represent uniquely significant steps in the preparation of other documents.

4. Stocks of blank forms.

5. Surplus copies of mimeographed, multilithed, printed or processed circulars and memoranda.

6. Routine requests for publications, and acknowledgments.[3]

The first step in gaining control over records is to determine what records are necessary to efficient administration and what form they should take. Until after these facts have been determined, it is advisable to forget about existing files. A review of present files to determine their effectiveness will then be in order. The first step in the official planning of the files should be to list the duties of the department and the manner in which the law specifies this duty shall be performed, also what records are specifically required by law to be kept. Having in mind the divisional organization of the department, which it is to be hoped is both a logical and effective division of functions, the planner should decide on a theoretical basis what files should be created. While doing this he should be mindful of how long the respective records need be kept in original form, which records may be reduced by microphotography, and which records can be destroyed completely after what respective intervals. In planning his filing units he should arrange for a complete and automatic segregation of records in the respective disposal periods. When nonpermanent records are filed with permanent records the amount and quality of the labor involved in weeding them out is so great it becomes necessary to preserve the entire file. This admixture of ephemeral and permanent records is the greatest single factor in the unwieldy growth of records.

A second point to be considered in connection with the outline of the records system of the department is what records parallel to them are required to be kept by some other department. If the records are duplicated elsewhere, which is the official permanent copy? If the original and legal copy is in some other department, then your copy may be required to be preserved only so long as it serves the administrative purposes of your own office. If, on the other hand, your copy is the copy which would be taken to court, you owe it to other departments involved that that copy be preserved if not permanently at least so long as it could possibly affect any other department. If the original and official copy is required to be kept in an institution under your or some other department, it is wise to treat the copy in the main departmental office as if it were the official copy. Judging by past experience, heads of state institutions are apt to be less record conscious than departments at the capital, and they are more likely to be the victims of so-called "efficiency experts" who order promiscuous and ruthless destruction of "that trash" without any realization of its importance.

After the theoretical organization of filing units to be set up has been completed, but not before, the commercial filing experts may be called in. Their business is to devise efficient filing procedures within the individual filing units. They can sometimes make helpful suggestions for organizing those financial and personnel records which are common to all private and public business offices. They cannot be expected to know the intricacies of administration of a department which has duties different from those of other department in this or any other state. Even though there seem to be parallels in administration, there are differences in details which affect records quality as to contents, lengths of time records should be preserved, and so on.

No one but a person who understands all the technicalities of each administrative unit should presume to set up future filing units. Our military occupation authorities are even now handicapped because after World War I a filing expert recommended a "consolidation" of the files of one division of the U.S. War Department. This reorganization of the files was along subject lines, a beautiful example of logic. But, unfortunately, that particular line of division is not the way the War Department operates.

One other point should be borne in mind in employing these filing experts. Some, though not the best, install filing systems that have been tailor-made by their companies which require the purchase of their own folders, guides, and the like, and which may or may not be the most efficient kind of filing for a particular type of record. The ease of filing by a particular system is used as a selling point, but this sometimes ignores the more important point of ease and speed in finding a document once filed. A filing system is inefficient that requires too many cross references; that encourages a file clerk to file under the name of the individual who happens to sign a letter, rather than under the institution or corporation involved; to file alphabetically when reference to the file is always geographical or chronological. There is no substitute for the experience and knowledge of the executive who is going to use the file. Neither is it true that filing is the job for a clerk who does not fit into any other part of the organization. Logical organization of filing units and a good system of filing within each unit are the most important elements in getting control of records.

2 / Controlling Administrative Records

There is relatively little opportunity to control the bulk of records made primarily for purposes of recording—the records of records, registers, proceedings of boards and commissions, and judicial files. . . . Fortunately such records in most state offices occupy comparatively little space. The records which present the problem of bulk are those administrative documents which are made not primarily as records but as a lubricant to the machinery of administration, the principal ones being bookkeeping and personnel records (often referred to as "housekeeping records"), correspondence, and that "silent organization" which expresses itself largely through the use of printed forms. Of course, in practice, there are no such sharp distinctions between the various types of records. . . . If the purposes for which the records are made are kept in mind, however, the procedures recommended for dealing with records will be found to apply.

In.the field of "housekeeping records" alone, government officials can get much help from precedents set by private business. Retention schedules have been drawn up for various forms of financial and personnel records. Discussion of these subjects can readily be found in books on office management and other publications on business practices. In this connection it should be pointed out, however, that the statute of limitations does not apply to state government and that recommendations to destroy certain categories of records periodically, based solely upon that body of law, cannot properly be made the basis for disposition of government records.

The number and complexity of housekeeping records depend upon the size of the department. The average state department will have as a minimum the following bookkeeping records: records of receipts from fees and taxes collected by the department; record of deposits in state treasury; record of expenditures charged against appropriations; record of administration of funds furnished by the federal government. Of these records the records of fees and taxes collected give details not to be found elsewhere and are generally considered permanent records. However, it is probable that only such records of this category as are recorded in ledger form need be preserved indefinitely. The record of deposits in the state treasury are like other receipts, of diminishing importance as time goes on but even so generally preserved indefinitely. The same is true of the records of expenditures of federal funds insofar as these funds are controlled by the department. Records of expenditures, however, particularly duplicate vouchers, are useful for only a short period of years—for making up budgets and for ordering supplies and equipment.

The records of receipts into and disbursements from the state treasury kept by the state treasurer and the auditor of public accounts are the official records of these transactions which have value as legal evidence. The auditor of public accounts has legal permission to destroy vouchers of no historical significance after twenty years; the Departments of Finance and Revenue have discretionary powers to destroy their financial records in from three to five years after the conclusion of the transactions to which they refer. Other state departments should review their holdings of financial records in the light of how long these records are actually useful to them and seek relief through the State Records Commission for disposing of duplicate vouchers, requisitions for supplies, and the like. It should be noted that the law giving powers to the auditor of public accounts and the Departments of Finance and Revenue to destroy certain original records does not apply to the duplicates of those same records held by other departments. Departments which do not realize that fact have already destroyed their duplicate records, and they should legalize this procedure through the State Records Commission.

Personnel records may be very simple or very elaborate. Each department should at least keep a payroll record indefinitely. To be sure, the auditor of public accounts and the state treasurer have an official record of payments made but their records do not always show the department or the title of the person. It is no uncommon occurrence for a department to receive a request from a former employee for the exact salary received and dates of employment for twenty-five or more years back. Right now the state architect is trying, in vain it is feared, to learn the number of employees in each office of the state in 1836 as a guide to refurnishing the old capitol at Vandalia. The first extant payroll for the secretary of state's office is 1884. In 1836 state employees were paid, not by individual warrants, but from lump sums vouchered for by the respective state officers.

What personnel records other than payrolls need to be considered permanent records is a moot question. The Civil Service Commission keeps the record of initial and promotional qualifications of civil service employees. Some record of the background of non-civil service employees is desirable. From a historical point of view it is valuable to keep a permanent condensed biographical record of all employees. Efficiency ratings and records of leaves of absence are necessary to current administration but of doubtful utility after a few years. Recommendations based upon such ratings are occasionally called for, but it seems futile to try to estimate a person's present value from what he was like fifteen or twenty years ago.

Correspondence files are the most bulky and otherwise troublesome records to control. The first question which arises is whether to have one central file where every piece of correspondence will be thrown into one alphabet, or whether to permit each division or operational unit to set up its own file. Theoretically a central file permits closer control over official records. Practically, divisions tend to hold back important correspondence particularly if the divisions are located at some distance from the central file—either in another building or possibly in another town. The decision as to whether to have a centralized or a decentralized file is largely a matter of internal organization. Most of our Illinois code offices seem to lean toward the idea of a central file.

Whether correspondence files are centralized or department-alized, certain principles of management hold good. The first of these is that access to the files should be controlled. No documents should be removed from the files without leaving a memorandum giving sufficient indication of the identity of the document, the data taken and the name of the person who has the record. Preferably one clerk should be assigned to charge out all files removed for office use. No document should be refiled by anyone except the file clerk responsible for that section of the files. This procedure is desirable in the case of all records, but a failure to observe it spells certain chaos in the case of a correspondence file.

The carbons of letters filed should be true copies of the letters actually sent. That should be self-evident, yet it is not a rare occurrence for a letter to go out with handwritten corrections or post-scripts which have not been entered on the carbon.

When both the first and final drafts of a letter are filed, a frequent occurrence when one person drafts a letter for some one else to revise and send out over his signature, the carbons should be marked in such a manner that it is possible to tell which is which.

The quality of paper stock for the carbon is also important. The carbon copy of a letter retained for his files gives the writer's side of an issue. How absurd, therefore, to mail out the original on expensive paper retaining for oneself a smudged carbon copy on flimsy paper. We have had the not infrequent experience in finding that the official carbon copy of an important letter has faded to illegibility or disintegrated into dust.

Another matter almost universally neglected is the signature of important carbon copies. What is to prevent a person so minded from getting access to the files and substituting a false carbon for the original? All state officials deal with persons who try to resort to such tricks.

Whether the correspondence is filed by subject, by number, by code, or alphabetically, it should be impressed upon the clerks to file under the name of the corporation or institution on behalf of which the letter is written, and not under the name of the individual who happens to have signed it. This seems like a matter too obvious to mention, yet it is the cause of more waste of man-hours in the state archives than any other one item. . . .

The first step to be taken to control the bulk of correspondence files is to segregate the ephemeral from the permanent records. Some persons advocate that replies to routine requests for publication and similar matters be made on the original letter which is returned to the sender. This may be efficient, but it is irritating to many recipients. If any reply at all is made most persons would prefer a form letter if not an individual reply. Carbons of such letters, if preserved at all, should be filed in a cabinet plainly labeled as temporary, nonrecord material.

Routine recurring letters on the same subject can often be reduced to form letters. Carbon copies are not necessary for form letters if the original incoming letters are stamped to show the date of reply, form letter number, and the initials or name of the person signing the outgoing letter. It is important, however, to be sure that copies of each form, accurately numbered, are on file.

One of the problems inherent in correspondence files is the separation of personal from official correspondence. When a discussion of office business is followed in the same incoming letter with political or personal gossip, it is quite natural for the recipient to want that letter filed in his personal file. Often official business correspondence is of a nature that the official has an interest in preserving a copy for his own use. It is highly desirable, therefore, to maintain double correspondence files, one to be the official file, the other a personal file. Care should be taken to ensure that originals or copies of any letters pertaining to official business shall be found in that official file. Some department heads have two carbons made of every letter sent, also a copy of important letters received, one carbon on a distinctive color, to be filed in the personal file.

Reduction of the bulk of correspondence seems to involve a certain amount of tedious weeding of files. Even after all obviously nonrecord material has been excluded from the file there will remain some letters which can be discarded after a certain length of time—six months, one year, five years, and so on. The convenience of having all the year's correspondence in one alphabet makes it impractical to try to keep the correspondence in files segregated according to date.

Matters of record to which correspondence is incidental should be excluded from the general correspondence file. For example, in the Archives Department we file our correspondence concerning assignments of vault space, authorizations for transfers of records, permits for departmental clerks, and such, relating to departmental vaults in the separate departmental vault file, not in the regular correspondence file. Routine letters transmitting duplicate passes, however, are filed with other correspondence.

Only the executive can decide whether or not a letter is likely to be of temporary or permanent importance. It is certain that he will not go to the trouble of weeding his correspondence files himself. The simplest procedure we have found for semiautomatic weeding is for the executive, at the time he signs a letter, to designate by code, on his carbon, the retention period, as six months, one year, five years, permanent, or the like. All letters are kept together in one file. At the end of the normal transfer period, usually at the end of the year, some clerk is designated to go through the files and discard obsolete documents. If a piece of correspondence, coded as temporary, has increased in importance by the addition of other letters to and from the same person on the same subject, that folder is referred back to the executive for reclassification. The disadvantage of this procedure is that someone does have to handle thousands of papers, piece by piece, and it is a temptation to neglect that duty. However, an office boy or low-grade clerk can do the preliminary sorting; and it does make for convenience to have all correspondence for the year in one file.

At this point it is proper to ask how much weeding and discarding of files is permissible. The answer is pragmatic. It is generally considered proper to weed files to remove documents which should not have been filed in the first place or which obviously have no record character, also duplicate copies filed.

It is proper to set up new filing units plainly labeled as temporary files of nonrecord character, subject to informal destruction later. Documents needed to support other documents or which form the legal basis for official action should not be filed in such a unit and should not be destroyed without legislative sanction.

Filing units created prior to the adoption of a records control system, particularly if such files have been kept over a period of years, or if they antedate the present administration, should not be destroyed in whole or in part without seeking permission through the State Records Commission.

In other words, individual documents of nonrecord character may be removed from files, new files may be consciously created as nonrecord units, but it is unsafe to assume that a filing unit already in existence is not a record subject to the law which prohibits the destruction of records.

Printed forms, both for intraoffice conduct of business and in the form of questionnaire reports required from persons, firms, and corporations, play a large part in governmental as well as business organization. The cheapness and ease of use of printed forms makes them particular offenders in the matter of excessively bulky records.

Some years ago, the Hammermill Paper Company commissioned a firm which specializes in problems of business management "to conduct an unbiased investigation into the use of printed forms and stationery, and the opinion, practices, and experiences of users of this material." The report, written from the viewpoint of the executive in the commercial field, emphasizes the use of records, particularly forms, as an aid to business management, the "silent organization" as the authors phrase it.[4] The principles laid down here coincide with the archival view that the best record system for a government department is one which best answers the questions, "What is the department supposed to do, how does it function, and to what extent is it succeeding or failing?" Much, though not all, of what follows is a condensation of this volume. A shorter article on the same subject, by Lt. Comdr. Willard F. McCormick of the Department of the Navy has also been used.[5]

"All forms needed by a business should be so designed that they will readily fit into the complete 'silent' organization, they should dovetail with the other related forms; they should be reviewed and approved by major executives; and no substantial change in the form organization should be made without executive sanction."

The first step in getting control of records kept on forms is to assemble and study all the forms already in use by the department. Then ". . . examine the forms in each group with the general attitude that every form, and every item on each form, must prove its usefulness or get out. You will probably be amazed to discover how much clerical work of questionable value is being done. Superfluous records are called for by this or that item; entries made on one form are duplicated on others; complete files of nearly useless information are being kept—no one knows why, except that 'we've always done it.' When this first step has been taken, new groupings of essential items will suggest themselves. One form may be prepared to replace two; clerical operations can be combined with substantial reductions in the work required; an additional copy of a form and a piece of carbon paper can be used to take the place of a clerk's time. Studying related forms together also usually brings out ways in which they can be dovetailed to speed up work and to reduce the possibilities of error."[6]

In this connection the suggestion should also be made that in redesigning old forms and adding new ones, consideration should be given to the desirability of segregating information of permanent record value from that of transitory interest, wherever that is practicable.

The following questions are useful for this review of old forms:

"A. What can be eliminated?
1. It this form essential?
2. Is it duplicated elsewhere, in whole or in part?
3. How many copies are made of this form, and what use is made of each copy?
4. Is each item on this form necessary?
5. Are any of these items duplicated elsewhere?
"B. What time-saving improvements can we make?
1. In the form itself?
   a. Can we combine forms to reduce work?
   b. Are the items arranged in the order in which the operations are (or should be) performed?
   c. Are the important items placed so as to permit easy reference in the files or binders?
   d. Are the items spaced horizontally and vertically to conform to the mechanical requirements of typewriters or other equipment in which the forms will be used?
   e. Is writing eliminated as much as possible through the printing of recurring answers or data which can be checked ($\sqrt{}$) instead of written?
2. In the work controlled by the forms:
   a. Can we combine operations to reduce work?
   b. Can we make more copies at one time to avoid duplication of work?
   c. Do the forms divide the routine into the best work-units for the individual workers?
   d. Can we change the sequence of the operations with advantage?"[7]

All requests for the introduction of new forms should clear through the same central executive control which his reviewed existing forms. Commander McCormick suggests that, "A complete survey of the need for a new record can be made by getting true answers to six questions: (1) Why is the item needed? (2) Who needs it? (3) What will it contain or consist of? (4) When will it be required? How often? (5) Where will it be prepared or distributed? (6) How will it be prepared or produced? Proper consideration of these questions will determine whether or not the item recommended is necessary."[8]

Butler and Johnson suggests the following questions as an aid to preparing the form:

"Is this form to be filled in by hand, by typewriter, or both?

"Is it to be run through any kind of machine?

"Is it to be filled in with data from other forms, or are other forms to be filled in from it?

"Are the same data, or answers, going to recur frequently enough to justify their printing upon the form itself, so that checkmarks will be sufficient to record the information desired?

"The answers to these questions will help to determine the size of the form and the surface of the paper, and perhaps the placing and arrangement of some of the items. They will affect the spacing of the items, both vertically and horizontally. Forms which are closely related in use should be designed in parallel so that the transfer of data from one to the other is made as easy and as error-proof as possible."[9]

The design of forms has a very important bearing upon their record quality. Commander McCormick points out in this connection, most pertinently, "In my opinion the greatest weakness of form and system designers is their lack of understanding of filing problems and how the forms they devise affect filing. In selecting sizes of forms, for instance, the element of correct filing is often overlooked completely. Forms that are one-half inch too large to fit in standard equipment have to be filed in cabinets several inches oversize. An interesting point with respect to correct filing size is the fact that the sizes that are correct from a filing standpoint provide for the most economical consumption of paper when cutting from mill sheets and for the most efficient use of printing presses."[10]

This matter of the relationship of size to filing is ignored by Butler and Johnson in their otherwise excellent discussion of form designing. . . .

The smallest practicable standard size paper should be used.

The quality of the paper (percentage of rag or sulphite) should be gauged to the relative permanence of retention for the form.

As Commander McCormick points out, "The weight of paper in relation to its size is important in filing. A 16-pound bond in letter size is satisfactory for filing, but if the form is increased to 9½ by 12 inches or 11 by 14 inches, it becomes awkward to handle and reduces filing productivity. The weight of paper used has a direct bearing on filing space. A 16-pound sheet is about three-thousandths of an inch thick, whereas a 20-pound sheet is close to four-thousandths. In translating this to the filing and storage of records it means the difference between 300 sheets and 250 per filing inch. Filing space is often overlooked by form designers when deciding on paper specifications."[11]

Bulter and Johnson call attention to other factors in deciding on paper specifications. "Letterheads and envelopes, and occasionally other forms, should suggest the quality and stability of the company they represent. Weight is one means of creating the desired impression.

"Weight is also an important factor in durability and in making for ease of handling. The number of carbon copies to be made has a bearing upon the weight selected. Moreover, not only typewriters, but many other machines have definite requirements or limitations which must be kept in mind in adopting standards for weights of paper.

"As a rule, forms bound together in books can be printed on lighter paper than those forms to be used singly or loose. On the other hand, the larger the form the heavier should be the paper. Postage and mailing requirements must also be considered. Forms may have to fall within definite weight limits to avoid unnecessary increases in mailing costs.

"Colors should be standardized, not to reduce their variety, but to give useful meaning to the variety. Selected with care, colors can be made to speed up routing, sorting and filing. They may be used to designate departments, branches, or other divisions of the business; to direct attention to 'rush' orders or other urgent communications; to indicate any other useful classification, such as the months, days of the week, manifold copies, and the like."[12]

The arrangement of the form is important to filing. McCormick points out that "Having the repeating references such as order numbers, alphabetical names, and other key filing factors in easy filing positions is essential."[13] Butler and Johnson add: ". . . the sequence and grouping of the items on a form will have much to do with the speed and accuracy with which the form is filled in. . . .

"The items on a form should usually be arranged in the order in which the work of filling in can best be done. If the information entered on one form is taken from another, the sequence of those items should be the same in both forms. If the information to be entered comes from a number of different forms, the items coming from each form should ordinarily be kept together in a group rather than scattered about, even though the scattering would seem to give them a more logical arrangement on the form as a whole. There are, of course, two points of view on the arrangement of a form: that of the person filling in the form, and that of the person who must read it. Both viewpoints must be considered. Often there is no conflict; when there is, the work of filling in will probably prove the more important.

"Ease and accuracy of reference can usually be secured without disturbing the best sequence of items. The items on most forms fall into natural groups. If these groups are made to stand out by the judicious use of rules, type, and white space, the eye will naturally go to each of them in their relative order of importance. For reference purposes, the upper right quarter of the form is the most valuable; then follow, in order the upper left, the lower right, and the lower left quarters.

"Perhaps the most common shortcoming of the thoughtlessly designed form is poor spacing. Some items are given two to ten times as much space as they need. Other spaces, particularly those calling for handwritten entries, are much too small. Many forms that are to be filled in on the typewriter have been designed without reference to its space limitations. The effect is to make the typist do a lot of hand spacing, resulting in a serious loss of time. It is much easier and more profitable, to adapt the form to the typewriter."[14]

Paper and Printing Digest says that "Rules should be set two picas apart to conform to double-spaced typewritten matter. This distance between rules is the minimum suitable for the average handwriting."[15] The paper specified should be sufficiently sized to take ink without feathering. This is an important point because paper preferred for printing generally does not take writing ink well.

An office manual detailing procedure and policies and containing samples of all forms used with notations as to suggested future improvements is recommended by Butler and Johnson. From an administrative point of view this manual should be revised frequently to keep it up to date. From a historical point of view a series of such manuals, compiled at stated intervals and whenever a notable reorganization takes place, is highly desirable. One of the reasons why certain records have to be retained indefinitely is that they throw light upon the history and method of administration at certain periods. Some of these records could be destroyed if there were somewhere a detailed statement as to procedures and policies as of definite dates.

The practice of keeping a diary is commended to officials. In this should be briefed all office matters worthy of note and especially résumés of all important personal and telephone interviews, particularly when such conversations involve matters of policy. It is an increasingly common practice to make stenographic or dictaphone recordings of such discussions, though the storage problem for the latter is discouraging. Perhaps the wartime instrument which permits hours of sound recordings on a small roll of wire may be the answer.

A monthly report on all important office matters detailing decisions reached pro and con certain procedures and policies will be found valuable historically as well as from an administrative point of view. These reports should be far broader in scope than the formal matters recorded in biennial reports. Biennial reports are aimed at the public and naturally strive for a favorable impression. The chronicles recommended here are for the benefit of the administrator and should record happenings and problems impartially. Such reports should be made a matter of record and should be required to be handed down to one's successors. They may properly be regarded as confidential records not open to unrestricted public inspection, at least until they have become noncurrent records.

8

Physical Properties of Archives

1 / Paper

It may seem futile to discuss standards for the materials
from which records are made—paper, ink, typewriter ribbons, and
carbon paper. Most of the literature on these subjects is technical
and little has been written from the point of view of the official who
creates or the archivist who preserves records. A popular work on
papers and inks is Julius Grant: *Books & Documents: Dating, Permanence, and Preservation.*[1] Two other books are also of interest
in this connection: William Bond Wheelwright: *Printing Papers;*[2]
and Dard Hunter: *Papermaking: The History and Technique of an
Ancient Craft.*[3]

Fifteen thousand types of paper are said to be manufactured.
Of these we are concerned here only with papers suitable for hand
and typewriting—the papers usually known as bond and ledger
papers. Book paper—that is, paper designed for printing—differs
from writing paper chiefly in its finish and mineral content, writing
paper having a harder texture and finish largely but not entirely
controlled by the amount of sizing used. The qualities which make

Part 1 of this chapter, "Paper," was originally published as
"Record Materials: Paper" in *Illinois Libraries* 27 (May 1945): 270–74.
Part 2, "Inks," was originally published as "Record Materials: Ink" in
Illinois Libraries 27 (October 1945): 438–44.

for permanence and durability are the same for both types of paper, hence much that has been written about quality in book papers is also applicable to writing papers.

"Paper consists essentially of fibers matted together. In addition they are usually sized (*e.g.* with alum and rosin, or with gelatin) to prevent ink 'running,' and loadings and colouring matters may also be added. The principal chemical constituent of the fibres is cellulose.... [and] pure cellulose is very permanent. Unfortunately cellulose does not occur in the pure state, and the processes of removal of the undesirable impurities which cause lack of permanence not only tend to weaken the fibre, but may also degrade the cellulose into other substances which themselves cause deterioration."[4]

Paper properties are largely determined by the composition of the paper; that is, its cellulose fibers or pulp as it is generally called; but also the care and skill with which its material has been prepared and manipulated during manufacture.

Rags and wood are the principal sources of paper pulp. Prior to 1840 when ground wood pulp was introduced, all paper was made from cotton and linen rags. Rags are still considered the most durable and permanent raw materials for paper. Cotton and linen fibers are made up of long curly fibrillae or tendrils that cling and mesh together to make a strong, uniform, closeknit web. The cellulose fibers made from wood lack those clinging and meshing qualities. In the process of spinning thread and weaving cloth most of the impurities are eliminated, and the alpha cellulose content of new rags may rate as high as 99 percent. If it were not for the cost and scarcity of usable rags, all papers would probably still be made from rag pulp.

The best source of rag pulp is cuttings from new white cotton and linen rags obtained from garment factories. Linen rags are little used today because of their scarcity but are mixed with cotton fibers in the finest grade of papers. Soiled or colored rags must be bleached with strong chemicals which attack not only the coloring matter in the rag, but also assail and irreparably damage the cellulose fibers. Also destructive, especially as to permanence, is the fact that a powerful chemical residue always stays in the finished paper. The pulp is made by macerating the clippings with dull knives and dissolving the material in water.

The best rag and rag-content papers are always watermarked, and those sold for permanent records attach a certificate to the wrapping, stating that all new linen and cotton rag clippings have been used. . . .

The terms "all rag," "rag content," and "linen finish" tell nothing about the quality of the paper. "All rag" may mean pulp made from such an inferior type of rag that the paper is less durable than sulphite paper. The term might even mean rayon rags which are themselves a form of chemical wood. "Rag content" merely means that some rag pulp was used, but not how much. "Linen finish" merely means a surface having a linenlike texture.

Cotton linters—that is, cotton as it comes from the cotton boll —can also be used in papermaking, but because of the relative cost of processing, rag cuttings are preferred.

Wood pulps are classified as ground wood pulp and chemical wood pulp, which in turn is subdivided according to the process of preparation as soda pulp, sulphite (or kraft) pulp, and sulphite pulp.

Ground wood or mechanical wood pulp is made by merely pressing peeled logs against a grindstone and screening out the knots and slivers. The pulp resulting contains nearly 50 percent of lignin and the other natural contents of wood with which the fibers are associated. These impurities rapidly discolor under sunlight, and their structure breaks down causing the paper in which they exist to become brittle and finally to disintegrate. The strength of ground wood pulp is so low that a certain percent of higher-grade papers has to be mixed with it to hold the paper together. Newspapers, cheap books, and magazines are generally printed on ground wood pulp. Cheap filing folders are often made of this substance and should be avoided because the impurities in the folder will discolor and cause decay of the papers which come into contact with it. Much of the prejudice against all forms of wood pulp stems from popular experience with rapidly disintegrating newspapers.

Most writing papers and the better grades of book papers are made partly or wholly from chemically purified wood.

Soda pulp uses wood from deciduous or broad leaf trees such as popular, chestnut, bass, and gum. The wood is heated under pressure with sodium hydroxide to separate the cellulose fibers. The pulp produced is white and may be from 68 to 78 percent pure cellulose, but the fibers are short and not very strong. Because the fiber is soft, the ink would run if used in writing papers. Soda pulp is now used chiefly as a filler for sulphite printing papers.

Sulphate or kraft pulp is made from coniferous woods, such as spruce and pine, using sodium sulphate as the solvent. The resultant pulp is strong, but it cannot be brought to a good white without weakening bleaches. It is used chiefly where strength but not color is essential—for wrapping papers, bags, envelopes, and the like. For the record department it is used in the making of folders. The acid effect of poor folder material on papers has already been mentioned. Good rag bristol would make the best folders, but because of its cost it is not stocked.

In purchasing folders, the Illinois archives has found that the darker the color the less is the chemical reaction on the papers filed in the folder. This is presumably due to the larger proportion of sulphate pulp used. Before World War II, the best grades of folders contained manila hemp, a very strong fiber used for ropes, textiles, and papers obtained from a Philippine tree related to the banana. The term manila as used in the paper trade, however, no longer means that manila fiber is used, but merely refers to the buff manila color. Wheelwright gives the following definition: "Manila Tag. Sometimes called document manila, a stiff, rigid sheet basis 24x36 —100 to 200 [pounds], of good folding and tearing strength and a light buff color. The color shade varies according to the grade. Ground wood is used together with sulphite in the cheaper qualities, sulphite or sulphate pulps, in the better, and more or less manila rope in still higher grades."[5]

Sulphite pulp is made from coniferous trees—spruce and hemlock especially—treated with bisulphite of lime. High yields of pulps of good color and fairly good strength are obtained; they can be bleached, though with some loss in strength. Sulphite pulps have a high degree of alpha cellulose content—as high as 86 to 94 percent —and are very resistant to light, heat, and aging effects in general. Sulphite papers have almost superseded rag paper for all purposes except the making of permanent records. Accelerated aging tests indicate that the best grade of sulphite papers is probably at least as permanent as a low quality of rag paper. The process was first used in 1856. Because this paper has not been on the market long enough to show positively what its life expectancy actually will be, paper made from all rag stock is still recommended whenever permanent records are necessary. Even though the cellulose content may be as pure as in all rag paper, the fact that sulphite fibers do not intermesh as throroughly as the fibers obtained from rags would seem to indicate that sulphite paper will not prove as durable as rag paper. Although it is difficult to judge sulphite papers by appearance, an easy way to recognize quality is to remember that the two best grades, and those grades only, are always watermarked.

Reworked paper pulp—that is, paper made from wastepaper— is not made up into writing paper, though it is sometimes employed as a filler for book papers.

Paper is formed from the pulp which is about 98 percent water, to which gelatin or rosin sizing, coloring, fillers, and so on, have been added. This treated pulp, then called stuff, is flowed over a slowly moving fine copper wire screen which acts as a sieve for draining out the water, then passing the mat which forms through a series of rollers which dry, roll, and polish the resultant sheet of paper. Papermaking is described as an art, because the quality of the paper can be affected at every step taken in the manufacture.

If the flow of pulp over the screen were entirely in one direction, all the fibers would lie longitudinally in the sheet. The screen is, therefore shaken sideways, to intermesh the fibers. In handmade paper there is little grain because the screen is rocked equally in all directions. In the machine-made paper of today, however, there is always a decided difference between the longitudinal and cross grain. The more slowly the papermaking machine is run, the greater the intermeshing of fiber and the less the difference in grain.

The direction of grain is very important, especially where binding is involved. Everyone has noted that some paper in ring binders tears out more easily than other sheets of apparently the same weight and quality. That difference is due to the direction of the grain of paper. This may be compared to a piece of cloth in which the crosswise threads are fewer or of lighter weight than the lengthwise threads. Needless to say, the cloth tears more easily longitudinally than crosswise. The same is true with paper. The grain of paper should run parallel to binding so that the paper will turn easily and lie flat; also, the paper is less likely to tear away from the binding, whether sewn or on a post binder, because the pull is against the strong dimensions of the paper. With cards, the grain should go around the typewriter platen, though the cards would stand up better in the file if the grain ran crosswise. A simple test for direction of the grain is to moisten the paper. Damp paper rolls along the length of the grain and also tears more easily in that direction.

In selecting paper for records, the two matters to be considered are permanence and durability. Permanence relates to the length of time the paper will endure without disintegration. That is a matter chiefly resulting from the quality of the fibers used and of chemical residues in the paper. Durability relates to the way paper stands up under handling—whether or not it dog-ears too easily, tears, breaks on folds, or tears out of binding. The principal signs of a breakdown in paper are discoloration (yellowing) and brittleness, indicated by breaks on folds and along edges.

One of the principal tests for permanence is the accelerated aging test. This test is made by exposing the sample in a receptacle for seventy-two hours at 100 degrees Centigrade (212 degrees Fahrenheit). The paper is tested for folding endurance, and the like, both before and after heating and the results compared.

There are a number of standard tests for papers and for physical characteristics. But, as the L. L. Brown Paper Company points out: "The true quality of paper cannot be determined by testing for any *one* property. Nor are tests of *all* properties dependable unless the analysis is expertly made under controlled atmospheric conditions.

... An increase of but 15% in relative humidity causes some tests to change 100%."[6]

In selecting papers it is necessary to be guided chiefly by paper experts. That is one reason why the certificates of quality which are attached to record papers are so important. There are, however, some simple examinations which the amateur can make for himself.

The two kinds of writing paper under consideration here are bond and ledger papers. Bond paper is used for most records up to and beyond legal size (8½ by 14 inches). Ledger papers are intended primarily for accounting records. They are generally heavier and smoother than bonds and are particularly made to stand erasures.

Four grades of sulphite bonds and ledgers are recognized by the paper industry. Two of these are watermarked and two are not. Rag content is indicated in watermarks by symbols, as stars, or by statements such as "25 percent rag."

Papers are graded further by weight. Writing-paper weight means the weight of a ream of five hundred sheets, 17-by-22 inches in size. Book-paper weights are computed from the 23-by-38-inch size. Hence a twenty-pound bond paper and a fifty-pound book paper are the same weight. Unless one realizes that difference, one is apt to run into difficulties in drafting printing specifications, particularly for printed forms.

Experience suggests that for loose sheet manuscripts sixteen-pound bond paper is satisfactory, but if the pages are punched for binding twenty-pound will be found more durable. If the notebook is likely to be used repeatedly, twenty-four-pound stock will prove still better. The larger the sheet the heavier weight paper should be used.

The writing qualities desired for both bond and ledger paper are a smooth glareless surface which promotes writing ease; the ruling and writing must be clean cut without spreading yet showing a suitable degree of penetration; it must be possible to write over erasures. Rag-content paper is less opaque than sulphite bonds. Thus, two samples of the same weight and finish may be distinguished as either rag content or sulphite by laying samples over a block type, placing the samples to be compared side by side.

Ledger papers being made with a view to erasability, the samples should be tested with a steel eraser and the fluff scraped off and examined. The lower grades show a lint which is less powdery in character, and the cheapest give off a somewhat fibrous lint, leaving behind a rougher scar which refuses to take fresh writing without getting fuzz in the pen. A high-grade ledger can be written upon over the erased area quite satisfactorily, especially if it is first polished with the bone handle of the eraser. There will be little if any tendency for the lines to spread, because of the superior sizing qualities of high-grade ledger paper.

Card stock for permanent indexes should be made of 100 percent rag index bristol. Ninety-pound bristol stock is recommended for 3-by-5 and 4-by-6 cards as being the most economical of filing space but durable as to handling. Cards should preferably be die cut, with rotary cut (two knives) second best. Straight guillotine cuts result in feather edges. Edges must have snap and must not scuff from handling. The card stock must be made on the fourdrinier machine, not the cylinder cardboard machine. The latter does not have the lateral shake which intermeshes the fibers. Cylinder-made cardboard does not take erasure well. Sulphite bristol with no rag content should be used in tabulating machines because rag paper may contain minute particles of metal which cause static and interfere with accurate operation of the machine. . . .

Officials sometimes excuse their failure to use the best quality of paper for permanent records by saying that first-class all rag paper is too expensive. An analysis of the qualities of papers used for other records in the same offices frequently shows that paper has been selected haphazardly—many records and memoranda of only temporary value are written on paper of a much higher quality than necessary. Surprising economies, sometimes as high as 25 to 30 percent, can be effected through selection of papers on a basis of the length of time the records are to be preserved.

Too many factors enter into the question of selection to permit more than a vague generalization here as to what papers to specify for what types of records. The amount of handling and the thickness of the paper to be used are factors. In general, paper experts recommend that for documents to be preserved for from five to ten years 50 percent rag should be used; 75 percent rag for documents to be kept for fifteen years, and 100 percent rag for documents to be preserved for fifteen years or longer. A 75 percent rag paper (that is, 25 percent sulphite) is preferable to a secondary grade of all rag (stock made from bleached or old rags). Records destined to be preserved for periods shorter than five years can be made on progressively cheaper papers, with ground wood pulp paper used for scratch pads, work sheets, and minor intraoffice memoranda.

2 / Inks

Since the typewriter has almost superseded pen and ink for making today's records, it may seem unnecessary to devote space to the subject of inks. However, it is just as important as ever that signatures and other handwriting which occurs on legal instruments should be permanent. File clerks, manuscript curators, and archivists who have the custody of older records need to understand something about the chemistry of inks, lest they employ unwise repair or unfolding methods which may cause the ink to run or to fade. As with the subject of paper, there are few nontechnical discussions of inks.[7]

Writing inks in common use today are chiefly of three types: carbon inks, iron gallo-tannate inks, and dye inks.

Carbon inks are made from a finely ground carbon or a similar substance (as soot or lampblack) used as the pigment. The best carbon inks, known as india or Chinese ink, are made from lampblack or soot obtained by burning vegetable oils such as sesame or wood (tung) oil. Carbon cannot be bleached by any amount of exposure to intense light and it resists attack by chemicals that quickly destroy paper. If carbon could be dissolved in water, it would be ideal material for making black writing ink. India ink is not a solution, but a suspension of carbon in water containing glue or gum. Carbon ink is too thick to be free flowing and it tends toward annoying sedimentation. Therefore it is used in record work chiefly for engineering and architectural drawings. Most colored drawing inks are clear solutions of dyes and as such are fugitive in color. Pigment inks, that is those made with an insoluble dry coloring matter such as dye lakes, are more permanent but are seldom used today because of a tendency to "settle out."

Iron gallo-tannate, or iron gall inks as they are often called, are the most satisfactory permanent writing inks. The principle upon which they are based is that a dark-colored compound results when tannic acid reacts with an iron salt. Tannic or gallic acids are dissolved in water to which a solution of ferrous sulphate and hydrochloric acid is added. To this mixture is added just sufficient coloring matter (preferably indigo blue) to give the ink a temporary color as the pure gallo-tannate ink, without coloring matter, will write with a dirty gray-green color when the characters are first formed. Upon exposure to the atmosphere oxidation occurs, precipitating a tannate of iron and making a black record which possesses a very high degree of permanency. This is the principle back of the familiar blue-black inks.

The chief advantages of iron gallo-tannate inks are the permanence of color, the penetration of the paper by the ink, and the fact that the ink is comparatively free flowing. Permanent iron gallo-tannate inks can even be made for use in fountain pens. The chief disadvantage is that these inks are acid in their reaction, not only corroding steel pens but being very active toward paper. It is no uncommon occurrence to find old records in which the ink has eaten away the paper so that letters or even whole words have dropped out.

Because the iron oxide in the ink penetrates the fibers of the paper, it is impossible to remove all traces of the ink by erasure, ink eradicators, water damage, or even by burning. Charred or faded manuscripts written with iron gallo-tannate inks can be deciphered by the use of violet and infrared rays, by certain chemical fumes, by prolonged exposure to photographic plates, or by the use of a microscope.[8]

Dye inks are coming into increasingly greater use because they keep almost indefinitely, are noncorrosive, and being much more dilute than iron inks they do not form thick deposits on pen points. Dye inks are fugitive, as everyone knows who has had experience with records made partly with ordinary red ink. When the ink is a solution of a dye, there is no possibility of restoration when the ink fades. Oxidation of the dye forms volatile products which escape into the air, or maybe small amounts of other substances which remain in the paper but with which there is no certain way of forming colored compounds. For these reasons dye solutions are not regarded as suitable for record inks. The fad of signing documents in green, red, or purple ink should not be indulged in where permanence is necessary. . . .

Printing inks concern us here because writing frequently occurs in association with printing, especially in connection with printed black forms. Ordinary printing ink is prepared by grinding a pigment with boiled linseed oil or varnish. Carbon black is the usual pigment used for black ink. The average good black printing ink, therefore, has a degree of permanence far superior to that of any paper on which it is likely to be used; and, moreover, it has little or no effect on the paper. Colored printing inks are more fugitive than black inks, and should not be used where permanence is a first consideration. Red ink is occasionally used to call attention to instructions for filling out a form. It should not be used as a part of the information making up the contents of the form itself. . . .[9]

Since most records of today are made on the typewriter, the quality of typewriter ribbons used is most important. Modern typewriting ink is compounded on similar lines to printing inks, that is, finely ground insoluble pigments (including lakes) are used. Carbon is the medium used for making black ribbons, and this is very permanent. Blue ribbons use Prussian blue and reds use antimony-cinnabar; the two latter are fugitive to alkali and acid, respectively. Black typewriter ribbons should be used exclusively for permanent records. The carrying medium for the pigment is vaseline or a mixture of heavy oil and paraffin wax which is well mixed with a fatty oil or oleic acid. The problem of manufacturing is the necessity that the ribbons should remain moist as long as possible, and glycerine is sometimes added to solutions of dyestuffs in water to ensure this end. The early typewriter inks were unsatisfactory chiefly because of the nature of the dyestuffs used. The acidity of the mix is an important point to watch on account of its effect on the paper.

In the manufacture of typewriter ribbons, the two materials to be considered are the fabric and the ink. The fabric should be good quality cotton [or nylon] cloth, free from waste and imperfections of manufacture. The thread count, or fineness of weave, is of importance because if the threads are too coarse and the fabric is too loosely woven, the writing will not be sharp and cleancut. The thread count per square inch should not only be sufficiently high but also the differences between the warp and filling counts should be small. An equal number of threads in the warp and filling produces the maximum number of points of contact of the ribbon with the paper as the blow of the typewriter key forces the ribbon against the paper. The closer these points of contact are the clearer the writing. The thickness of the ribbon also affects the sharpness of the writing. The present U.S. specification requires that the number of threads per square inch shall be at least 300 and permits the number in one of the directions to be as low as 148. . . .

The great majority of typewriter ribbons used today are cut from fabric forty-two inches wide and in lengths of 144 yards, cut by a special machine into strips one-half inch wide, with a narrow band of adhesive applied to each cut edge to keep the warp yarns from coming loose. The cost of weaving is not only less, but ribbons with selvages are said to be not quite so uniform in width as cut ribbons. Some special office machines put such a great strain on the ribbons that the extra strength of the selvage is needed. Waviness of the edges caused by poor cutting or uneven gumming may fray in the typewriter and cause trouble.

Typewriter inks are a special form of printing ink—that is, they are fluid mixtures that consist essentially of a liquid portion or vehicle, and a solid coloring material or pigment. The vehicle may consist of mineral, animal, or vegetable oils, or a mixture of them. Sometimes a liquid wax such as sperm oil is included. Carbon black is the most important pigment. Because of the slightly brown color of carbon black, blue or violet "toners" are put in the ink on the same principle as bluing in the laundry to make clothes look snow-white instead of yellowish. Specialized inks are made for ribbons having two colors, for instance, black and red, running side by side, so that the colors will not diffuse or "bleed" into one another.

There are many things to be considered in judging the quality of a typewriter ribbon. The ink must be applied to the fabric in sufficient quantity to give writing of good intensity of color, but not enough to cause blurring or to clog the type. The ink must not be so thin as to smear the paper nor so thick that it will not flow through the fabric. By writing several times with the same portion of the ribbon, the ink is partially depleted. If the ink is right, it will flow to this portion of the ribbon if allowed to rest for a short time. A satisfactory ribbon should show good "recovery" within one hour. It will have a longer useful life, other things being equal, than a ribbon that is made with too thick an ink.

Perhaps the greatest fault of a typewriter ribbon is that the ink contains too much oil in proportion to the amount of pigment. This oiliness greatly increases the amount of writing that can be done with a ribbon. The more fluid the ink the greater the recovery, and the greater the probability that the ink is too oily and will show on the reverse side of the paper. Excessive oiliness makes it harder to erase misprints without smearing. When testing ribbons, it has been noticed repeatedly that when the ink is too oily it does not contain enough carbon black. As the ribbon becomes more worn, the successive lines become paler and begin to have the distinctly purplish color of the toner. The ink is colored with dye and not with carbon black. If the ink contains enough carbon, the lines change from intense black to light gray by degrees, and are not purplish. This ink almost never shows on the reverse side of the paper.

When ink does not contain a sufficient amount of carbon black the writing done when the ribbon has been in use for some time will fade when exposed to bright light. Carbon black itself will not fade when exposed to direct sunlight, and it is not changed in any way if the typewritten matter happens to be kept in such a damp place that the paper becomes moldy and falls to pieces. Treating the paper with chemicals that will bleach the dye or even destroy the paper has no effect on the carbon black. Typewriting done with a properly inked ribbon ought to last as long as the paper holds together. . . .

Ribbons for computing and recording machines are of the same general nature as typewriter ribbons. They require a fabric of high-breaking strength, as there is considerable strain in operation, especially in the automatic machines. They are usually rather heavily inked. Permanence is not so important a factor as in typewriter ribbons. . . .[10]

Before the days of the typewriter and carbon paper, business letters and other important documents were written longhand with a special copying ink and press copies were made for filing. To make a press copy, a blank sheet of paper is laid upon the writing, and the two are strongly compressed between damp cloths or blotting papers for a short time. The water squeezed out of the cloths dissolves enough of the ink to make a copy of the writing on the blank sheet. Because the writing is reversed in the copy, the blank sheet is of thin translucent paper so that the copied writing can be read on the reverse side. Writing done with ordinary typewriter ribbons will not yield press copies because the pigment and dyes are not soluble in water. Special ribbons are needed for this purpose. A favorite combination seems to be a ribbon that gives black writing and blue press copies. Part of the pigment of the ink is a finely powdered blue dye which is usually dark brown when in this form, and does not noticeably affect the color of the ribbon copy. In the letterpress, the water from the damp cloths penetrates the film of oil on the particles of dye and dissolves enough to make strongly colored copies. In the early days of the typewriter, glycerol inks were used but were soon abandoned for oil inks.

Ordinary stamp-pad ink consists of equal parts of glycerol and water in which is dissolved varying amounts of the dye. "At ordinary temperatures glycerol is practically not at all volatile, and it is hygroscopic, or attracts moisture from damp air. This keeps the ink from drying on the pad, even in winter, when the air in heated buildings may be of desert aridity. In summer, when the air is of high humidity much of the time, the ink takes up water, and sometimes the pad is too wet." In neither case is the change in the ink sufficiently great to affect its use. Tests are made by saturating disks of white felt with the standard and a sample, then making impressions on the same sheet of white paper with a clean rubber stamp. Rapidity of drying, sharpness, and intensity of coloring are compared. A comparative fading test and a test for absorption of moisture or drying of the pad after exposure for ten days concludes the test. Black stamp-pad ink should always be used for file marks, not only because of the fastness of color but also because colored inks, particularly reds and purples, do not register in photographic reproductions.[11]

Because carbon copies are the official and only records of outgoing correspondence, it is appropriate to give some attention here to the qualities of good carbon paper. Carbon paper is paper covered on one side with a thin even coating of a mixture of colored pigment with waxy and oily materials. The general name is given because most carbon paper is black and is colored with carbon. As in typewriter ribbon ink, a blue or violet tone is added to neutralize the brownish tone of thin layers of carbon ink. Only the carbons made with black carbon ink may be considered permanent.

Typewriter ribbons must be thin, so as to give sharp writing. There is even greater reason for making carbon paper thin, because the blow of the type is spread more or less by being transmitted through the ribbon, the first sheet of paper, and the carbon paper itself before it can make a copy. This spreading of the force of the blow is increased a little for each additional carbon copy made. In the trade, carbon paper is known by the weight of the tissue on which it is coated. The four-pound paper is used for making a large number of manifold copies: five and seven-pound papers are suitable for ordinary correspondence and reports; and the heavier papers are intended for pen and pencil work. The better grades should consist entirely of tag, manila, hemp, or jute rope stock or a mixture of these. Cheap carbon papers made with ground wood pulp deteriorate very quickly.

There are numerous grades of typewriter carbon paper which differ in weight of tissue and in the hardness of their coating. Hard, soft, or medium finished papers are produced by varying the proportions of the ingredients used. The terms are only relative since each manufacturer establishes his own standard.

The hardness of the coating to a great extent determines the suitability of the carbon paper for a given kind of work, but there are other factors that influence the results; among these are the thickness and stiffness of the first and copy sheets and of the carbon paper itself, the number of copies made at one time, the size of the type, the hardness of the platen and other characteristics of the typewriter, and the touch of the operator.

If only one to three copies are made at one time, hard carbon paper is best because it makes sharper copies and is cleaner. If a large number of copies must be made at one time, the carbon paper should have a soft coating. Too many users of carbon paper prefer the soft coating for ordinary work in which only one or two copies are made. Because it makes blacker copies, they ignore its faults. It soils the fingers easily and smears badly when erasures are made, and although the copies are blacker they are not as sharp and legible as those made with harder paper. Because there seems to be no method for measuring the hardness of the coating, the best way to find out whether the carbon paper is suitable for a given class of work is to make writing tests, first noting general physical characteristics. As in the case of typewriter ribbons, the Bureau of Standards warns against selection of brands on the basis of single tests, because carbon papers have unavoidable variations in inking and in the foundation paper.[12]

A good carbon paper should be clean and nonsmudging. The coating should be applied evenly and smoothly and there should be no pinholes or other imperfections. The paper should lie flat on a smooth surface for ease in handling by the operator. . . .

Copies made with black carbon paper should not fade when

exposed to direct sunlight, though they will become brownish on account of the destruction of the toner. A carbon copy suffers more from handling than does a ribbon copy because most of the color of the carbon paper lies on the surface of the paper and can be rubbed off. The fluid part of the ink in a ribbon sinks into the paper, and part of the carbon goes with it and adheres to the fibers of the paper. Much of the ink is thus protected against being rubbed off.

9

The Handling and Repair of Fragile Documents

1 / THE REPAIR OF MANUSCRIPTS

Few public libraries have important manuscript collections, but librarians are frequently appealed to for advice as to the best means of conserving family papers and other documents. Paper breaks where it has been folded, it often becomes mildewed, and especially in the case of newspapers it disintegrates because of poor quality. This article . . . makes . . . a few suggestions as to the usual methods of preserving and repairing manuscripts.

There are three commonly used methods of repairing documents: framing, coating or spraying with a reinforcing liquid, and covering with paper, cloth, or cellulose acetate made to adhere to the document.

Framing. The earliest, simplest, but costliest method of preserving manuscripts is to frame them under glass. One or two plates are used depending on whether it is desired to show one or both sides of the paper. This is perhaps the most satisfactory method to use where a single document is to be kept on permanent exhibit,

PART 1 OF THIS CHAPTER, "The Repair of Manuscripts," was originally published in *Illinois Libraries* 21 (February 1939): 5–6. Part 2, "Handling Fragile Documents," was originally published (in two parts) in *Illinois Libraries* 29 (November and December 1947): 410–13, 460–64.

as in a home. Especial care should be taken to seal out dust which might infiltrate through the frame.

Naturally glass is both too expensive and bulky for use in collections of any size. Manuscripts may be enclosed in celluloid or cellophane envelopes which may be purchased through stationers or made at home. Celluloid is preferable to cellophane, since it does not stretch and has more body. Edges can be sealed with scotch tissue. One firm manufactures cellophane envelopes with a deep paper border which can be bound into a post binder locked at both ends, both as a protection against loss of papers and protection against fire which would rarely penetrate beyond the border.

The advantage of celluloid and cellophane envelopes is their cheapness, protection against marks of handling when documents are exhibited, and the fact that anyone can make his own envelopes. The disadvantages are bulk, a flexibility which may cause further breakage of the paper, and a possible chemical reaction on the paper. If cellolose acetate and not cellulose nitrate forms the base, there is no additional fire hazard since the first named melts but does not flame or explode.

Coating or spraying with a reinforcing liquid. Various liquids have been devised which act like varnish in stiffening the paper. The most satisfactory of these is gelatine made by soaking parchment. The proper type of gelatine is almost impossible to get in the United States. Although extensive experiments have been made along these lines in Europe, American archivists frown upon their use. Most of them attract insects, are inflammable, or become brittle with age. They are mentioned here merely as a matter of record and because from time to time such liquids are advertised in this country and librarians should be warned against indiscriminate trials.

Covering with paper, cloth, or cellolose acetate made to adhere to the document. American curators have found the most practical method of manuscript repair to be to affix a reinforcing agent by paste or thermoplastics. The simplest and easiest method is to paste a paper or cloth backing on the manuscripts. This method must not be used on official records because writing might be concealed by so doing. Paper mending-tape such as is commonly used in repairing leaves of books should *never* be used to repair manuscripts because of future discoloration and certain further breaking as the tape becomes brittle with age.

The most difficult and at the same time most artistic method of manuscript repair is to split the paper and insert a strengthening sheet of paper between the two pages. This is done by pasting the manuscript between two sheets of linen, letting it dry, and then tearing the sheets apart, half of the paper adhering to each sheet. The linen is then soaked off and the two sheets of paper mounted on the reinforcing paper. This process requires great skill and delicacy and is seldom employed except in deluxe work done abroad.

The most commonly employed method of manuscript repair is the so-called crepelin method. The manuscript to be repaired is dampened and a very thin silk gauze pasted on both sides, then dried under pressure. This silk gauze, commonly called crepelin, is sold under a trade name; one yard will cover six single legal size sheets. Although the process is simple to describe, it requires considerable practice and skill to do a satisfactory job of crepelining. If the paper is soft and the workman proficient, the crepelin is almost invisible. Experiments at the Illinois State Library indicate that legibility either in ordinary scanning or in photography is not impaired. For manuscripts which are very soft or charred, this is almost the only practical method of repair.

Japanese tissue is extensively used for covering newspapers. The method of repair is the same as for crepelin, but it is far less expensive. Legibility is markedly decreased and photography difficult. Japanese tissue paper is used only when cost is the major consideration.

The most recent method of repairing manuscripts, generally called lamination, makes use of thermoplastics. The manuscript is placed between very thin sheets of cellulose acetate and put under intense pressure in heated plates, resulting in a fusing together of the cellulose acetate and paper. The process is being developed at the National Archives and at least one laminating machine is on the retail market.

The proponents of this new method point to its cheapness, speed of operation (which may be questioned), no loss of legibility in scanning or photography (including infrared and X-ray processes), and the absolute protection against tampering with the contents of the manuscript. Critics of the method object to an unpleasant glaze, the loss of the "feel" of the manuscript with its implications as to possible forgery, and the fact that if the manuscript should slip in going through the press, the manuscript would be ruined, since the cellulose acetate cannot be removed. At present, the machinery used is expensive, bulky, and crude. . . . Undoubtedly, however, this new process when perfected will replace all other present methods of repairing manuscripts.

2 / Handling Fragile Documents

A well-known manuscripts collector once publicly excoriated the writer for having had some of the state archives of Illinois crepelined, a standard method of repair. Upon being asked how he would prevent further decay of damaged papers, the gentleman airly replied, "Every manuscript in my collection is in perfect condition. I won't buy one that isn't, and if by chance a document comes into my possession that is torn or broken I throw it out." Unfortunately for the archivist, however, such a simple solution is impracticable because the processes of decay affect, without discrimination, those manuscripts which are valuable as well as those which are worthless. Not only is it necessary to keep fragile materials, but even worse it is often necessary to produce decaying documents for use before it is possible to have them repaired. Every curator of manuscripts has frequent occasion to cringe when he observes the criminal carelessness with which not only his patrons but even, alas, his own staff members handle and further damage fragile papers. By and large these actions are due less to indifference than to ignorance about how to handle manuscripts properly. Many a scholar never guesses why he always has more difficulty in getting access to manuscript collections than some of his colleagues.

We shall discuss here, first the preparation of manuscripts for reference use and second, explain how to use manuscripts in the manner which will result in the minimum wear and tear. Most discussions of the subject of preparation assume that the curator will have available all the most modern equipment for proper processing. This article is aimed particularly at the librarian and custodian of small collections who must do the best he can with what he has at hand. . . .

Paper manuscripts only are dealt with in this article, not only because parchment, papyrus, palm leaf, bark, and other types of writing material are less frequently encountered, but also because these materials require quite different techniques.

The most important matter for both the curator and the patron to grasp is that a manuscript, whether it be of private or of public origin, must be neither added to nor subtracted from. That means that care must be taken to prevent loss of contents by breaking or flaking off of the paper itself; also that the original text must not be tampered with by overwriting, added notes, marks, and blots. These points will be elaborated upon below.

An elementary knowledge of the chemistry of paper and ink is useful to anyone handling manuscripts. . . . Basically paper is manufactured from short vegetable fibers suspended in water and agitated sidewise to mat them together while the water is being drained and squeezed out in the process of manufacture. Prior to 1820, all paper was made of cotton or linen rags, still considered the best fiber for the purpose. Later other substances were also used, the most common being ground wood, the cellulose fibers of which are leached out by caustic chemicals. Today practically all paper except that manufactured for records is made chiefly from wood pulp, though the better grades of sulphite paper are reinforced by adding 25 or 50 percent rag content. Theoretically, sulphite paper can be made as durable as all rag content paper, but practically speaking it is not considered permanent.

Paper has so many inherent weaknesses that one wonders that it does last so long. During manufacture the paper stock may be weakened by strong leaching and bleaching chemicals; the water used in manufacturing may hold impurities in suspension, such as small quantities of iron to cause foxing later; fibers may be imperfectly matted; residual chemicals may gradually weaken the paper. The basic fibers themselves, being of vegetable origin, tend to decay, pulp made from wood faster than that made from good white rags. The animal sizing used to give a smooth finish is attractive to insects and to mildew spores; in fact, it is the identical culture medium employed in the manufacture of penicillin. Too much heat and dryness accelerate chemical action which turns paper yellow and makes it brittle. Too much dampness encourages the growth of mold and softens the pulp to the point of dissolution.

For centuries the best and most widely used permanent writing ink has been iron gallo-tannate, made from acids which eat into the paper. Even where ink has apparently been completely erased chemically or mechanically, there is such a permeation of ink into the fibers of the paper that the original can be deciphered through the use of black light or chemical reagents. Not infrequently, manuscripts are encountered which have letters or even whole words completely eaten out by acidity of the ink.

Understanding somewhat the inherent weaknesses of paper, one can realize how very carefully and tenderly fragile manuscripts must be handled. If there is one cardinal rule for this it is to be slow and deliberate in lifting and turning pages, always supporting them from underneath.

The following instructions outline the procedures recommended for preparing manuscripts for use, followed by suggestions for handling manuscripts for purposes of consultation.

Upon receipt of a box of manuscripts, attention is first given to the destruction of any insect life in the papers themselves and to preventing the infestation of other material in the building from this accession. A large manuscripts department generally has a fumigator and a compressed air-vacuum cleaning machine. Where such equipment is lacking the following procedure will be a fairly adequate substitute.

The container should be removed unopened to a well-lighted table out of the breeze, somewhat distant from the stack area. A clean light-colored plain paper should be spread upon the table and the box opened. Most collections which come in, especially if transferred from an attic or basement storeroom, will be infested with silver fish and perhaps also with roaches or termites. Book-worms are not encountered in this country except in shipments from abroad. A good precaution is to open the box and spray the immediate vicinity of the work table with a good mist insecticide, either a bomb sprayer of the type used by the army or, better yet, the type of atomizers recommended for restaurant use. If possible leave the room closed overnight, but do not attempt to work in it without a thorough airing out for this type of spray employs either a cyanide solution or DDT, both of which are harmful to human beings as well as to insects. Care should be taken to avoid direct contact between the spray and the manuscripts because an oil is used and this would spot the paper. Although we have not seen a scientific report on the subject, we have not heard of any other deleterious effect of such sprays on paper and ink. The regular fumi-gation vaults employ chemicals which are harmless to paper, but these are not effective as sprays. Further suggestions concerning simple fumigation procedures may be found in Mrs. Minogue's bulletin.[1] If deemed expedient the spraying recommended above may be repeated while the box is being emptied.

The manuscripts should be removed from the box, a small handful at a time, and gently cleaned by blowing upon them and dusting with a small camel's-hair brush or a soft clean cloth. No attempt should be made at this time to remove more than the loose surface dirt. As each group has been dusted it should be laid down, in inverted order, on another table or in a clean carton several feet away from the table on which the cleaning is being done. Two tables placed parallel to each other with just space between to swing around in a swivel chair is a convenient arrangement. At in-tervals and always when work on the collection is halted, the paper on which the dust and dirt have been collecting should be carefully rolled up, destroyed, and fresh paper laid down. Great care should be taken not to disturb the order in which the manuscripts were packed even though they may appear to have been dumped into the box promiscuously, because that original order may later prove to have a significance which ought not to have been destroyed.

The next step is to sort the manuscripts into enough order to permit the taking of such inventory as may be necessary for the receipt and accession records. Each document as indicated by separate folding should be numbered in the order found in the box, very lightly in pencil, preferably on the part bearing the endorsement as to contents if there be one. It is then safe to refile these little packets as seems logical, because they can always be returned to the original order if desirable. It is generally preferable to do the preliminary filing before starting to unfold, partly because it is easier to handle documents in this more compact form and because it is less damaging to fragile papers. Advice on filing procedure would involve a discussion of classification principles which would be confusing at this point. It is generally safe to file chronologically if no other order is obvious.

Cleaning of individual leaves and unfolding of documents come next and are best performed as one operation. Because the addition of moisture is sometimes necessary in connection with the process of unfolding and because cleaning should be done before humidification is started, we shall start with a discussion of the removal of surface dirt and mold, rather than with the subject of unfolding. "First of all," as Mrs. Minogue explains, "it is necessary to remove all pins, clips, and rubber bands. . . . If rubber bands or clips are left in contact with records in storage, the rubber will deteriorate, leaving a brown stain on the paper, and the clips may corrode, making them difficult to remove and causing rust stains."[2] If, as often happens, it is later necessary to use clips to hold sheets of paper together, extreme care should always be taken to superimpose a sheet of paper between the clip and the manuscript and to avoid contact between the clip and adjacent manuscripts.

As each manuscript is unfolded it should be cleaned as thoroughly as possible without adding to the disintegration of the paper. There is nothing better for this purpose than a soft camel's-hair brush about one-half to three-quarters of an inch wide. The small pads of surgical cotton sold for dressing table use are also useful, especially for blotting up mildew. Each document should be dusted on the outside, within the folds and at the top and bottom. Great care should be taken to remove all loose mildew. Bleaching and removal of spots by chemicals, even gentle washing in warm water and mild soap suds, should be left to the know-how of the repair expert. Amateur dabbling with any liquids is too apt to damage rather than to improve the manuscript.

Documents often have an accumulation of dirt, especially in the folds and on the wrappers, which can largely be removed by a gentle brushing and careful use of art gum or soft bread crumbs. One might think of wallpaper cleaner in this connection, but that should not be used because of a slight tackiness which is likely to damage the writing. Test the softness of the paper and the ink on an inconspicuous part of the manuscript before cleaning the paper. It is better to produce a soiled document than a clean one with ink lightened by erasures. Most rag papers and many modern papers can be cleaned satisfactorily by the art gum and bread crumb method. Lay the document down on a hard smooth surface and clean with a light upward stroke in a direction away from the operator along the length of the grain. If the location of bad spots in the paper seems to call for some other direction, clean at a diagonal to the grain. Strokes across the grain may cause a slight fuzzling of the paper. Be careful to stop well short of brittle edges and folds and soft spots.

Mildew . . . seems to take two separate forms—a black powdery substance which turns the paper purple as it rots away and a white powdery but more moist substance which dissolves paper back to pulp. The black mildew can be brushed off and if all the powder is removed and the paper exposed to dry air for a few hours and then kept under normal conditions of humidity, there seems to be no spreading of the infection.

White mildew acts very much like a cancer. It generally starts as a hard powdery white spot about the size of a pinhead. This can be brushed off; but if not completely removed the mold soon eats into the paper and spreads, literally dissolving it. This type of mildew is penicillium, the same substance as the "miracle" drug of similar name. Both types of mold are strongly acid. Once established in paper we have found no really effective way to stop the growth except through lamination which seals off the paper from the spore-laden moisture of the air. The cellulose acetate used in that repair process seems impervious to mold, though the manufacturer of one of the lamination machines on the market advocates neutralization of acids in the paper prior to repair.

One treatment for mildew is to sponge the spot lightly with denatured alcohol, then to scatter an absorbentlike French chalk on the paper, brushing it off after two or three days. The use of the absorbent is particularly helpful in the case of bound volumes. The alcohol will remove surface stains of the purple variety but is not effective after the fibers of the paper have been attacked. It may dissolve printing ink and cause it to run, but it is harmless to ordinary writing fluids. Needless to say, precautions should be taken against the flammability of alcohol fumes. The British advocate exposure of manuscripts to thymol fumes in a tight container. Direct sunshine is as good a check for mildew as can be found, and violet rays are also effective. The bleaching effect of both upon ink limits the practicability of those remedies. In addition to its corroding effect upon paper, the penicillium or white mildew attacks inks like a chemical ink eradicator. Indeed the first symptom of its presence noted may be a fading of the ink accompanied by a bleaching and softening of the paper.

Mildew is a fungus growth spread by airborne spores and will again attack the paper if the moisture content of the air in the storage space becomes high enough. The best degree of humidity is 55 percent, but it does not become dangerous until the percentage rises above 75. In the absence of air conditioning, the simplest and cheapest room humidity control can be had by the use of sodium chloride, sold in handy containers by paint and drug stores for drying out basements. Paper which shows signs of softening from mildew should never be subjected to a flattening process that involves dampening of the paper.

In unfolding documents, all clips, pins, and rubber bands should be removed, but until repairs are made it is advisable to leave the original staples and lacings which hold the sheets together. Each document should be flattened by opening carefully to its full extent. Clerks quickly discover a knack of seizing the top and bottom of the sheet and jerking the document flat with a slight snap. This shortcut should be discouraged, because of the strain it puts upon the paper, especially at the folds.

Most writers on the subject advocate unfolding every document at the same time, but if the manuscript is very soft or very brittle it is preferable to leave it folded until complete repairs are made. Paper which is apparently intact often seems to disintegrate upon exposure to the air. An experienced manuscript curator learns to know instinctively whether or not it is safe to unfold, but it is impossible to reduce that to rules.

Sometimes several documents have stuck together. It is best, at this stage, not to try to separate them. Often a part of a document, usually the inside pages, is in good condition while the outside leaves are very brittle or very soft. It is common sense to leave the whole document folded until repaired rather than to risk confusion from separation of the parts. If the folded documents are in very bad condition, a sheet of white onionskin paper endorsed with necessary notes of identification can be folded around the document. The reshuffling involved in filing is then possible with minimum damage.

As each document is unfolded the sheets should be clipped together, using a small piece of folded paper (about two by three inches) between the manuscript and the clip, for all clips will eventually rust and leave a mark on the paper even if they do not stick together. . . . Rough edges on the ends of the wire should be avoided because of danger from tearing; also clips made of either very thin or very heavy wire are unsatisfactory. Pins and wire staples should not be used. The documents will lie flatter if the clips are affixed at different points on different documents, but if this is done, extra care must be taken to avoid contact between the clip and the adjacent manuscript. Usually it is best to attach the clips at the weakest point in the paper, as the paper holding the clip acts as reinforcement. Any pieces which fall off during the processing of the paper should also be put under the paper surrounding the clip. As an alternative to small pieces of paper under the clip, we sometimes attach the manuscripts to a piece of legal sized paper turned up about two inches from the bottom. The name of the collection, the date, and a description of the document are typed on the flap of this paper which serves as a support for the whole document. Patrons should be instructed to reattach all clips and papers just as given them, and the reference clerk should check on this.

Ordinarily documents will tend to flatten each other when superimposed upon one another in a pile. Heavy binder's board or smooth pieces of plywood should be laid at the bottom and on top of each pile while working on the records. The piles should not be stacked more than four-to-six inches high lest they topple or skid. Papers filed in upright folders held tightly by drawer compressors will ordinarily need no further flattening process. If the compressor is too loose, however, there is some danger from sagging and curling. We do not advocate upright filing in drawers where the manuscripts are very fragile or where they are larger than legal size. For unmended fragile manuscripts of normal size we use pamphlet boxes just wide enough and tall enough to go in our cabinet drawers, and about four inches in depth. The manuscripts are on end but prevented from slipping about by crushed paper. We find less abrasion from this method of filing than from horizontal filing in boxes because there is bound to be a certain amount of shuffling of the contents of the box when it is pulled from the shelf. For oversize manuscripts, shallow boxes laid horizontally on the shelf seem the most practical equipment. Acid-free folders, readily obtainable commercially, should be used. Ordinarily the loaded folder should not be over half an inch thick, but with fewer manuscripts to the folder if the documents are fragile. Each folder should be plainly labeled as to contents and numbered or dated in a manner to facilitate refiling. Folders should be separated by guide cards about every four or five inches.

If thick documents have been deeply creased or rolled tightly it will usually be necessary to add moisture to complete the flattening process. The National Archives has a special humidifying vault in which such documents are spread out on stainless steel shelves until thoroughly permeated with moisture. The documents are then removed and the separate sheets run through a household type electric mangle or ironed with a hand electric iron. We have on occasion placed dampened sheets of paper between waxed paper and run them through our photographic print drier with fair results. This process requires that multileaved documents be taken apart, which is not always possible or desirable. Mrs. Minogue comments upon this process as follows: "Because some residual moisture remains even after ironing it has been found that the process of flattening actually adds to the strength of papers that have become embrittled from age and exposure to dry air. If the flattened papers are subsequently stored under the suggested 50 to 65 percent relative humidity the moisture will remain and the papers will have become permanently more flexible." Our experience, however, points definitely away from the advisability of using any heat in connection with the flattening process.

Mrs. Minogue tacitly admits as much in her next paragraph, "If, as occurs in rare instances, papers are extremely weak or fragmentary, it may be advisable to flatten them by direct pressure without the use of heat. The humidified sheet must be very carefully flattened by hand on blotting paper, covered with another sheet of blotting paper, and subjected to light pressure in a binder's press for 24 hours. This method of flattening is always safe, and may be used in the treatment of any document, but as it requires much more time and labor than ironing, it is not recommended for any but the most delicate items."[3]

In the absence of mechanical humidification such as that available at the National Archives, various methods are used to add sufficient moisture for flattening papers. Because of the danger of causing ink to run or of weakening the fiber of paper it is not advisable for any but a skilled repairer to soak the paper itself. We have found the following method the easiest and safest procedure. The first process consists of laying a wet towel down on a binder's board, protected on both sides by waxed paper, then superimposing the documents, then topping with another wet towel similarly protected and another board putting all under heavy pressure in a letter-press. After a few hours the towels are removed, fresh waxed paper is put in place and the documents left in the press under lighter pressure. The second method consists of placing blotters covering pieces of soaked newspapers cut to size, interspersed between every inch or so of manuscripts, putting all between pieces of binder's board and under heavy pressure for a few hours. The blotters and newspapers are then replaced by pieces of waxed paper and the pressure slightly lessened. Both of these processes can be used for multileaved documents, but they have the disadvantage of taking several days, also there may be a slight risk of mildew when documents are allowed to remain damp too long. If the work is done in a dry room, however, this danger is not great—at least, we have never had any trouble of that sort. We have had a little difficulty with ink running where the newspaper-blotter method was used carelessly.

Brittleness results from acidity inherent in paper, a condition which increases with age, and like all chemical processes is accelerated by too much heat and too little moisture. Breaking occurs first on folds and at the edges. It is for that reason that flat filing is considered the only proper way to keep manuscripts. Increasing the humidity in the paper helps, and some manuscript experts report improvement from giving manuscripts a bath in sizing, which should be done only by a person experienced in such work. If the paper has actually broken, there is nothing to be done except to repair the document. Since we are not discussing repairs in this article, nothing more need be said here on this subject except to warn against "temporary" repair by strips of mending tissue. These mending tissues turn brown, discolor the paper, dry out and crack, often increasing the original damage by pulling away surrounding paper. The best repair strips now on the market are made of cellulose acetate with a slow drying self-incorporated adhesive. This adhesive, like other types of plastic mending tissues, has the additional disadvantage that the adhesives invariably "bleed" at the edges in warm weather, sticking to adjacent paper and causing tears and peeling off of writing. Removal of these mending tapes when the manuscripts are later being prepared for lamination or crepelining is difficult and nearly always adds to the amount of broken surface.

When manuscripts are broken on the fold we separate the sheets of a document but leave each broken leaf folded, protecting the edges by inserting the sheet in a wide fold of paper clipped to the original. Any detached pieces are carefully laid inside the fold directly under the clip. Consultation of such a manuscript before it has been repaired is strongly discouraged, but if it becomes necessary to produce it the patron is cautioned to preserve and to return to the desk any piece, however small, that falls off as he is handling the document. Few people realize how skillfully these fragments can be pieced together in the repair shop. The pieces that break off always seem to be key words, parts of signatures, or essential seals.

Theoretically every document should bear a stamp showing ownership. Practically, most archivists find it impossible to affix such a mark to every document. In the case of archives, if such a stamp is used, it should be a file mark showing date of filing in the archives and the accession number. Such a stamp should preferably be of metal using printer's ink which cannot be effaced. This file mark should be stamped on the back of the document where it will not efface any writing, preferably on the part of the document bearing other identification endorsements.

It is desirable in the case of all manuscripts and essential in the case of those in bad condition to number the manuscripts and the parts thereof in such a manner as to facilitate refiling and keeping them in order. Such numbers should be written with a soft pencil so that erasure can be made when the document is repaired and put together in permanent form. The marks should be placed on an inconspicuous part of the manuscript but in a uniform style to show what they represent. Generally these marks include numbering by digits, to show the place of the document in the file, plus letters to indicate parts of each manuscript. Thus the mark on the cover might read 101 A–D; that on one page 101 A 1–2 (indicating that the page is broken into two segments), while 101 A 2 indicates that the fragment is the second part of page A.

The above ownership and pagination marks are the only marks

which the manuscript curator should ever add to the document. Above all he should not presume to retouch the writing in the manuscript. All numbers and other identifications should be used on the folders only. If any additional marks or notes seem necessary or if any mark is made on the document after it comes into his possession, the manuscript curator should either remove the mark or attach to the document an explanation authenticated by his signature and the date; or he may do both as appropriate to the situation.

Much wear and tear on originals can be eliminated through the use of transcripts filed with the original. These transcripts may be typewritten or photographic or a combination. These transcripts should be dated. Transcripts should be made whenever a manuscript is found to be fading or disintegrating and should always be made before sending it to be repaired. Transcripts made by a camera give more detail than photostats, but both methods often leave the reader in doubt about overwritten passages, imperfections in the paper, and so on. The handmade transcripts help in those cases, but of course are subject to inaccurate interpretations. For that reason the transcript should bear the name of the person making it, together with some indication as to who the person is. . . .

10

Protection of Records from Disaste

NEXT TO THE PHYSICAL PROTECTION of people in wartime, the preservation of records essential to citizenship and property rights is the most important duty of the state. The chaos resulting from total war in Europe will be enhanced or diminished in the postwar era in direct proportion to the success of the officials in protecting those records vital to rehabilitation. The status of the refugee unable to establish his citizenship identity is pitiable indeed. Stories from France tell of people drifting back to their old homes only to find their property in the hands of German looters. That is always the fate of people in conquered countries, but after the war is over and peacetime civil government is restored adjustments will undoubtedly be made. The success of these adjustments from the point of view of the French will largely be dependent upon their being able to prove their title to lands and other possessions.

The people of the United States hope and pray that war will

PART 1 OF THIS CHAPTER, "Archives and War," was originally published in *Illinois Libraries* 23 (February 1941): 17–19. Part 2, "Protection of State Records," was originally published as "Establishing Priorities for State Records: Illinois Experience" in *American Archivist* 5 (January 1942): 18–27. Part 3, "Protection of County Records," was originally published as "County Records and the War" in *Illinois Libraries* 24 (March 1942): 41–43.

not bring mass evacuations of our cities and countryside as has happened in Europe. If such a catastrophe should overtake us, greater chaos would result here than in Europe for Americans are a nomadic people and cannot, like Europeans, call upon their neighbors to testify that their families have lived in the locality for generations. It is high time for archivists and other officials to consider what records are most essential for the protection of individuals, whether such records are now in existence, and what can be done to improve and preserve them. . . . Librarians and others [should know the social significance of government records, particularly county archives in order to] . . . cooperate intelligently with local officials in planning safeguards for their records.

First of all, every person needs proof of his identity as a citizen. He needs records of the date and place of his birth and, if he was foreign-born, proof of his legal entry into this country and of his naturalization. The first Illinois act requiring registration of births and deaths (with the county clerks) was not passed until 1877, and registration was not strictly enforced until the Division of Vital Statistics was created in 1915. Unquestionably, thousands of children of foreign-born parents will be treated as aliens because they cannot prove that they were either born in the United States or that they were minors when their parents were naturalized. Women married to aliens prior to 1922 must prove their American birth in order to regain their citizenship. Men must be able to prove whether or not they are of draft age. Proof of age and citizenship is required not only for passports but even in the case of persons going across the border of Canada.

Every social worker has a repertoire of pitiful stories of cases where Old Age Assistance would not be given because of insufficient documentation. The State Division of Old Age Assistance reports that old-age pensions were denied twelve hundred aged persons in Illinois during the year ending June 30, 1940, because they could not secure proof they were sixty-five years old or older. These persons comprised more than 12 percent of all applicants who were ineligible for pensions and totaled nearly 4 percent of all applications for assistance received during the year.

Where birth records are not in existence, it is necessary to prove age in some other way. The following proofs of age are acceptable under the Illinois Old Age Assistance Act: "(a) a duly attested transcript of the applicant's birth certificate, furnished free by the State, filed according to law with a registrar of vital statistics, or other officer charged with the duty of recording birth; or (b) a photostatic copy of a Bible record; or (c) a certificate of record in an application for membership in a fraternal order; or (d) a certified photostatic copy of an application for insurance made prior to January 1, 1920; or (e) a certified copy of a school record containing the date of commencement of such school terms, and the name, age and date of birth of the applicant; or (f) a certified copy of enlistment in the army or navy service of the United States or any state thereof; or (g) a certified copy of record of application for marriage license; or (h) a certified copy of any other public record made prior to January 1, 1920, which contains therein a statement of the age of the applicant."[1]

Other records which might be used as proof of citizenship are voters' registration cards, draft board records, naturalization papers, and such. The 1900 and 1920 federal census schedules have been indexed and may be used as legal proof of age. For information about this index address the . . . Bureau of the Census [Personal Census Service Branch, Pittsburg, Kansas 66762]. . . .

The second type of records needing special precautions against destruction are those involving property rights. Plats showing boundary survey lines and records of deeds and mortgages in the county recorder's offices are the most important documents in this category. It is unnecessary to go outside the history of Illinois to show the disastrous results from the lack or destruction of such recorded instruments. After the French surrendered the Illinois country to George Rogers Clark, a horde of land speculators descended upon the inhabitants pointing out that there were no records to substantiate their claims as to real estate holdings. When the United States government several years later sent commissioners to take testimony as to those land holdings and to confirm titles, they found that most of the French had in despair sold their land claims for a pittance and removed to Missouri.

The other well-remembered example in Illinois history is the destruction of all Cook County records in the Chicago fire of 1871. The General Assembly in a special-called session passed laws providing for the recording of land title papers held by individuals and for legal procedure for the reproduction of destroyed county records where that was possible. One abstract company, the Chicago Title and Trust Company, was able to save its records from the fire and as a result has enjoyed a very profitable monopoly in providing title abstracts to Chicago real estate.

Most county recorders are very well aware of the importance of the land records in their custody. In pitifully few of the courthouses, however, are these records kept in vaults which would withstand even minor fires, not to mention bombardment and other war hazards. As a matter of insurance, the land records of every county should be copied on microfilm and these copies deposited in the state archives or in bank vaults outside the county seat. The cost of microfilming would be infinitesimal in comparison with the monetary loss which would come to citizens in case the originals were destroyed. European record offices adopted this form of insurance several years ago. The Netherlands, for instance, filmed all documents dated prior to 1600 and deposited copies in important libraries all over the world. The British Public Record Office made a special survey of bank vaults in the provinces and directed that certain specified records not adequately provided with vaults be removed to approved bank vaults in case of war.

The two categories of records—vital statistics and land records—must be preserved as the absolute minimum. One other set of records—the state constitution and the enrolled laws—upon which property rights are based are microfilmed and the copies deposited elsewhere for safekeeping. Other state records too numerous to list here in detail are also of great importance. Among these, to mention only a few at random, are the registers of professional licenses (for some fifty professions), corporation records, insurance records, legislative papers, mine maps, election records, military service records, supreme court cases, and intrastate commerce cases.

The "archives" frequently mentioned in European war despatches are generally not archives in the usual sense but diplomatic and military records in the current files of government departments. The protection of such records from the hazards of war is more the province of the departments to which they appertain than of the archivist.

The records mentioned above as requiring particular protection against the hazards of war are all business records, preserved for their practical rather than for their sentimental or historical value. The importance of history as a moral weapon should not be undervalued. One of the standard methods of subduing a conquered country is to attempt to destroy or belittle its historical memories. Thus, the Russians before the First World War attempted to stamp out the Polish language. The revival of the obsolete Erse language was a deliberate attempt by Irish politicians to foster patriotism. The recent return of the body of Napoleon's son to Paris was an attempt by Hitler to win French converts to the Nazi cause. If little is said in this and succeeding articles about the preservation of historical archives, it is because so much has already been written on this subject it should be unnecessary to urge the importance of that work.

Many problems confront the archivist in wartimes. First is the matter of selecting and classifying records in the order of importance for preservation, including provision for making and distributing copies as a matter of insurance and planning evacuation if that should be necessary. Although the vaults of the Illinois state archives building are largely above ground, their steel construction is believed by engineers to afford reasonable security against destruction from the air. The inland location of Springfield also makes it unlikely that evacuation will be necessary.

2 / Protection of State Records

Illinois officials have as yet made no plans for evacuation of state records in case of a possible wartime emergency. However, priority ratings for the state's archives have been established in connection with the program for making the most effective use of the new Illinois state archives building. Although located in Capitol Park near the center of Springfield, the archives building is well isolated from other buildings. The steel skyscraper construction of its vaults, which rest upon their own caissons, is the type which has proved most effective against European bombings.

The Illinois state archives building was designed to provide scientific care for the following categories of records (a) those records of such great legal value that they should never be allowed to be removed from the building—such as the constitution, deeds, and abstracts for state property, enrolled laws, and the like; (b) noncurrent records of permanent legal and historical value, no longer needed in ordinary current state business; (c) the most important permanent legal records which need the physical and moral protection of the building, but which because of semicurrent use must occasionally be withdrawn for departmental use.

Classes (a) and (b) are kept in the archives vaults which are under the exclusive jurisdiction of the Archives Department. Class (c) records are housed in a separate series of departmental vaults in the archives building, the records in these vaults remaining under the exclusive jurisdiction of the state departments to which they belong, except that no records may be transferred to the departmental vaults until the department has submitted inventories of records proposed for transfer and has received written authorization for same from the Archives Department.

General regulations relating to transfer of records to the archives building are as follows:

What Records Will Be Accepted

The Archives Department for housing in its own or in the departmental vaults will accept only official records.

Records must be of permanent value. No record subject by law to periodic destruction, no duplicate records, no duplicate stock of printed reports or other departmental publications, and no stationery supplies can be admitted. . . . The decision of the state librarian or assistant state librarian as to the suitability of records proferred for transfer is final.

In general it may be said concerning Illinois archives, "If a record is in the archives building, it is important." The converse, that records not in the archives building are unimportant, most emphatically is not true. Many records of extreme value—to cite as one example, corporation charters still in the capitol vault of the Corporation Department—are needed for such immediate departmental reference that they cannot be transferred. Other records of great legal importance are retained in the offices of the respective departments for one reason or another, properly or not. In the following discussion of priorities, no distinction is made between records which the archivist merely thinks ought to be transferred and those which have already been taken to the archives building. In a time of emergency such distinctions would be forgotten.

Certain records should obviously receive priority ratings; many records are duplicates of originals kept by other departments, or are records of little legal value kept chiefly for administrative convenience. Great masses of records, usually of recent date, are on the borderline of importance as permanent records. Examples of each type and general principles followed in assigning ratings are discussed below. The reader should remember, however, that these are Illinois records, studied from the point of view of Illinois legal requirements, which may be quite different from those of other states. Also in Illinois many important records which may seem to have been forgotten here are kept by the counties, and over such records the state has no control.

Primary Records

I. Records which establish rights of citizenship or of property owned either by the state or by individuals, including authorizations to do business.

A. Vital statistics. The records of births, stillbirths, and deaths kept by the Department of Public Health are the chief state records which affect citizenship rights. Other state records may of course be so used incidentally in individual cases, as for example, a certificate in an old application for a pardon which was accepted as a proof of age for Old Age Assistance. Such individual records cannot, of course, be considered in making priority ratings.

B. Land records. In the case of Illinois these comprise:

   1. Records of the old federal land registrations in Illinois and include surveys record of sales, and so on. These are duplicates, in part only, of the records in the General Land Office in Washington, and certified copies of these Illinois records are by law recognized judicially.

   2. Records of lands once owned by the state and later sold or donated to individuals and include patents to the state and records of patents issued by the state.

   3. Deeds and abstracts for real estate now owned by the state. Contract records of the state and specifications are in this category.

C. Charters of domestic corporations and authorizations for out-of-state corporations to do business in Illinois. Also, copies of bylaws, amendments, and other records subsequent to incorporation or authorization which affect the legal status of the various companies operating in Illinois.

D. Registers of licenses to practice professions, issued by the state. In case of evacuation of records probably only the actual registration lists would be removed. However, of almost as much importance are the supplemental files of applications, with credentials, examination and other records proving eligibility for licenses, also minutes of the various examining boards. Files on complaints investigated are not authorized for transfer to permanent archives except when the licenses are revoked. Court and other proceedings justifying the revocation are properly regarded as archives.

E. State civil service records are in the same category. For licenses issued by the state for such subjects as automobile registration, liquor sales, hunting, and the like, the register of licenses issued is sufficient for archival purposes and applications and other records can generally be destroyed after a period of years.

Authorizations issued after hearings, as in the case of regulation by the Illinois Commerce Commission, are quite different and of course full records are kept. These are considered under the heading of court records.

II. Records involving safeguards to life. The most important record that comes to mind in this connection is the mine maps, required to be kept up to date, which are filed with the Department of Mines and Minerals for use in mine rescue work.

Routine reports of factory, fire, food, lodging house, and other state inspection services are not regarded as archival documents, especially since the information of permanent value contained in these reports is usually tabulated in statistical form.

Investigations by special committees or commissions, particularly those records ordered by the governor and the General Assembly, are of great historical importance and should be preserved.

III. Records specifically required by law to be made or to receive judicial notice, especially if the forms to be used are described. This includes proceedings and minutes of official bodies, registers of official acts and sworn reports required to be filed with an official. For example, the auditor of public accounts is required to "keep a fair record of all warrants by him drawn, numbering the same, in a book to be kept for that purpose."[2] The secretary of state is required "To keep a fair register of all the official acts of the Governor. . . . To keep a register of all . . . commissions [required by law to be issued by the governor], specifying the person to whom granted, the office conferred, the date of signing the commission, and when bond is taken, the date and amount thereof and the sureties."[3] "The Adjutant General shall . . . keep a record of all orders and regulations of the Commander-in-Chief and all matters pertaining to the unorganized militia, the National Guard and the Naval Reserve. He shall keep a record of all appointments, elections and commissions of officers, and appointments of non-commissioned officers. He shall . . . record all enlistments and discharges, and keep the necessary military history of each member of the state forces."[4]

Such registers of official acts create no problem for the archivist. They should, of course, receive high priority ratings. When it comes to the rating for reports required to be filed with the various state officials, the archivist runs into the problem of bulk. These records are required by Illinois law to be preserved permanently unless specific legislation permits their destruction after a period of years. A detailed study of Illinois statutes reveals only twenty-three categories of records authorized to be destroyed and not all of these are state records. Most of these reports are required to be certified by the parties filing the same. (Reports not required to be certified can generally be classified as nonpermanent records.) The records are required as an aid in enforcing the laws regulating the matters involved in the reports. Back reports are required for purposes of comparison. Theoretically, such reports should be . . . [given the same treatment] as current records. But when the archivist is confronted with the monthly reports required to be filed by practically every business house of Illinois in the administration of the retailers' occupation tax, he must refuse priority ratings lest such bulky records crowd out all other records.

In some cases the departments can tabulate the information contained in the reports and ask permission to destroy the originals after a period of years. This is dangerous since the courts cannot recognize these tabulations as primary evidence. In other cases, microphotography or a combination of microphotography and tabulation is the answer. In the case of some of the newer departments, and these are the ones which tend toward the greatest bulk in records, experience has been too short to permit a decision as to whether it will be necessary to keep all these reports indefinitely. In Illinois, the archivist is reluctant to authorize the transfer to departmental vaults of reports filed with departments which have not had about twenty years' experience in the use of the particular files in question.

Reports under seal of office required to be filed by one government official with another are considered permanent records and given an "A" rating.

IV. Court records. Docket books and records of decrees are, of course, given the highest rating but case records containing pleadings and evidence are considered permanent records suitable for transfer as archives. Included are records not only of the supreme court, but also of such fact determining bodies as the Illinois Commerce Commission, the Industrial Commission (workmen's compensation), State Claim Commission, and State Tax Commission.

V. Minutes of various state boards and other officials. These minutes are important as showing the history of the department and decisions as to policies. Included in this category are rules and regulations promulgated by the departments and office manuals.

VI. Current bonds of government officials. Records of privately owned securities deposited with state departments (as in the case of state banks and insurance companies). These records are never in the custody of the archivist in normal times. In case of emergency they would probably be entrusted to him for safekeeping.

VII. Historical documents and other records important to public morale. Present and former constitutions, territorial and early state records (especially legislative records), and enrolled laws are closely tied up not only with the administration of state government but also with public morale and are given high priority ratings. Confronted with an actual or sudden emergency the archivist might hesitate about some of these records, which are generally in print, and he might wonder if other essential records might not deserve prior evacuation. Given sufficient warning, however, he would probably evacuate such records ahead of the actual emergency since the printed copies could be used for administrative purposes. It has been proposed to make certified film copies of the Illinois enrolled laws. The printed session laws are certified and can be used in court in all cases except where errors in proofreading can be claimed. The original enrolled laws will not, of course, be destroyed but in case of hasty evacuation the film copies might be taken instead of the originals, thus releasing transportation and storage space for other important records.

VIII. Noncurrent records in general. Prior to the common use of the typewriter (about 1890 in Illinois), the making of records was a tedious hand process not undertaken lightly. It is safe to assume that any record more than fifty years old is probably worth keeping from a historical if not from an administrative point of view.

Secondary Records

In case of emergency, every effort would be made to save first the records discussed above. This still leaves the problem of the excessively bulky records of present-day government all of which the officials say are necessary for proper administration. This is a problem for which Illinois has not as yet found a solution. A description of the problem would take too much space here. However, it has had to be dealt with albeit with grave misgivings in selecting records for transfer to the departmental vaults. Some of the rule of thumb tests which have been applied in Illinois may be suggestive:

I. In general, departments are advised to retain in their office vaults records less than three years old. For the archives proper, no records less than three years old nor records covering the years of the current administration are accepted. Records less than ten years old are accepted only when they have become noncurrent in the sense that no further official action will be involved in their use, other than the mere issuance of certified copies. Outside of those limitations the department heads decide when records become noncurrent and suitable for transfer to the archives department.

II. When it is necessary to choose between parallel sets of records proposed for transfer, these two questions are asked:

A. If you were required to produce one of these records in court, which would you take? This question, correctly answered, solves 90 percent of priority questions since generally but one record on a given subject is acceptable as evidence.

B. Suppose your entire personnel were annihilated, which records would be the minimum essentials for an outsider to have to carry on the business from where you left off?

A strict policy as to the quantity of records accepted has several times led to a redesigning and condensation of report forms. In one case four forms, each covering the same information as the other three plus one or two additional items, was reduced to one form, saving one-fourth of the bulk of records to be stored. The archivist should be alert for opportunities to reduce the bulk of records at their source.

III. Historical versus legal records. Sometimes officials in discussing transfers remark that one set of records is the official legal file, but they wonder whether certain other records which they make, or could make, might not be more interesting historically. To this the archivist can only reply that the official is an administrator, not a historian and that consciously created history is too close to the border line of propaganda to be trustworthy historical evidence. Legal rather than historical documents are the province of the state official. Jenkinson lays down basic principles on this subject which are commended to other archivists as sound in American as well as in British practice.[5]

IV. Printed documents, especially reports, are on the borderline between archival and nonarchival material. . . . In Illinois, printed state documents are not accepted for the archives, except where they bear an official file mark or are special reports submitted in printed form. The Documents Department of the Illinois State Library (housed in the archives building, but not a division of the Archives Department) keeps a file of every state publication. One copy is filed in original binding for preservation only and is not produced for patrons if other copies are available. Printed reports are not archival, as a rule, in that they have no evidential value in court since they are a compilation from legal records, not the records themselves. Because they offer condensed information about the department, every archivist should see to it that his state library keeps a complete file of state documents, both printed and mimeographed, if he does not do it himself.

V. Correspondence files are among the most bulky records offered for transfer to archives. It is easy and superficially efficient to drop carbon copies into each of several files, but these increase the bulk to extremes. In Illinois, correspondence files are not accepted unless they have been well weeded—duplicate copies of the same circular letters, form letters, requests for copies of departmental publications, applications for jobs, and other ephemeral matter must be withdrawn from the file. Letters which set the policy of the department and correspondence between officials involving interdepartmental relations are extremely valuable and it is preferable to accept the chaff, if necessary, to risk the loss of these by refusing all transfer. One state department was able to reduce the bulk of its correspondence files by two thirds through judicious weeding. The difficulty with a weeding process is that only the executive is capable of judging what should be kept and executives have neither the time nor the inclination for such work. Preventing the original accumulation of trash-filled correspondence files is the only solution to this problem. Some of the Illinois departments keep three sets of correspondence files: a file for temporary correspondence to be discarded automatically after a suitable period; a "director's file" for the most important correspondence; and a "personal file" containing, among other correspondence, copies of those official letters which the department head might wish to take with him on his retirement.

VI. The Illinois Archives Department arbitrarily refuses to accept financial records kept by any department other than those kept by the auditor of public accounts and state treasurer, except fee books. While this rules out many records which are essential to efficient administration of the various offices, when analyzed it will be found that these records are made for office convenience only and have no legal status before the courts. They are apt to be very bulky, and they are seldom referred to in office business after five or ten years.

VII. Loose-leaf and card files offer grave administrative problems to the archivist in that insertions and subtractions can be made so easily and are so difficult to detect that certification of them as records is risky. The archivist, however, in deciding upon their value as archives should be governed by their legal status rather than by their form. Because of their bulk and weight, he would recommend that important files which should be evacuated in times of emergency should be reproduced on film.

One form of card file which has caused some questioning as to its archival status is the tabulating card. Many departments, the Illinois Departments of Public Welfare and of Public Health, for instance, use their case records for statistical purposes chiefly and reduce the contents onto tabulating cards. Is it necessary to keep the bulky originals when every item has been condensed onto these cards? In case of evacuation, the tabulating cards would probably be the records preserved but from a strictly legal standpoint they do not have the validity of the certified originals. But of how much value are those originals as permanent legal records? The answer, admittedly unsatisfactory, is that time alone can tell and that the records must be preserved until the answer can be given even though they may not be transferred to the archives for the present.

VIII. Temporary records are excluded from the archives building, but they would have to be considered in case of emergency evacuation. Just as a merchant might not particularly care whether his ten-year-old closed accounts records were saved in case of a fire but would be ruined if his current account records were lost, so the state official also has records of pending business which would have to be preserved in an emergency. With such records the archivist is concerned only so far as he might be expected to cooperate with the department in such circumstances.

It would obviously be impossible to mention and evaluate every type of record kept by the state. Some of the most important Illinois records have been omitted from this summary. Enough of the basic considerations have been mentioned, perhaps, to help other archivists to make similar studies for their own states. By and large, the various state departments can be expected to know which of their current files should get priority treatment. Only the archivist and the department head, in close collaboration, can determine which of the older and less frequently consulted records are the most valuable. Such a study as has been made in Illinois takes time, but it is immensely worthwhile. . . . The archivist's knowledge of his state's government organization and his educational contacts with other state officials make him immeasurably more valuable as a public servant, and he will be in a much more favorable position for securing better care for his state's archives.

3 / Protection of County Records

Sixty million native-born American citizens cannot prove their citizenship through acceptable legal records, according to estimates by the U.S. Bureau of the Census.[6] What that means to persons of foreign descent can well be imagined. . . . Thousands of needy persons have had their applications for Old Age Assistance rejected because they could not prove their age. This critical situation is due chiefly to late and inadequate laws and lax enforcement of birth registration requirements, rather than to carelessness about preservation of records already created.

Not only citizenship rights but also ownership of all real estate and some personal property must be established through county records. The importance of deed and mortgage registers is fully appreciated by county recorders, but in very few courthouses are these vital records protected by adequate vaults. Citizens should insist that neither the county government nor the individual shall again suffer loss because official records are missing. They will not achieve this goal unless influential persons such as attorneys, teachers, and librarians back their county officials in efforts to provide adequate care for county archives.

Most county courthouses are already crowded, and . . . it is increasingly difficult to find adequate storage space for records. The demand for wastepaper, also, is likely . . . to result in indiscriminate destruction of records despite the law which makes destruction of legal records without legislative authorization a criminal act. The following list of types of records, grouped according to their use value, may be helpful to county officials and their advisers in selecting records to receive preferential care.

So long as the county is able and willing to provide adequate vault space and to take proper care of its records, original records of local historical and legal interest should be kept in the county. Historical county records which would otherwise have to be destroyed may be deposited in the state archives to be held until such time as the county can provide adequately for them or they may be deposited permanently.

County records recommended for especial protection against the hazards of war:

I. Records which protect rights of citizenship, life, and property
   A. Vital statistics—registers of births, marriages, and deaths
   B. Naturalization records
   C. Adoption records
   D. Records of legalized changes of name
   E. Records of persons adjudged incompetent as spendthrifts, drunkards, insane, and feebleminded. Court decrees later pronouncing them again sane or otherwise competent
   F. Records of commitments to and releases from state charitable and criminal institutions
   G. Probate records, particularly for unsettled estate, guardianship, and conservatorship cases. Wills and inventories of estates; reports of administrators, executors, conservators, and guardians; court orders and decrees
   H. Land records, including survey records, registrations of deeds and mortgages, records of tax sales, and of sales of school swamp lands
   I. Mine maps
   J. Current chattel mortgage records
   K. Certain authorizations by state departments which do not go into effect until recorded in the county: registers of
      1. Licenses to practice certain professions
      2. Corporate charters
      3. Authorizations to foreign corporations to be business in the state
   L. Marks and brands for livestock

M. Registers of licenses issued for "shanty boats," peddlers, fishermen and hunters, butter and cheese cooperatives, ferries, mills, toll roads, and bridges

N. Court records, including petitions, appeals, dockets, transcripts of evidence, judgments, decrees, and orders, bonds, reports and documents filed with the court, records of unfinished business

II. Records which affect the property rights of the county government

  A. Deeds and abstracts to real estate owned by the county

  B. Leases in current effect

  C. Contracts, including drawings, specifications, contract papers, bonds, and so on

  D. Current inventories of county property

  E. Official bonds and oaths of office

III. Essential administrative records

  A. Election records

    1. Official lists of county officials (from organization of the county)

    2. Abstracts of election returns, particularly those not certified to the secretary of state, as, referenda on commission form of government for cities; annexation and separation of territory from cities, towns and villages; local officials not commissioned by the governor

    3. Registration of voters

  B. Records relating to boundaries and organization of special districts, such as drainage, wildlife conservation, park, high school, tuberculosis sanatorium, soil conservation, public health, and mosquito abatement districts

  C. Records establishing governmental policies, such as proceedings of the board of supervisors or county commissioners, attorney general's rulings, order books, court decrees, official reports (printed and manuscript)

  D. Correspondence, limited to that establishing policies, official business with other officials. Routine requests for publications, and the like, should not be filed with official correspondence

   E. Financial records

      1. Receipts into and expenditures from the county treasury; authorizations and account books in particular

      2. Assessment and tax collection records

   F. Highway department and surveyor's engineering records

   G. Jury lists

IV. Noncurrent records chiefly of historical interest

All county records are historically significant because county business affects every individual in the county. For the history of the pioneer period, county records are indispensable to the historian because county government was the one cohesive element of community life

In general it may be assumed that county records have historical value if:

   A. A record has survived for at least fifty years

   B. The record has been transcribed or entered in a bound volume

Ledger volumes are expensive, handwriting tedious and time consuming

   C. The miscellaneous unbound files are the fuller and original documents on which the bound records are based

Examples of a few of the types of historical materials to be found in county archives:

   A. Minutes and proceedings of the county commissioners' court or board of supervisors (the most valuable single set of records)

   B. Records associated with famous persons, notably Lincoln

Records of court cases in which Lincoln and his law partners were associated, also other documents signed by him or in his handwriting. One of the earliest known Lincoln autographs was recently found in a Macon County stray record

   C. Court records, particularly those of the early circuit court

D. Probate records, particularly proceedings of the probate justices of the peace (–1849), wills, and inventories of estates
E. Land records
F. Militia rolls
G. Census schedules
H. Registers of marks and brands; stray registers
 I. School reports
 J. Early petitions
K. Road reports
L. Election poll books
M. Early assessment and tax collection records
N. Marriage records
O. Apprentice records
P. Bills of sale. Much information concerning treatment of Negroes and evasion of antislavery laws will be found in apprentice records and bills of sale
Q. Records of early criminal trials

11

Photographic and Microphotographic

Reproduction of Records

1 / MICROPHOTOGRAPHIC REPRODUCTION OF COUNTY RECORDS

THE MICROPHOTOGRAPHIC EQUIPMENT and personnel now engaged in copying V-mail and engineering and other records for defense plants, will, at the close of the war, be released for civilian work.[1] It may be expected that a number of commercial firms, some responsible, many other fly-by-night outfits, will be seeking large-scale microfilm projects. That state and county officials will be solicited for the business is evidenced by the fact that identical bills to permit government officials to substitute microfilm copies for originals have recently been introduced into the legislatures of a number of states, presumably at the instigation of commercial interests. Two such bills, one applying to state records and the other

◄§ PART 1 OF THIS CHAPTER, "Microphotographic Reproduction of County Records," was originally published as "Microphotography and County Records" in *Illinois Libraries* 26 (December 1944): 505–9. Part 2, "The Preservation of Local Records by Microphotography," was originally published as "The Place of Microphotography in the Collection and Preservation of Local Archives and Historical Manuscripts" in Jerome K. Wilcox and A. F. Kuhlman, eds., *Public Documents with Archives and Libraries: Papers Presented at the 1938 Conference of the American Library Association* (Chicago: American Library Association, 1939), pp. 327–34. Part 3, "Reproduction of State Records," was originally published as "Photography for State Records" (in two parts) in *Illinois Libraries* 28 (February and March): 151–55, 180–87.

to county records, amended at the suggestion of the state librarian to make them conform to good record practices, were passed in 1943 by the General Assembly of Illinois.[2] It is likely that county officials will be subjected to high-pressure salesmanship based upon profitable business for the commercial companies rather than upon an intelligent study of needs or applicability. A discussion of the ways in which microphotography is used in record work is therefore in order.

The first application of microphotography is for direct recording. An example of that is to be found in the state treasurer's office which records state warrants by photographing them on 16-mm film. Formerly the pertinent information contained in each state warrant issued was transcribed in tabular form into bound volumes. From September 1943, to January 6, 1944, this record required 540 one-hundred-foot rolls of 16-mm film, each roll containing facsimiles of between 6,500 and 7,000 warrants. These rolls are arranged, four rows wide, in five shallow file drawers, each holding 108 rolls. The five drawers occupy between six and seven cubic feet of filing room, as against space required for between eighty and one hundred standard-size ledger volumes which have resulted from the old system of recording. Thus the advantages of direct recording by microphotography are indisputable accuracy and tremendous saving in space, labor for transcribing, and cost of materials.

The cameras used in this type of work are automatic, not requiring the services of a skilled photographer. The rolls are sent to the company supplying the film for developing, thus requiring no darkroom. Copies can be made as fast as the work can be fed into the camera. Because of the cost of the camera, whether leased or purchased, it is uneconomical to attempt to use this method except for records of very considerable bulk and for documents of uniform size. Direct recording by microphotography is recommended only for records infrequently consulted because of the inconvenience of the necessary use of reading machines and the danger of damage to film (that is, to the contents of the document) from careless handling.

Film copies are often used for closed indexes, especially where duplicate copies are needed in different places. For instance, the indexes to certain war service records of the federal government are kept on film, one copy being on file in the U.S. Veterans' Administration and one in the National Archives.

The second common application of microphotography in record work is to reduce the bulk of records by substituting microfilm copies of back files for the original records. Storage space amounting to as much as 90 to 98 percent may be saved. To date this procedure has been used by government officials chiefly for reducing the bulk of administrative records of temporary or questionable value. So far it has not been used for the type of records kept by county officials.

The 1943 Illinois act permits any elected or appointed officer of any county or clerk of any court to "cause any or all public records, papers or documents kept by him to be photographed, microphotographed, or otherwise reproduced on film." Provided these photographic reproductions conform to certain standards, these reproductions "shall be deemed to be an original record for all purposes, including introduction in evidence in all courts or administrative agencies. A transcript, exemplification or certified copy thereof shall, for all purposes recited herein, be deemed to be a transcript, exemplification, or certified copy of the original." Original records thus reproduced, dated later than 1870, may then be destroyed provided due notice of intention to destroy the records is filed with the county board and posted in a public place in the office of the county clerk and in the office of the officer or clerk of the court signing such statement, for at least thirty days before a regular or special meeting of the county board to hear and consider objections. Authorization to destroy the originals may then be granted by the county board. "Original records, papers or documents created prior to 1870 may not be destroyed. If any county cannot provide adequate housing or storage space for such original records, papers, and documents dated or executed prior to the year 1870, any such officer or clerk may deposit such records, papers, and documents in the Illinois State Library archives. The Illinois State Library shall provide counties depositing any such records, papers, and documents with it, a photostatic copy or microfilm of such records, paper, or document."[3]

Despite the legal authority to destroy original county records permitted under this act, officials are warned to be very conservative about such destruction. Well informed county officials who have been consulted and studies made by the Archives Division indicate that very few, if any, county records, certainly not those in the four major offices of record—county clerk and court, probate court, circuit court and recorder—are records which could safely be destroyed. Most county records are "true records," by which we mean records which the law requires to be stamped with an official file word, and/or otherwise recorded by registration or transcription before the matters referred to in the record can take legal effect. Examples of such records are wills and other probate records, adoption and naturalization papers, marriage, birth, and death registers, and records of deeds and mortgages. The probate clerk of Cook County keeps two copies of his records—the original documents and copies for public use. He proposes to keep film copies of older records as the duplicate copies for public use. It is proper so to substitute copies of county records for office use to prevent tampering and wear, but the originals of such important records should be preserved.

The use of microphotography for reducing the bulk of records has certain limitations which are often ignored by persons who are urging adoption of the process. First of all, microphotography is not as cheap as some people suggest. The film itself is inexpensive —from one cent per frame of two pages and upward, depending upon the quality of the film used and the rate of reduction. The overhead is very high, however. Cameras can be either leased by the month or purchased. Purchase price of suitable cameras ranges to four thousand dollars or more for the larger automatic type. The salary and expense of operators must be taken into consideration and the cheaper the camera the more highly skilled the photographer must be. Film may be processed either by the photographer or sent to the film company for development. Processing by the photographer is about a dollar and a quarter a roll cheaper, but it requires darkroom equipment and considerable skill. If a considerable amount of work is to be done, commercial companies should be called in to do the work. Prewar companies apparently, to judge from price quotations which we have seen, tended to charge what the traffic would bear. Improved equipment and competition will force these prices down to more reasonable rates. Unquestionably the relative quality of copies made by responsible firms will justify the relatively higher cost.

A second limitation of microphotography for reducing bulk is that courts still prefer the original record to a copy, no matter how accurate. Tests for authenticity of a document from a study of paper, watermarks, ink, and other external evidence cannot be made from a photograph. Interpolations and words written over other words do not show up in such a manner as to indicate which was the interpolation. A hole in the paper may look in a photograph like a letter or a figure and so lead to erroneous inference. A scratch in the film made either through carelessness or by malice may destroy a signature or other essential part of the document. Where microfilm copies are to be substituted for the original record, two film copies should be made—a master copy and a working copy. This does not double the expense, for the second copy can be made much more cheaply than the original.

The size, form, and manner of consulting records has a decided bearing upon the convenience of the use of microfilm. Very large volumes such as plat books cannot be copied successfully by standard microphotographic cameras because the ratio of reduction cannot be much more than sixteen to one. The more expensive precision cameras can do the work, but the standard reading machines cannot enlarge the images enough for them to be read easily. Records which are frequently consulted for purposes of comparison with other records cannot conveniently be used in film form unless several reading projectors are on hand, and even this is unsatisfactory as it is slow and confusing to have to handle a number of rolls of film. Case files to which additional documents must be added from time to time should not be kept on film because such additions would require splicing, and a spliced film cannot be accepted in court. The probate files, for instance, of closed cases could be micro-filmed but inasmuch as these are often held open as long as twenty years, especially in cases where there are minor heirs, the more recent and most bulky files can hardly be reduced by this method.

Records most appropriate for filming (speaking of convenience for use on film rather than suitability from a legal standpoint) are those records generally kept in register or record volumes or un-bound records filed in numerical or chronological sequence—for instance, county collectors' books, proceedings of board meetings, hearings, and closed indexes.

Before filming any records, arrange them in proper sequence and in the most convenient form for use on rolls, which may differ from the old arrangement. Be sure that the filing is accurate.

The great application for microphotography, particularly for county records, is for making copies as insurance against loss of the original. Fires, floods, and deterioration take a heavy toll of records. At least 80 percent of Illinois counties have lost part or all of their records, at some time or other, through courthouse fires. The most spectacular and costly example is the complete loss of all Cook County records in the Chicago fire of 1871. The one abstract com-pany which saved its records has had a profitable monopoly ever since. River counties have suffered heavy losses from floods. The Pulaski County records, for instance, rescued from the flood waters of 1937 and promptly and carefully cleaned have now begun to fade so fast that nothing will be left in a few years. . . .

The cost of filming records, great though it may seem to the county finance committee, is infinitesimal in comparison with the cost of trying to reconstruct the records. Only by photographic processes can facsimiles of the original records be made available for use, and of all photographic methods this is the only one not prohibitive in cost. Insurance films should be filed elsewhere than in the courthouse. The Illinois State Library offers free housing for such films in its air-conditioned film vault in the archives build-ing. Facilities for making enlargements of the film as needed are also available there. . . .

A fourth application of microphotography to county records is for centralizing research material. Early county records are the richest, often the only, vein of source material for the pioneer history of the state. County archives have not been exploited to any extent so far because the county seats are too far apart and too inaccessible to many scholars. County officials have neither the time nor the facilities to accommodate research students, either in person or through correspondence. These older records, because of infrequent use, are most apt to get crowded out of the regular courthouse vaults into attic and basement storerooms which results too often in their ultimate destruction. Because they are of little current interest from a legal standpoint, county boards are often unwilling or unable to go to the expense of microfilming the older records. It has long been the hope of the Archives Division to secure microfilm copies of all such records. The Illinois Bar Association is also interested in transcribing early court records and has already started filming those records in some of the older counties.

Microfilm copies are also the cheapest form of note-taking for patrons. These persons may be allowed to use their own portable cameras for copying records they wish, or where microfilm copies have already been made, copies of the films can be supplied at nominal cost. In either case, it is proper to impose the restriction that these copies must not be used for legal purposes without paying the fee collectable by law for certified or uncertified copies of public documents. Courts should not accept such copies in evidence without a certificate of certification or a receipt showing payment of the fee. It is also proper and customary to reserve the right to inspect and approve any proposed publication quoting the documents at length.

The Illinois State Library has neither the equipment nor the personnel to do extensive insurance microfilming of county records, nor has it any intention of competing with commercial firms. Many problems, especially those involving certifications of films, have not been given adequate consideration in the past by persons making such copies. . . .

2 / THE PRESERVATION OF LOCAL RECORDS BY MICROPHOTOGRAPHY

The Public Archives Commission of the American Historical Association, the progenitor of the present Society of American Archivists, was created in 1899. One of the first matters discussed by this group was "Should local archives be centralized or should they be left in the communities in which they were created?" This question is still debated as one of the vital issues in archival economy.

Local government, especially county government, touches so closely the lives and property rights of all citizens that the proper preservation of local archives is of immeasurable concern to all. American history and the social implications thereof can and should be rewritten on the basis of research in this vast reservoir of unexploited source material. Political economists, especially tax experts, are already using this material in their studies looking toward the elimination of overlapping governmental agencies.

Historians and social scientists in general are demanding vociferously that this material be collected at research centers. They point out that many records have already been lost through fire, flood, disintegration, and thoughtless or wanton destruction. County seats are widely scattered, inconveniently located for scholars wishing to make comparative studies or to do extended research. Many courthouses and town halls are not fireproof and practically none have adequate vaults. None have accommodations for research, either in the way of physical space and equipment, trained personnel, or scientific catalogs and indexes. Frequently the oldest and most valuable historic records are to be found in backward counties from which population and wealth have receded. This is notably true of the states of the Ohio River valley. These counties have neither money nor appreciation for the proper care or for the preservation of their records. The older records relating to some of the newer and now urban counties are frequently found in small and relatively unimportant county seats. Some of the early records relating to Chicago, for instance, are to be found across the state in the county seats of Pike County (Pittsfield, population 25,000), Fulton County (population 44,000) and Putnam County (Hennepin, population 5,000). When it is remembered that all official Chicago archives (including land title records) were destroyed in the 1871 fire, the significance of the fact that the records of one county were rescued from a city dump several years ago is readily apparent.

Included in the group of social scientists interested in the preservation of local archives are the various state, and to a more limited extent, federal departments whose work now ties in with or supersedes the functions formerly exclusively those of local governing bodies. The most striking example is, of course, the various records upon which social security boards depend. In Illinois, for instance, birth records having been kept only since 1878, marriage records and probate records must often be resorted to in proof of age. These are county records which for the most part quite properly should stay in the county.

In brief, all these people doing research in local archives are asking: "Unless your records are transferred to some safe central depository, what assurance have I that I can get access to them when I need them?"

To this question the local official replies: "We admit all that you have said. Most of us regret and deplore the dangers to which our records are exposed, and are doing the very best we can with the resources we have. We realize that the records might be safer in the state archives. But we cannot send them away. Our records relate almost exclusively to the property rights of our citizens. Our records of deeds, mortgages, court decisions, marriages, probate matters, etc., are inextricably woven together with our administrative and judicial functions of enforcing those property rights. Copies you may have; but originals, no."

And to this the state archivist, himself harassed for want of space adds: "Suppose we should get all these originals? Where would we find a place for them?" Even Illinois with its magnificent archives building blanches at the thought of having 102 counties ship the contents of their vaults to Springfield.

At this juncture in the discussion of centralization versus localization of archives, the question is put: "What services can we count on from microphotography as a means of photographing the local materials of significance that should be brought into a central place of records?"

The obvious reply that microphotography is the answer to the whole problem requires qualification. Although microphotography is the cheapest means of copying available, it is not inexpensive. County record volumes average about six hundred pages each. At two cents per page (the usual commercial rate), this gives a basic cost of twelve dollars per volume. Unbound manuscripts which require unfolding and careful handling cost more, duplicate copies much less. Parenthetically, our own experimentation indicates that while we can lower the cost when the records can be photographed in our own laboratory, for fieldwork this two cents per page is a reasonable figure. We expect in the future to have most of our fieldwork done commercially but shall make duplicate copies, compilations, and enlargements ourselves. . . .

The use of microphotography in collecting local material is admittedly practical, but since the cost places an obvious limitation upon our definition of "materials of significance" it is necessary to suggest policies for selection, methods of reducing the original overhead cost by duplication of the film in part or in whole for other institutions or individuals, and methods of exploiting the film collected.

Microphotography can be used in all fields of historical interest. Pictures can be taken of historical events or places and pictures can be copied in the same manner. The National Archives has a department devoted to making and collecting sound and silent cinema of historical events. Newsreel items of local interest can be obtained without great expense through the motion picture companies.

Film copies of newspapers are becoming commonplace in libraries. Some metropolitan newspapers are sold in film editions with the publisher usually meeting the cost of the master film. The Illinois State Historical Library purchases two Illinois papers this way. In addition, it has had its file of two Springfield papers copied for the years 1885 through 1910—the period of greatest disintegration. Other historical libraries are following similar policies. Since the cost of film copies is largely if not entirely offset by the cost of binding and shelving originals, this practice will be increasingly followed, even though the total cost of filming local newspapers may have to be borne by one institution.

Manuscripts in private hands are peculiarly suitable for microphotographic copying, for most owners will permit institutions to make copies when they would be unwilling to sell or donate the originals. The use of copies to save originals is too common a practice to require comment here. The use of infrared ray and X-ray photography in detecting forgeries or reading faded or deleted copies and particularly for recapturing the writing on charred manuscripts, while not particularly pertinent to our subject, should be kept in mind when salvaging apparently hopelessly damaged records. . . .

It is in the field of county archives that microphotography can make its greatest contribution to the preservation of local source materials. There are several points of approach to the selection of material for copying. Should all records be copied as an insurance against fire, flood, earthquake, or other catastrophe? Should the state archives limit its copying to archives of purely historical interest, and if so, what should be its basis for selection? Should all records of a series prior to a given date be copied, or should selections of more spectacular items only be copied? Should the state archives be responsible for making copies of those records required for research by other state departments? To what extent can the cost of overhead for copy work be reduced? And finally, how best can the copies be exploited by the archivist?

Much has been made of the insurance aspect as a basis for copying local records. Fires in local record repositories have been so numerous that one wonders that any records have survived. Many records in our southern states were lost by war. Floods have taken toll, the most destructive being the 1937 Ohio River floods which destroyed the records of several counties in Indiana and Illinois.

The Indiana State Library fortunately has copies from which the Indiana records could be partially replaced, but two Illinois and perhaps some Ohio counties lost all their records. It is unquestionably desirable that copies be made as insurance against loss. However, this insurance feature is and should be the responsibility of the local government rather than of the state. Overhead expense can be saved by sharing in the cost of copying records desired by both the county and the state. It is probable that a county might have many records which it would not feel necessary to insure but which, because of their historic interest, the state archives would wish to copy. On the other hand, the county might wish insurance on current records such as assessment rolls in which the archivist would have little present interest, or perhaps better stated, would not feel could be included in his selection of records for immediate copying. At least one commercial microphotographic company is selling insurance on county records, protecting its policies by film records. A number of private abstract companies are copying land records for their own use.

Many state departments are interested in obtaining copies of local records for use in their own research work. The Illinois State Tax Commission, for instance, copied county records in connection with a study of overlapping taxing units. The copies made by state departments are apt to be selections of material covering limited ranges of topics and involving comparatively recent records for use in one piece of research only. The archivist, therefore, should no more assume the financial responsibility for doing this copy work than he would for underwriting the cost of hand note-taking. However, by keeping in touch with such work being done, he can often save overhead by having his own field work done at the same time. He can often get whole volumes copied for little more than the cost of copying scattered items wanted by the research department.

The question as to what the archivist shall select depends upon his budget and the amount and type of material available. On the basis of the number and nature of inquiries received, Illinois has decided to copy county records created prior to 1860, starting with the twenty oldest counties. We intend to copy practically all bound records and a selection of unbound material. Most of the older records, such as wills, inventories of estates, of interest to the historian were transcribed *in extenso* into volumes, making it necessary to copy unbound originals chiefly for their autograph value or occasional omission of contents from the volume records. We plan to copy all county commissioners' and board of supervisors' proceedings to date, this being the general administrative unit. We shall probably also copy other records of a later date such as vital statistics. Other states will choose other dates or subject limitations. On the basis of such inventories as are available, we expect to have to copy between one and two hundred volumes per county. . . .

Microphotography also plays an important role in the exploitation of the copies collected. The original film copy should be used only as a master copy, and duplicate copies made for use in projectors or for making enlargements. Film copies are used as extra editions of the original. In addition, compilations can be made of related material, such as for example, all available material on the Black Hawk War or the expulsion of the Mormons from Illinois. Films and enlargements therefrom can circulate on an interlibrary loan basis. In the centralization of materials for research we can at the same time decentralize the research work by giving the scholar the opportunity to borrow copies of his materials for use in his hometown.

3 / REPRODUCTION OF STATE RECORDS

Photographic processes play an increasingly important role in record-making. In order to use photography successfully it is necessary to understand not only what the various types of equipment can do, but also their limitations when applied to records problems. . . . The filing expert can establish efficient procedures for organizing records within an established file but only the policymaking officials of a department are qualified to decide what records shall be created, for what purposes they shall be used, and how long they shall be preserved.

The situation as regards applications of photography to record making is analogous. The salesman should demonstrate what his equipment can and cannot do from a mechanical standpoint, but he is not qualified to advise as to whether or not a specific type of photography will result in records adequate for the purposes for which the records are created and preserved. That statement is particularly true for microphotography. The mere fact that courts would accept a photographic record (a frequent sales point) will not compensate for the inconvenience and delays resulting from having to thread a microfilm into a reading machine a dozen times a day in order to consult a frequently used record. On the other hand, the department should take advantage of the 90 to 98 percent saving of storage space and filing equipment obtainable from the reduction to microfilm of bulky records infrequently consulted and of limited permanence as to the necessity of preservation.

Three photographic processes are in common use in connection with records: 1. infrared and violet ray photography; 2. photocopy; and 3. microphotography. Those who wish a more extended description of available equipment than can be given here, and also of processing methods, will find a useful guide in H. W. Greenwood, *Document Photography: Individual Copying and Mass Recording.*[4]

Of these three processes the first, infrared and violet ray photography, is used chiefly for the scholarly examination of old manuscripts and in crime detection. Specially sensitized film or paper, exposed to infrared light through the use of filters or ultraviolet light through violet ray mercury lamps can reveal hidden, overwritten, faded, or charred writing; detect forgeries and interpolation; and aid in the taking and study of fingerprints. For routine work its most promising use would be for the restoration of records damaged by flood or by fire.

By photocopy is meant photographs made directly on sensitized paper without the intervention of a photographic plate or film. "Practically all document photography in which original size reproduction is involved uses paper as the recording material. Paper is used also in other cases where some reduction is called for, particularly in the case of the photographic recording of large documents such as drawings and the like. Paper in general is used in all cases where the copy or documentary photograph will be larger than half-plate (6½ x 4¾ in., 16.5 x 12 cm)."[5]

. . . .

Photocopy methods are used for direct recording and for making copies for office or patron use. Photocopy is most frequently used for recording in county courthouses. Deeds, wills, soldiers' discharges, and many other records are required to be recorded verbatim. The secretary of state, for example, records contracts and other matters affecting charter rights in this fashion. Photocopy recording is authorized by Illinois law and is recognized as valid evidence by courts because it is a facsimile copy which permits of no possibility of misinterpretation, interpolations, or erasures. The speed of the process is also a great economy over typewritten or manual transcription. The first or negative copy is used as the record since it would be possible to retouch the negative in a manner that could not be detected in making a positive print. . . .

The photocopy process is used even more extensively in record work for other purposes. Its use for making certified and noncertified copies of documents for patron use has largely superseded typed or handwritten copies, again because of the speed and economy of production. . . . Photocopies of records are frequently used as replacements for the originals for patron use. The purpose may be to save wear and tear on the original record or to obviate any possibility of tampering with the original record. . . .

Photocopy is the process of copying documents at full size, or if at a reduction, on a scale which permits reading the prints with the naked eye. It is employed where quick reference or consultation by the public is indicated. Microphotography is the process of copying documents on film sixteen or thirty-five millimeters wide at a scale of reduction so great that mechanical aids are necessary to enlarge the image enough to be legible. It is employed where consultation of the documents will be infrequent; where the saving in bulk overbalances the advantages of preserving the original documents at full size; or where facsimiles are wanted at a low cost. . . .

The custodian of records has a twofold problem. He is likely, first, to need to copy documents of a variety of shapes and sizes (many being quite large), in varying shades of paper and ink, bound and unbound, many in fragile condition. Second, he is likely to need to copy thousands, perhaps millions, of records of more or less uniform size and speed is essential to keep down the cost of doing the work. . . .

It cannot be overemphasized that only the official responsible for record policy or an experienced records consultant such as the state archivist is competent to decide whether or not a microfilm record can in the long run most efficiently achieve the purposes for which the record is created. The records officer should decide to what extent microphotography meets his needs and then decide which of the various pieces of equipment offered to him can do the work proposed most quickly, efficiently, and economically. Under present trade conditions the records officer should demand an ocular demonstration and a written guarantee of quality and performance before purchasing any equipment or contracting to have the copying done for him. . . .

Government agencies which plan to use microphotography in any quantity sufficient to justify going into that field at all should turn to the commercial type cameras—the "universal" and the specialized cameras. Some of this equipment can be purchased outright, some can either be purchased or leased, some may be leased only. Most companies will contract to copy a large backlog of accumulated files, but it is cheaper for the department to do all its work with its own labor. All commercial type cameras are sufficiently mechanized and automatic as to controls that anyone can operate them successfully after brief instruction and a little practice. . . .

The "universal" commercial cameras come in a number of sizes. . . . Large cameras can copy any type of document, bound or unbound, up to a maximum of 37½ by 52½ inches. They use nonperforated film that gives a maximum reduction of 1:30, which is about the limit of legible reduction possible with present-day film. A greater reduction results in a blurring of letters and figures, as explained by Greenwood: "When reduction is too great the effects are first noticed in the loops of a's and e's which become filled. This is first noticed at a reduction of about 1:20. Above 25 diameters reduction the text becomes difficult to read, and above 40 diameters it is practically illegible."[6] The ideal reduction ratio is considered to be 1:12. The best library film readers will bring documents back to original size at a maximum of 1:23. Where copies are needed of documents requiring a greater than 1:30 reduction, they may be copied sectionally on 35-mm film or if that is not practicable they may be copied on cameras which will take larger size film. . . .

The maximum speed of the "universal" cameras is about thirty-five exposures per minute, but it should be noted that actually it is seldom possible to copy at that rate since the original document must be adjusted by hand on the copying frame, and unless there is uniformity of color of ink and background as between pages, there must be frequent checking of focus and timing. An attempt to go too fast, particularly in turning the leaves of bound volumes, will result in blurred images since there is a tendency for static electricity to cause a slight movement of the paper as the hand is withdrawn. Claims of great speed for this type of camera should be regarded with skepticism.

Many modern records which come in long files of uniform or nearly uniform size lend themselves to high speed copying on fully automatic cameras. First used by banks for recording checks, these machines are now used for a wide variety of records. Document placing, focusing, and timing are all automatic. . . . The speed of copying depends upon the length of the original. Six to eight thousand documents of check size can be copied per hour, whereas papers of correspondence size reduce the rate to perhaps two thousand or less per hour. Some makes of cameras limit the length of the original document which can be copied; others, working on a rotary principle, can take documents of any length up to the capacity of the one-hundred-foot roll. . . .

Most, if not all, of these specialized high speed cameras use 16-mm film. Here again, commercial development of film is desirable; most of the camera companies require it.

Bound records cannot be used in these high speed cameras. Fragile documents and those which have sharp fold marks should not be run through these machines because of the danger of tearing. . . .

Before deciding to make extensive use of microfilm, one should weigh carefully the implications of the physical properties of film (its degree of permanence and its weak points), how and where it is to be stored, and the limitations set on its use by the fact that it cannot be read without mechanical enlargements.

Cellulose acetate is used as the film base. Unlike the highly flammable nitrate base used for motion pictures, this so-called "safety" film is slow burning—it will melt but will neither explode nor burst into flame. . . . Accelerated aging and other tests indicate that the cellulose acetate film base if kept under proper temperature will probably prove as durable as the best grades of paper. . . .

The weakest point in microfilm is the relative softness of the emulsion that carries the photographic image. It is easily scratched. When it is remembered that a sixteen-letter word on microfilm may occupy less space than a single letter of the original, it is easy to see how an almost unnoticeable scratch, made either maliciously or by accident, might destroy a signature or other vital part of the document. Atmospheric dust particles, abrasive materials or oil from the reader, or finger prints may damage the film. An enlargement of a dust particle lodged on the film might obscure a letter or be taken for a letter not actually there. To avoid these hazards as much as possible, it is customary to use the original negative microfilm copy as master copy only, kept in reserve storage, and to use positive prints for office and patron use. In estimating the cost of microfilming records, the expense of making these duplicate film copies must also be figured. To get satisfactory copies it is advised that they be made commercially, at a cost of approximately five to six cents per foot.

There is one other weak point in microphotography. The

emulsion used in photography is a silver compound. Unless very carefully processed there may be residual chemicals which will cause the image to darken over a period of time. This calls for periodic inspection to avoid the possibility of eventual loss of the copy. Under first-class commercial processing, however, there is far less danger of this happening than there is in the case of photographs made on paper. . . .

Magnifying glasses, microscopes, or the various "viewing" apparatuses on the market can be used for scanning microfilm but for satisfactory use some form of reader or projector must be used. . . . For departments employing microfilm for office use, a reading machine is necessary. Most of the manufacturers of the commercial type cameras build reading machines for use with their equipment. In order to keep down the cost of the machines, these readers are often usable for limited sizes only. . . . The small, inexpensive individual or portable readers are unsatisfactory for record use. They are intended either for use with short strips of film or else for the low magnification required for reading printed books of standard size.

It is frequently necessary to make copies of a part or all of a film. Positive contact prints for scattered or a few pages can be made in the office darkroom, if there be one, but for long runs it is best to have the work done at one of the microfilm laboratories.

The most frequent need, however, is for copies of occasional pages at anything from contact to full or even greater size. Where these copies must be numerous it must be admitted that there is apt to be a serious bottleneck of production. A device is available which synchronizes the movement of paper and film to make enlargements of an entire roll of film at a fixed enlargement. What is needed is an attachment which would permit a person using a microfilm reader who finds one page of which he needs a copy, to press a button and to have a full size enlargement, fully processed, drop into the waiting basket. Such a machine has been produced in an engineering model, but there is apparently no prospect for its coming into the market very soon. . . .

The most frequently used apparatus for making enlargements

is the type of enlarger used by photographers. Several on the market provide spool holders and film-advancing mechanisms permitting convenient use of rolls of film. This process is also a slow process requiring a darkroom, manual developing, and thorough washing in running water. . . .

One other point sometimes neglected in making microfilm copies is the desirability of inserting one or more frames at the beginning and end of each roll, giving in letters large enough to be legible to the naked eye the number of the film roll, the title of the record, and the inclusive pages covered by the film. At the Illinois archives we use for this purpose, celluloid letters one inch in height arranged on a slotted board like those used for hotel announcements.

Microfilm used for record purposes should also be certified. . . . It should also be noted that microfilm copies should be checked for retakes needed because of omissions or imperfect copies before the original records are destroyed.

One other element of cost, often overlooked in estimates for microfilming is overhead beyond that of the equipment used. George A. Schwegeman of the Library of Congress, reporting at a meeting of the Society of American Archivists, stated that a cost analysis of photographing twenty-four million documents indicated that the operation of taking the pictures and developing them had amounted to within two and a half and two and seven-eights cents per hundred but that the overall costs ranged from nineteen to sixty-eight cents per hundred.[7] Among the factors often neglected in estimating costs are the time required for checking for accurate filing as a preliminary to photographing; for unfolding and flattening documents; for correct placing of broken or fragile papers; for the weighting down of each page in a bound volume; for refocusing for different thicknesses of the book as the pages are turned; for variations in timing of exposures for different shades of paper and degrees of fading; for checking of retakes; and for putting away the records after they have been copied. . . .

12

Records Disposal

1 / THE DISPOSAL OF RECORDS

THE STATUTES OF THE UNITED STATES and of many states make it a criminal offense to destroy any government record without specific authorization. This regulation is necessary because certain property and other civil rights can only be proved through records filed with or compiled by government officials. Administrative records establish the government's side of its transactions with individuals, corporations, and other government agencies. They record administrative policies and procedures in connection with law enforcement, such data being particularly necessary because of frequent changes in officials. Furthermore, government records are the richest and most important source materials for social and political history. In this country the demands of historians for documentation have been the chief influence in the creation of archival agencies.

Thus far American archivists have devoted themselves primarily to the task of preserving all government records. The increasing complexity of government organization and the ease and cheapness of multiplying copies of documents have resulted in a

꿍 PART 1 OF THIS CHAPTER, "The Disposal of Records," was originally published in *Illinois Libraries* 26 (March 1944): 120–24. Part 2, "Reducing the Volume of Records," was originally published as "Reduction of Records" in *Illinois Libraries* 26 (April 1944): 152–57.

stupendous growth in the bulk of government records—federal, state, and local. It is obviously no longer possible for any governmental agency to preserve all records which result from its activities. The emphasis of archives work has shifted from preservation of records to selection of records for preservation.

This problem of selection places tremendous responsibility upon both the archivist and the government official in whose office the records originate. It is more necessary than ever for a man to be able to produce legal proof of his ownership of property, of the place and date of his birth, of his family relationships, or his qualifications to practice his profession or to drive his car, of any number of matters. The government is taking over more and more responsibility for the regulation of trade and industry and protection of public health and social welfare. All of these matters involve public records which must be adequate, perfectly preserved, and accessible. Haphazard destruction of public records in the past has cost inestimable pecuniary losses both to individuals and to the government and created irreparable gaps in historical data. The proper selection of records for preservation and for destruction calls for almost superhuman judgment. It is not surprising, therefore, that this task has been shirked by all concerned until all available storage space was exhausted and administrative efficiency curtailed by chaotic record conditions.

The archivist of the United States calls attention to the critical nature of this problem: "Just before Pearl Harbor a hasty survey of Federal records in the District of Columbia indicated that the quantity of such records had more than doubled since 1936 and that their bulk was increasing at a rate approaching a million cubic feet a year. The situation outside Washington is unknown, but it is believed that as many Federal records exist in the field as in the Capital. In size alone, therefore, the records problem of the Government is already staggering. What it will be at the end of . . . [World War II] is not pleasant to contemplate."[1]

Although the ratio of expansion of records is less for state and local governments, it is still so great that the necessity for a policy for reduction of their records is as pressing as in the case of the federal government. The county clerk of Cook County (Chicago) adds over 600 folio volumes a year for tax collectors' books and has 1,200 current volumes of tax sale records. The circuit clerk of that county has over 1,310,000 files on current cases in his vault plus a rented warehouse filled with semicurrent records.

The Retailers' Occupation Tax Division, reporting in 1942 as one of the eleven divisions of the Illinois Department of Finance, stated that during the previous fiscal year it had received and filed 1,789,954 tax returns, an average of 152,294 per month. Obviously neither state nor county can afford the equipment for filing nor the space for housing records piling up in such astronomical quantities.

Private business also has this same problem of excessive bulk of modern records. As a result of comparative studies of similar records in the same industry, a number of schedules have been published suggesting the length of time certain categories need to be kept. Recommendations as to the disposal of business records are generally conditioned upon statutes of limitations. Governmental agencies are less able to profit by such studies. In the first place, the statute of limitations does not apply for the most part to public records. Attorneys frequently go back as far as the territorial records to document their briefs. Secondly, there is less opportunity to compare similar records. Most government agencies keep similar "housekeeping" records of a financial nature, but their important records result from unique laws applicable only to the one department. Even as between states there is no uniformity of law or procedure to give a satisfactory basis of comparison.

Reduction of the bulk of government records is being attacked from three angles: first, prevention of creation of unnecessary accumulations at the point of origin; second, reduction in size by the application of photographic processes, particularly microphotography; and third, through scientific selection of records which can be destroyed as having no further value for administrative or research purposes.

Record creation and preservation to be effective should be deliberately planned and executed and this scientific organization of records should be made at the time they are coming into being. Primarily this planning is the responsibility of the department in which the records originate.

Creation of records involves a study of what records are needed as well as how to avoid unnecessary bulk. The matter of providing for the actual recording of important data deserves careful consideration. A department head and often the so-called efficiency expert whose advice he seeks tend to evaluate records from the standpoint of temporary and current use. Financial records which would exonerate the official in case of an investigation will be kept meticulously, while other records of far greater importance from an administrative point of view—such as statements establishing and explaining policies or registers of procedure—are often kept sketchily or not at all.

The archivist as the ultimate custodian is also interested in the creation of records. After the records have been transferred to the archives it is difficult to weed the files and too late to supply gaps where necessary records have not been properly made. The more effectively the records have been organized before coming into the archives the more quickly and efficiently he will be able to service them. The archivist has specialized training and experience as to the long-range applications of records which can often be helpful to his fellow officials.

The federal government recognizes the necessity for scientific record-making as well as for record preservation, and a number of departments, notably those of the Treasury, State, War, and Navy have appointed records coordinators to plan and organize their files. The law also recognizes the interest of the archivist of the United States in records from the time of their creation to the time of their deposit in the National Archives or their destruction as useless records. Section three of the National Archives Act reads in part as follows: "All archives or records belonging to the Government of the United States (legislative, executive, judicial, and other) shall be under the charge and superintendence of the Archivist to this extent: He shall have full power to inspect personally or by deputy the records of any agency of the United States Government whatsoever and wheresoever located, and shall have the full cooperation of any and all persons in charge of such records in such inspections. . . ."[2]

The first step in creating a new record file should be to consider carefully the purpose and need for the record. Why is the record needed? Who will use it and how? What information should it contain? What is its relation to other records? Is it "an intermediary or subsidiary item, or is it an end-result record"? Does it duplicate information to be found in some other record, and if so can the two records be combined? Is this a permanent and essential legal record, or is it an office memorandum compiled for temporary convenience?

Having decided upon the true nature and contents of the record, consideration should next be given to the most efficient physical form for the record. Forms designed to use the most compact layout, size, and paper weight can accomplish striking reductions in the bulk of records. Lt. Comdr. W. F. McCormick of the U.S. Navy has pointed out that "the increase of a multiple form from two to three copies may increase filing labor and space required by 50 per cent. Changing the size of a form from 8½ by 11 inches to 8½ by 14 inches increases paper consumption and space required by about 18 percent. The Navy processes several thousand purchase orders a day. Imagine the seriousness of adding another copy to a purchase order set or increasing the size of the form."[3] He also calls attention to the fact that the difference between sixteen-pound and twenty-pound paper is, in filing space, the difference between 300 and 250 sheets per filing inch. . . .

Much can be done to prevent excessive record accumulation, particularly in the field of administrative records by procedures to insure the segregation and prompt elimination of documents known through experience to have no permanent value. Personal letters, advertisements, and routine requests for copies of printed matter do not belong in an official correspondence file. A formal definition of the term that could provide a clear-cut distinction between a true record and mere office memoranda is impossible because all memoranda have at least a temporary value or they would not have been made in the first place; and they must be preserved as long as they do have value.

The most effective means of keeping down the bulk of records is for the department head to determine on the basis of the work of his department what documents shall be designated as official records and what as unofficial files. Normally, duplicate delivery receipts and adding machine tabulations should not be dignified by the term records nor should duplicate records kept for mere temporary administrative convenience. The mere act of attaching a file mark or of placing a document in an official file gives it the legal status of a record. If a file has been kept on a certain subject over a period of years, that file though obviously worthless should not be destroyed without obtaining due legal authorization. Common sense, however, would indicate that it is proper to weed out individual documents which ought never to have been filed there in the first place, always provided that the discarded documents are conscientiously and honestly appraised by a responsible official as worthless.

Correspondence files are notorious collectors of ephemeral material. It is easier to drop an extra carbon copy of a document into each of several places than to decide the official location for the one copy. It is easier to file and produce all letters from one file than from two—an official and an unofficial file. Some control must be provided, however, if the bulk of the correspondence file is to be kept within reasonable limits. Only the executive is capable of weeding old files, and he neither can nor will take the time for this work.

There are several devices in common practice for restricting the size of correspondence files. One is to type the carbon copy of the reply on the back of the letter received. The second device is to set up three correspondence files, one designated as the official file, one as the director's file, and one for temporary routine matters. Into the official file go all correspondence relating to policies and law enforcement. Personnel and other important administrative matters may go into the official file but preferably should be set up as a separate file. The director's file contains duplicate copies of correspondence that the executive would want to take with him as personal files upon his retirement from office. The temporary files should be so designated and earmarked for periodic discard. A third and, for some departments, a more convenient and efficient method is to use a single file for the permanent and fugitive correspondence, but to have each letter code marked as permanent, subject to destruction after one year, five years, or whatever periods of time are most suitable. The executive makes this code annotation on the letter when he signs it. Clerical help can then be used to weed the files periodically. It will often happen that a folder labeled as temporary will expand unexpectedly because something apparently trivial develops into something important. Supplemental correspondence attached to a letter marked temporary will be the signal for the clerk to refer that file to the executive for a possible reclassification. Other devices for keeping down the bulk of records at the source will occur to alert officials charged with the creation of records.

Microphotography has been hailed by enthusiasts as the greatest invention since printing and the solution of all storage problems. Microfilm copies, they say, can be substituted for the originals, releasing from 90 to 98 percent of the storage space formerly required. Microfilm properly made and processed is as permanent as the best quality of rag paper, the copy is an exact facsimile of the original, it cannot be tampered with without detection, and the courts have long accepted recording by photostating, another form of photography. The federal government and several of the states, including Illinois, have passed legislation legalizing the substitution of microfilm copies for original records. The fact that microphotography has certain limitations has been underemphasized, however. Some of these limitations will be overcome with time, but officials should at present be conservative about destroying original records.

First of all, microphotography is not as cheap as some people suggest. The materials are very inexpensive, costing upward from less than a cent a page. The cost of overhead, however, is very high. Cameras, reading machines and other equipment, and the salary and expense of the operator can easily bring the cost of copying records to a much higher figure than the cost of constructing a warehouse to house the originals.

Second, the courts still prefer the original record to a copy, no matter how accurate. Tests for authenticity of a document from a study of paper, watermarks, ink, and other external evidence cannot be made from a photograph. Words written over other words do not show up in such a manner as to indicate which was the interpolation. A hole in the paper may look in a photograph like a letter or a figure and so lead to erroneous inferences. A scratch on the film may destroy a signature or other essential part of the document. Best practice is to have two film copies—a master copy and a working copy.

So far microfilm copies have been substituted for original government records chiefly in the case of administrative records which cease to be of much legal or historical value after a period of time. Original records which protect civil and property rights should not be destroyed after microfilming. Microfilm copies are the cheapest form of insurance in case original records are destroyed, and this is the most important application of microphotography to archival work.

The size, form, and manner of consulting records has a bearing upon the convenience of use of microfilm. Very large volumes such as plat books cannot be copied successfully by standard microphotographic cameras, though there are very expensive precision instruments which will do the work. Records which are frequently consulted for purposes of comparison with other records cannot conveniently be used in film form unless several reading projectors are on hand, and even this is unsatisfactory. Case files to which additional documents must be added from time to time should not be filmed because such additions involve splicing and a spliced film could not be accepted as evidence in court.

Records most suitable for filming (speaking of convenience of consultation on film rather than suitability from a legal standpoint) are those records generally kept in register or record volumes or unbound records filed in numerical or chronological sequence—

for instance, county collectors' books, deed and mortgage records, records of wills, record of proceedings of board meetings and hearings, and the like.

The treasurer was the first Illinois state official to make extensive use of microphotography. Formerly each warrant issued as a disbursement from the treasury was registered by hand or typewriter in tabular form in a bound record volume. Now this registration is done by copying each warrant on 16-mm film. Each roll of film, four inches in diameter and three-quarters of an inch thick, registers six thousand checks. This roll of film takes only about 2 percent of the space required for the volume registers formerly used and eliminates any possibility of error in the record because the register is a facsimile of the warrant issued.

2 / Reducing the Volume of Records

Careful planning for the creation of archives will do much to check the accumulation of unnecessary records. The necessity remains, however, for further reduction in the bulk of the files by systematic withdrawal of records after they cease to have further administrative, legal, or research value. As a matter of course all records should be preserved so long as they are potentially useful for the protection of property or personal rights. After their usefulness for purposes of administration is over, generally also before that time, most government records take on an increasing value for historical purposes. Theoretically, therefore, all government records should be preserved permanently. Even the historian realizes the impracticality of working from such an avalanche of records as would result from keeping everything.

The selection of which records should be retained and for how long, which can be destroyed and at what point, calls for exceptional judgment and knowledge of governmental organization. The British call it an art and provide additional compensation for members of the Public Record Office staff who are called upon to help decide.

It is comparatively easy to select records of permanent value, relatively easy to decide on those of no value. The great bulk of records are borderline. Take, for instance, the function of licensing persons to practice their professions. Certainly the registers of licenses are permanent records. But how long do we need to keep the other records necessarily created in connection with the administration of the licensing acts? These records include correspondence with and about each applicant; applications with accompanying credentials; examination records, recommendations of the examining board; complaints, records of examinations, hearings on and disposition of complaints; records of proceedings in relation to revocation and reinstatement of licenses; and records on renewals of licenses. That is one of the simpler examples of record creation. . . .

In making an appraisal certain questions should be asked. Is this the original, official copy of the record? Who made this record? Who uses it? What purpose does it serve? What information does it give? Who should be inconvenienced by the destruction? Is the information contained in this record obtainable elsewhere? If so, where, and in what form? If the information is found elsewhere is this record essential to establishment of the legality or authenticity of the information found in the other record? If two records cover the same ground, which would be the one taken to court?

A fundamental distinction should be made between a "true record" and a record which is a mere by-product of administration. By the term "true record" we mean a record which the law requires be stamped with an official file mark and/or otherwise recorded by registration or transcription before the matters referred to in the record can take legal effect. Most county records fall into this category. Wills and other probate records, records of deeds and mortgages, naturalization records, registers of marriages, births and deaths, and enrolled laws are examples of that type of record. It is perfectly proper (and the law permits this) to substitute for office use, certified transcripts of the originals when they wear out or otherwise disintegrate or if there is a possibility that some one might attempt to tamper with the original. It is the personal opinion of the writer that such basic records should never be destroyed but preserved in safe dead storage if there is no room for them in the regular vaults. There are too many possibilities of error in transcription or questions of authenticity only to be proved from the original to run the risks involved in destruction of such records.

Administrative records which serve as memoranda of transactions involved in enforcement of laws by government agencies may or may not be such "true records." The line is a tenuous one, felt rather than subject to definition. The law makes no distinction between such records.

"Housekeeping records," particularly personnel records and those relating to expenditures of appropriations (except those kept by the state treasurer and auditor of public accounts), are generally not of permanent value. It is not safe to generalize on this point, however, for these records vary in importance. It is important to keep fee books for as long a time as payment of the fees has any legal significance to the government or to the payee. In the case of fee books kept by the Illinois Corporation Department, for instance, that means that these volumes must be kept indefinitely. Likewise it is personally important to each employee that his payroll and efficiency rating records be kept at least during his lifetime. The scholar doing sociological or historical research might want such records kept indefinitely. Generally it is not difficult in practice to decide which of these "housekeeping records" need to be kept permanently and which may be destroyed after a suitable lapse of time.

A distinction should be made between "housekeeping records" and the records which relate to the technical aspects of the work of the agency. These latter records should be preserved so long as they aid in efficient administration of the department and protect against claims of all sorts. Generally speaking it is considered improper to destroy any records of a current administration, though Illinois laws permit the destruction of certain state tax records by the Finance Department after three years and automobile registration records by the secretary of state after five years.

In addition to temporary preservation for current administrative convenience, the objective should be to preserve permanently those records which would enable future administrators or persons interested in the history of the department to get a clear and somewhat detailed picture of the work that the department has been required to do at all periods, what it did, how it did it, and what measure of success or failure it had.

The most difficult phase of the selection of records for preservation and for destruction is to decide whether or not they have present or potential value as source material for the study of history, biography, genealogy, economics, sociology, or other forms of research. Literature is filled with thrills over the discovery of important facts in the most unlikely places and wails about the attics which were cleaned out just before the authors arrived.

A common and helpful device is to set an arbitrary date back of which records are to be considered historical and not subject to destruction. Historians criticize this method because they point out that some routine records (though such records are comparatively few) dating back to the 1840s are of no greater historical interest than routine records of the 1940s which everyone would recommend for destruction as valueless. They point out that some of the records which historians today find of greatest value are being used for purposes undreamed of by the makers of the records. For instance, the Abraham Lincoln Association has published a series of volumes entitled "Lincoln Day by Day" which accounts for a surprisingly large proportion of his daily activities throughout his lifetime, all compiled from obscure items buried in court records, newspapers, and correspondence files of his contemporaries.

Certainly there can be no justification in letting anyone get the idea that age is the only criterion for historical value, and that records before a given date must be kept while later records can be destroyed. The historian of the future will undoubtedly need the government records which tell the story of the social revolution exemplified by the New Deal and those which describe the incredible overnight conversion from peacetime industry to all-out war work.

There is a justification, however, for selecting an arbitrary date prior to which all records must be kept and subsequent to which records shall be selected for preservation. There is a pioneer period in every state from which comparatively few records have been handed down. Government records are generally not only the most informative on such periods, but often the only records there are. The few records which do not seem to be of much importance take up proportionately little space and can therefore be preserved.

The date 1870 has been informally selected as the close of the pioneer period for Illinois. That is the beginning of a new constitutional period and is a convenient breaking off place for administrative records. This date is acknowledged by law to the extent that destruction of any county records created prior to 1870 is prohibited. It is a great convenience to be able to state definitely, without further appraisal, that records prior to 1870 are acceptable for the state archives. Creation of the impression that those records, at least, are sacrosanct sometimes acts as a very definite check upon an official determined to "get rid of that old junk in the storeroom." The transfer of older records to the archives clears sufficient space to permit a more thoughtful appraisal of what is left. We are very careful to impress the fact that while saying that every record prior to 1870 shall be considered a permanent record, we are not implying in any way that later records should not also be preserved.

For later records the archivist can say definitely that "all records derived from an organization that portray the basic facts of its establishment, form, policies, and operations are of historical value."[4] Beyond that point the decision as to the retention of records as historical source material should rest upon a consideration as to whether the sort of information to be found in the records exists in some other, perhaps more compact or accessible form.

It is true that biographers have unearthed much otherwise unfindable Lincolniana from records of a type we might consider destroying if they were modern records. The possibility of some Lincoln of the future hardly justifies our retention of every record that mentions every person. As Philip C. Brooks, using Washington as an illustration, puts it, "obviously few of the millions for whom we now have those records will achieve any unique importance, and for those who do there are so many more sources of information than those we have for George Washington that minor ones such as leave cards become insignificant."[5]

Much of the scientific and sociological information to be found in modern records is tabulated by the departments from every conceivable angle as a matter of routine. The historian of the future will therefore have less need for consulting the original bulky case records. Furthermore, government records are no longer the chief source of information. Likewise, most government records are now made in such a routine manner on standard forms that there is little chance for flavor of personalities which make old records so fascinating.

Occasionally an official in discussing his records will remark, "This is the important record from the administrator's point of view, but from the historical angle I think this is the one we should keep." Sometimes they suggest adding certain information on their forms, which though not required for administrative purposes could be easily obtained and which they think would interest historians. The archivist can only point out that consciously created history is dangerously close to propaganda. The historians of the future will be best served if the records are well organized and present a true representation of the administrative purposes they served.

Prior to 1943 the only way by which an Illinois official could legally dispose of useless records was to present a legislative bill to the General Assembly asking permission for the destruction of specific categories of records. This method involved spending considerable time on the part of the official to nurse the bill through the various legislative steps; and on the part of the General Assembly committees to which the bill was referred, time and effort were required to determine whether or not such destruction would be proper and justifiable. To date, only a few such bills have been enacted into law. Some bills presented in the past have been ill considered, seeking permission to destroy records which though no longer of administrative use are historically valuable; or asking permission to destroy records too soon after their creation. Most state departments have large accumulations of useless records for which it has not seemed worthwhile to go to the trouble of getting legislation which would permit destruction. . . .

Two acts permit state and county officials, respectively, to use photographic methods, particularly microphotography, in the making and keeping of records. Provided that these photographic reproductions meet the minimum standards of quality, they "shall be deemed to be an original record for all purposes, including introduction in evidence in all courts or administrative agencies. A transcript, exemplification or certified copy thereof shall, for all purposes recited herein, be deemed to be a transcript, exemplification, or certified copy of the original." [6]

One purpose of these laws is to permit officials to record documents by photography. For instance, the state treasurer uses microfilm copies of state warrants as a substitute for the former registration in ledger volumes. The second purpose is to permit the destruction of bulky original records after microfilm copies have been made. In the case of state records the State Records Commission supervises the destruction in the manner prescribed in the act creating that commission. [7]

No original county record created prior to 1870 may be destroyed. However, any county official who is unable to provide adequate housing for such original records may deposit the same in the Archives Department of the Illinois State Library, which shall provide photostatic or microfilm copies for county use.

County records dated subsequent to 1870 may be destroyed through the following procedure: The county officer or clerk of court "shall file with the county board of his county a statement signed by him listing the records, papers and documents he desires to cause to be so photographed, microphotographed or otherwise reproduced on film and stating that, subject to the prior approval of the county board, he proposes to cause the records, papers and documents so listed to be reproduced on film and subsequently destroyed. A copy of such statement shall be posted in a public place in the office of the county clerk and in the office of the officer or clerk of court signing such statement. The county board, at any regular or special meeting held not less than thirty days after the filing and posting of such statement, shall consider said proposal and any objections thereto, and may authorize the officer or clerk of court signing such statement to cause any of the records, papers and documents listed in the statement to be photographed, micro-photographed or otherwise reproduced on film and to cause such records, papers and documents when so reproduced on film to be destroyed." Records should be photographed in such order that integrity of files is preserved. The authenticity of the copy should also be certified on the film by the head of the department in which the record originates. . . . .[8]

13

The Archivist and Records Management

1 / THE ARCHIVIST AND RECORDS MANAGEMENT

PRIOR TO THE ADVENT OF RECORDS management the archivist was not conceded a role in the creation of records. Perhaps it was the publicity given to the occasional discovery of a rare Shakespeare, Button Gwinnet, or Lincoln document in what appeared to be otherwise worthless records that earned the archivist the reputation of being a mere pack rat. Actually it was the archivist who spearheaded the drive for the creation of commissions empowered to authorize the destruction of obsolete records and who worked out such disposal procedures as sampling and retention schedules.

This article will not continue the discussion of the future relationships between the archivists and record managers which was the subject of Morris Radoff's 1955 presidential address before the Society of American Archivists.[1] Neither is it to be construed as either a commentary or a critique upon the records management survey conducted in Illinois. Actually the paper grew out of preliminary attempts to crystallize the thinking of the Illinois officials who were responsible for letting the contract for that survey.[2]

　　THIS CHAPTER, "The Archivist and Records Management," was originally published as "The Archivist Looks at Records Management" in *Illinois Libraries* 38 (October 1956): 222–33.

First of all, the archivist considers that the training of records managers in management engineering qualifies them to tailor records to fit the need of the administrator. The archivist's training in research methods, his intimate knowledge of the history of his government, and his experience with the various ways in which records are used for purposes other than administration qualify him to take an active part in the creation of government records. These factors have given the archivist some definite ideas as to desirable qualities for records, both as to their factual content and their physical format.

The archivist's primary concern is naturally with that "hard core of permanent records" of which he will sooner or later become custodian. Unfortunately, records management came so suddenly and so fast that the archivist, himself a member of a relatively new profession, has not philosophized about the kind of permanent records which should be created. When Illinois officials came to plan their own records management survey, they wisely realized that nothing could be done about existing records except to determine which to keep and which to throw away. They decided to spend the appropriation for their records management survey on an attempt to set up records systems which would prevent future accumulations of worthless records hopelessly intermixed with records which should be retained indefinitely.

Before records management consultants became available, state officials had turned to filing systems analysts for advice on the creation of records. With a few notable exceptions, these analysts were employees of firms manufacturing filing supplies and equipment. These persons had no incentive for keeping down the bulk of records for they were interested in sales of their companies' products. Their one aim was to devise the simplest filing system, and to them that generally meant one file in which every document of the office, whether important or trivial, should be filed in one alphabet. Filing systems intended to be simple, broke down from sheer weight, and an astronomical quantity of unusable records piled up in basement cubby holes and in outside warehouses.

Fortunately, the necessity for breaking up the files in accordance with their use has somewhat simplified the problem of setting up the more recent records into retention periods.

Practically all government records need weeding to segregate important from ephemeral records. The one man in each agency competent to do this weeding is the executive, but he has neither the time nor the patience to do the work. If the department head can find no time to weed the records for his department surely the archivist cannot be expected to do the work for all departments.

Unfortunately, no mechanical shortcuts have been devised for weeding government records. The archivist cheerfully votes "aye" on motions to authorize a department to destroy records which are obviously worthless. At the same time he remembers sadly the frustration of the scholar who could find no source materials in that same department when he attempted to write the history of one of its important sociological experiments.

The archivist's dilemma is to decide whether to take the responsibility for destroying historically valuable records embedded in a mass of irrelevant materials or whether somehow to find space for that bulk because it contains valuable data. No one questions the moral right of the attorney to demand that all of such material be preserved for so long as any part of it may be needed for legal purposes under applicable statutes of limitation. Likewise the accountant is supported when he demands that financial records be held for audit. The archivist should likewise be supported in his demand that records in question be held until such time as they can be sorted or until experience can prove definitely that they really are worthless. It is not difficult to decide the value of records two hundred years old, but it is a grave responsibility to try to make a correct decision about records only five or ten years old. The archivist is reconciled to having to house badly planned files already in existence, but he hopes wistfully that records management can avoid such problems for the future.

The records manager acknowledges this responsibility, but he asks the archivist to specify the type of records which should be considered as being of permanent value. The following paragraphs are tentative—thrown out for further discussion by archivists, other government officials, and records managers.

Perhaps it may be well to mention some negative premises with respect to the creation of permanent records. First of all, it can be assumed that modern governmental records will no longer be the chief source materials for the historian as is true of the records of the pioneer period. Then paper was scarce and expensive, comparatively few persons were literate, and facts did not get set down on paper unless it was important that they be preserved. Clerical work has undergone as much of an industrial revolution in the past seventy-five years as manufacturing. Today paper work, which we continue to call "records," is just as much a part of office machinery as are the typewriters and tabulating machines on which this paper work is produced. Paper work is one of the devices through which the administrator directs his staff. Very few of the records being created today have any permanent significance.

Every archivist can cite examples of hindsight in the selection of records to be destroyed. He remembers records which were destroyed that should have been retained; and he points out other records which, fortuitously preserved, have taken on significance for research or governmental use never dreamed of by their creators. However, it is possible to take a calculated risk and to decide that there is little likelihood that certain types of records will become important at some future date. It is possible that some presently obscure person may become another Lincoln, every scrap of writing about whom will become precious. Against such a possibility the sheer bulk of present-day records precludes the likelihood that sufficient material of biographical value will be located to justify the cost of storage.

The archivist is a pragmatist. Like the administrator, he considers that records are created for one purpose and for one purpose only, namely, to fulfill an administrative need; and if the records fulfill that need, the archivist considers them adequate. Government records document legal needs of the department itself or of the people or firms with which it deals; or they document policy or other decisions which affect those relationships. Some governmental agencies, notably certain county offices, function largely as places where documents of importance to citizens and associations can be registered as legal proof of the existence of certain rights and privileges. Records are created to facilitate business. If, as often happens in the case of government records, the documents tend to take on value for purposes of historical or other research, that is so much "velvet."

Another premise concerning government records is that the closer the government is to the people, the more likely it is that the records kept by that agency will tend to take on value as historical documents. Thus we find that county records, alas the poorest cared for, are the most important historically. State records fall in between county records and federal records in value. Quite often one state conducts a sociological experiment on a small scale which is later copied by other states and by the federal government. Documentation of that experiment is, of course, important. It is not safe to carry this point too far, for surely nothing comes so close to everyone as the Internal Revenue Service and the records of that department are not being preserved, probably more because of bulk than for any other reason.

Thus by indirection we arrive at a consideration of the positive side of documentation: what types of government records should be preserved permanently? First of all, it is obvious that records which document the legal right of the government or of its constituents must be preserved as long as those rights are enforceable through the courts. Some of such records, for example contracts for construction work, may have a further value for historical purposes. For instance, the contracts for the building and later remodeling of the old Illinois State House at Vandalia were very useful to the state architect when he restored that building a hundred years later. He only wished that similar data could have been found about the furniture purchased for the building. The archivist's training and experience is helpful in considering the retention values of such records. Certain other types of records have no legal terminal date and must be preserved indefinitely. Among such records, to mention only a few, are the legislative and constitutional convention records used so often to establish the "intent of the law," vital statistics, naturalization records, census records, land records, and court decrees.

A second need for documentation is for the history of the functioning of a department. Officials frequently submit as justification for the destruction of certain records the statement that "they have all been tabulated and written up in our reports." The obvious answer is "but your reports do not tell the whole story." So long as human nature is what it is and so long as muckrakers exist, officials will report their triumphs but gloss over or ignore their failures and weaknesses. No one disputes the fact that all records which would have significance for an official investigation of a department must be retained as long as there is any likelihood of an investigation arising or of the case being reopened. Many administrators feel an obligation to retain such records indefinitely.

Beyond the possibility of an investigating body demanding access to records which prove or disprove wrongdoing, each governmental agency should make and preserve as permanent archives such records as will enable a researcher to get a clear picture of the operation of the agency from the date of its creation to its termination or incorporation into a successor department. The policies of the agency in all stages of its life should be clearly shown by the records. These records should reveal whether or not the policies were successful, and if not, wherein they failed and what was done about it. They should clearly show what the organization of the agency was like during all periods and they should list the names of all key personnel. It is difficult to be dogmatic about the specific forms which such policy records should take because agencies differ so greatly in organization, powers, and duties.

It is generally agreed that minutes of governing bodies and of commissions, that proceedings and decrees of courts should be deemed permanent records. Other records which should generally be considered to have continuing value are directives from superior officers to their subordinates; rules and regulations of the department with subsequent amendments; regulations of other governing bodies (usually federal) which affect the operation of the agency in question; the attorney general's opinions on departmental problems; significant reports made to or by the department; and such correspondence or other documents as establish the policies of the agency (that is, those which lay down policies, not those which merely reiterate them). Office manuals, in both original and revised form, if sufficiently detailed, could often substitute for bulky records which otherwise must be preserved to show the history of the organization.

One of the duties of most governmental agencies is to investigate and prosecute violations of laws. There seems to be no consensus as to the value of hearings and other enforcement procedures. Archivists tend to believe that the factual contents of such records, though bulky, must be preserved if one is to get a complete picture of the way a department functions. Here they run into the bane of their existence, "security records." Departments claim that a large proportion of their investigations are "nuisance cases"—malicious compliants without adequate basis for prosecution. They maintain that public access to such records is improper since the records include documents which might be damaging to the reputation of individuals. They are unwilling to entrust these documents to the archivist even for controlled handling as restricted records under seal. It would seem reasonable to demand as a minimum that a permanent record should be made which would show for each investigation, perhaps statistically, preferably by descriptive summaries, the nature of the complaint, the names of the parties involved, the decision reached by the investigators, and the results of appeals or other legal action, if any.

The most valuable record ever kept, from the archivist's point of view, is the old type register which summarizes in tabular form on one sheet the essential information to be found on as high as perhaps eighty to one hundred original forms from which it was compiled. Such registers are particularly valuable in the case of licenses of one kind or another. Where such registers exist, the bulky originals can usually be destroyed after a suitable retention period with a clear conscience. Unfortunately, registers are out of style;

they are regarded as being an unnecessary duplication of work, subject to errors in transcription, and "too voluminous." Various substitutes have replaced registers—tabulating cards, summary index cards, and microfilm copies, each of which has objectionable features. One case has come to our attention in which a department, to avoid making a ledger entry in a register, has substituted IBM cards, only the first line of which has permanent significance; these tabulating cards are in turn copied onto microfilm. There may be sufficient saving in bulk to justify this, but two costly procedures have been substituted for one simple process; furthermore, there is the question as to whether information as vital as this happens to be can safely be entrusted to the physical shortcomings of microfilm. It is not intended here to advocate the return of the old registration system in its original form but rather to alert records managers and others to search for a practical substitute.

Some questions which need consideration in connection with the data contents of records are as follows: do the records now being created contain all the information needed for the efficient operation of the agency? Do the records contain superfluous or obsolete data? Who uses each series of records and for what purposes? Is use of these records confined to the unit in which they originate, and if not, who consults them and for what purposes? Does any other unit in this agency or in some other agency compile the same or similar data and to what extent is the duplication necessary? Which of such files is the most important legally? How long will each type of record information collected be of value for administrative purposes? Is the information obtainable from these records summarized elsewhere and if so, in what detail? For the solution of problems involving these and similar questions the archivist defers to the records manager.

The greatest improvement possible in record making comes in the field of the physical form of records. Here, again, the archivist looks to the records manager to keep the bulk of records to manageable proportions through segregation of records having various retention values by planned disposal schedules, by forms control, and by recommendations as to the applications of microphotography and other mechanization. The archivist expects these recommendations by the records managers to result in increased efficiency in the administration of the department in which the records originate, adequate documentation, and considerable reduction in bulk of those records which will come to the archives.

The archivist's interest in the physical quality of records is based upon the problems which face him after the permanent records come into his custody. Will they create problems in storage; will they require restoration in connection with their preservation; will they be in a form which will make it easy for him to locate data in the records? The interests of records managers and archivist are almost identical when it comes to desirable physical qualities of records. Both have contributions to make. The records managers are more proficient in such matters as forms control and filing systems; the archivist generally has had more experience with papers, inks, and rehabilitation of worn or otherwise damaged documents, and he may also have had more experience in qualities that affect the legal use of records in his own government.

The archivist is interested in sizes and shapes of records. He hopes the records will fit into standard containers if they are unbound or on standard shelving if bound. Some of the questions which both the archivist and the records manager consider are as follows: how effective is the size of the paper used? Is legal size paper used where correspondence size would be adequate? Could the number of pages be reduced by changing from correspondence to legal size? How effective are the form layouts? Are some blank spaces too large, others too small; is the spacing incorrect for typewriting; can attached pieces (resulting from improper spacing) be avoided? Is it possible to design forms so that all papers to be filed in the same folder shall be the same size? (Unevenly loaded folders are dust catchers; small pieces slip out of place, and it is hard to keep the file looking neat.)

One example of a failure to use forms that fit into standard sizes of equipment comes to mind. A certain department requires voluminous annual reports from a large number of corporations. Present practice is to bind these reports into annual volumes. To obtain comparative data for the same company over a ten-year period requires handling ten folio volumes. Based on the way these records are used, the most efficient system would be to combine all reports on a given company in one alphabetical file. The department in question is quite aware of this, but it is forced to use this inconvenient form because it is the standard report form adopted by other states having jurisdiction over the same type of corporation. It would impose an additional burden on the various companies to have to bother with a nonstandard form for one state.

Comparatively few modern records are kept in bound form, and, for the most part, the archivist is quite agreeable to this procedure. He wants to know what inherent records qualities call for binding rather than for filing in unbound form. If binding is decided upon, the archivist has much bitter experience upon which to base his recommendations. First of all, he wants the binding to be durable. He prefers buckram or canvas to leather because the latter deteriorates rapidly unless given frequent lubrication. The weakest spot in most volumes of ledger size and larger is the back spine which breaks off easily. He wants the sewing to be strong (hand-sewing through signatures rather than the machine oversewing to which most binders are addicted). He wants a careful balance of paper weight and quality so that leaves will not pull out or scuff on the edges. Particularly, he wants the pages to open flat to facilitate photocopying and exhibiting. He wants all four margins wide so that when rebinding becomes necessary the binder will not trim off some of the writing. The height and width of the volumes should, so far as practicable, be of standard ledger size so that they will fit the standard size roller or sliding shelves used where the books are consulted frequently. Ledger size is the largest size practical for housing volumes upright on library shelves. Plat books and engineering drawings, of course, require larger volumes but all outsize books kept by a department should be of uniform size for economy in shelving.

Volumes should be thick enough to stand upright on the shelves without warping, but they should also be kept thin enough so that a woman can handle them. Two to four inches in thickness is about right. Most departments now making records in bound volumes use some form of locked binder. Prebound volumes require handwritten entries whereas the binder permits typewriting or photocopy recording. If locked binders are used, the purchasing agent should be reminded that postbinders with protruding knobs may be priced less than the flush binding type, but the former are wasteful of storage space since they cannot be stacked.

More consideration should be given to the thickness of the volume in relation to the estimated number of entries. Archives are full of 350-page volumes of which 300 pages are blank. So far as possible volumes should begin and end with a fiscal period or some other logical break. It would seem axiomatic that each volume should have a firmly affixed or a stamped label indicating the title of the series, the volume number, and the inclusive dates. Archivists know (to their sorrow) that such labels are rare. Durable thumb index guides which permit the searcher to consult the volumes without turning many pages are also highly desirable.

The archivist judges the efficiency of a filing system by the ease of locating data after the series come to the archives. He dislikes complicated filing systems which require classifications keys. If an index to a series is necessary he asks whether a filing system could be devised which would eliminate that index. If the archivist criticizes the filing analyst for ignoring the problem of bulk, the latter has generally installed a filing system which works. Usually an efficient filing and indexing system which suits the requirements of the department creating the records will also meet the needs of the archivist. That is not always true, however, especially when the records are used in the archives for purposes other than administrative. The tract index which satisfies a land-office clerk, for instance, will have to be supplemented by a name index for the benefit of genealogists using the records in the archives. Sometimes the archivist finds that supposedly noncurrent records become very active after a more scientific filing system has been adopted. Fortunately, it is generally only the oldest records which have to be completely refiled.

Records transferred to the archives should come adequately

filed in good folders of uniform size; the documents should be accompanied by indexes with adequate guide cards and sufficient cross references, and the drawers should be correctly labeled. The archivist is unable to appreciate the economy mindedness of the file clerk who removes all folders and guide cards before sending the records to the archives with the thought of reusing those filing materials in his own office. Records managers could be helpful in pointing out proper etiquette on this score!

Most people assume that flat filing of documents is universal. Actually, however, a surprising number of government agencies, particularly county officials and court clerks, are still using the old fashioned "document files" which require documents to be folded. Folding makes papers brittle and in time they break on the folds. Folding the documents for filing in document files and unfolding for flat filing in the archives requires two processes. General Assembly clerks find folding a convenient device for keeping together the various sheets of paper which accumulate while bills are going through the legislative steps. Unfortunately, the use of "document files" is most often due to improper dimensions of vaults, particularly as to height, which makes this type of equipment the only economical way to use available space. So far as possible, however, documents should be flat filed.

The subject of papers and inks is one which has received insufficient study by those responsible for the creation of records. Everyone who has had experience with records knows that paper made before the nineteenth century is found in good condition except when exposed to improper storage conditions which have resulted in mildew. Papers made later than 1850 deteriorate rapidly, some becoming brittle in a matter of months. Most administrators dismiss this situation with the statement "you cannot get fine handmade paper today." Actually paper is being manufactured now that is as fine in quality as the handmade papers. The durability of paper depends upon the purity of the cellulose fiber from which it is made, and nothing has been found which is superior to cuttings of clean new linen and cotton cloth. It is the acid impurities on the wood fiber found in modern sulphite paper which causes loss of strength. All rag paper is expensive, but if paper qualities were matched to the length of time documents are to be kept, this economy would permit the use of all rag paper for permanent records. Paper manufacturers have recommended qualities of papers to be retained for a specified number of years. They recommend 100 percent best quality rag paper for a permanent record or for one to be kept at least thirty-five to fifty years; 50 percent rag for a record to be retained twenty-five to thirty years; highest quality all sulphite or 25 percent rag stock for records to be retained fifteen to twenty-five years. Records destined for shorter retentions can be made on progressively cheaper papers with ground wood pulp paper used for scratch pads, work sheets and minor intraoffice memoranda. Now that retention periods are being predetermined for records being created, it is possible to set standards for proper grades of paper.

There are other elements besides the chemical constituents of paper which need further study and standardization of specifications. Among these are such matters as weight, finish, color, and so on. Too often it is found that the letterhead mailed out is on very fine bond paper, whereas the carbon copy retained by the governmental agency is written upon very cheap, flimsy paper; the copy is often faint, made with wornout carbon. So long as all correspondence, trivial and important, was kept in one file, it was probably too much to ask that different grades of copy paper be used for the more important materials. Some Illinois departments, however, have long ruled that all carbon copies shall be made on 25 percent rag paper.

The study of proper quality paper should include cards and file folders. Many departments which keep important record data on index or summary cards are using poor quality of card stock which soon turns brittle, causing edges to become soft and scuffed. Rag stock cardboard can be obtained, and specifications should call for die-cut edges and punched holes. Weights should be coordinated with sizes and frequency of use. Furthermore, the weights of all cards in the same file should be uniform. The greater cost of good stock cards must be judged against the probable cost of reproducing worn cards. The retention period for the card file is of even greater importance than in ordinary paper work because of that cost.

Officials often assume that they are specifying correctly when they requisition "the best quality of manila folders." The word "manila" refers to color, not to quality of paper stock. Ordinary commercial folders contain a high percentage of ground wood pulp and have a high rate of deterioration. The life of the average wood-pulp folder used for records, a relatively   frequent use—such as those which reach the archives—is only from three to five years. Furthermore, acids from these folders migrate to the papers within the folder. The several sheets at the front and back of an ordinary folder show embrittlement and discoloration within a short period. Kraft cardboard folders, rated as having a low pH (acidity) content, equipped with reinforced tabs, and guaranteed for fifty years, are in regular commercial production at a reasonable price. Such folders should be recommended for all permanent files.

There are, of course, other features to consider in purchasing folders. These include such items as the number of cuts for the tabs, position of tabs, quality of tabs, how tabs are to be labeled (written in ink or typed directly on the tab, pasted labels, pre-printed labels and typed inserts), scorings for folds and built-in fasteners (preferably but seldom so found, rustproof). Proper and sufficient guide cards are also important. Proper use of folders, particularly uniformity in the placement of tabs in a significant position, not only make for neat-appearing files but also aid in locating materials within the files. Though advice on such topics fall more within the specialty of filing analysts than records managers, they are important and should be stressed.

The typewriter has superseded handwriting in the making of documents so that officials today have less need to be conscious of inks than their predecessors. However, inks are still used, particularly for signatures necessary to validate documents. Handwritten interpolations are also frequent. These signatures and other writings on documents are usually affixed by whatever pen happens to be handy. The current fad for indigo blue, green, and purple inks for signatures is inexcusable since these inks are fugitive in color and many do not reproduce well when photocopied for certified copies. Ball-point pens should never be used on records, not only because the inks are impermanent but also because the signatures can be lifted and used in forgeries. Contrary to common belief, fountain-pen inks can be used for record purposes provided the ink bottle is labeled "permanent" or "record" ink. Blue-black inks so labeled are not in the same category with the colored analine dye inks spoken of above. In this case, the iron gallo-tannic base of the blue black inks is pale in color as written but turns dark gradually as it oxidizes. A fugitive blue dye is added to bridge the period between the pale and the dark stages of the writing. The carbon black inks commonly used in engineering and other drawings are permanent but they are water soluble and must be protected from moisture. Sometimes fixatives are sprayed on them. Care should be taken in the use of colored inks on drawings for the reasons mentioned above in connection with signatures. Because these facts are not generally appreciated, the archivist hopes that records managers will call them to the attention of their clients.

Good quality typewriter ribbons are essential to ensure legible copy. A few of the earliest typewritten documents in the Illinois archives (1877–85) give evidence of fading. Some later ones which at first glance might appear to have faded have instead lost ink in the process of making letterpress copies. Fading does not seem to be a fault of modern typewriter ribbons. The importance of the ribbon comes from the need for clear legible ribbon copies. Good quality carbon paper is important. While the ribbon copy is deemed the original document, a carbon copy is often the record copy so far as the office of issuance is concerned. Smudged, faint copies can be dangerous.

Various copying and duplicating processes are on the market and are applied extensively to paper work. The archivist looks to records managers to apprise their clients of developments in the field. Robert Beeman's "Tools of the Office: Duplicating Equipment," in an objective manner explains the principles back of each type of copying and duplication process, gives comparative data on speed, costs, number of copies for which best suited, and on distinctive features; he lists all machines with the characteristics and limitations of each.[3] With such a guide the applications to specific records problems are simplified for the executive. From an archival point of view certain warnings are necessary. The duplicating processes listed by Mr. Beeman as azograph and chemograph, gelatin, offset, relief, spirit, and stencil, are intended to apply where quantity production (10,000 to 25,000 copies) is wanted, and do not appear to relate to the creation of records. Actually they do. Forms are increasingly being produced, particularly by offset, and some of these forms are intended for permanent records. Many reports, particularly those intended for limited circulation, are produced on these types of machines. At least one copy of each of such reports, particularly those which are monographs on technical investigations, must be deemed of archival value. Practically all these publications, commonly referred to as "processed documents," are made on an inferior type of paper. The archivist may find it possible to laminate the archival copy of these reports, but he is concerned over the quality of paper used for such forms as have an indefinite retention value. Apparently no research has been done on that phase of record-making.

Mr. Beeman lists as copying processes diazo, facsimile, photocopy, smokeprinting, Thermo-Fax, Verifax, and xerography. The common characteristic of copying processes is that copy is reproduced photographically by direct method on emulsion coated paper without the intervention of a film negative; the copy is the same size as the original, or in some models at relatively small ratios of reduction or enlargement. Only one copy can be made in a single operation. The oldest and most commonly applied type of copying process is photocopy, generally though inaccurately called photostat. (Photostat is the trademark name for the equipment of only one manufacturer.) The principal applications of these copying processes to records making is for producing copies (certified or not) for patrons and for recording legal instruments. Salesmen always claim that their equipment makes "permanent copies" though sad experience has made the archivists skeptical. In New York

State where recording by photocopy was first adopted, the state records examiners report that after a few years there is apt to be found a dangerous darkening of images due to the oxidation of residual chemicals. Recording by photocopying is desirable since not only is much time saved in transcription but the product is an indubitable facsimile of the original. These advantages are considered to offset the cost of recopying when legibility begins to show impairment, but they do impose upon the official keeping the records the duty of watching for the need for recopying and of seeing to it that the work is actually done. Manufacturers of photographic supplies can and do on request supply permanent rag papers, but they are not responsible for careless processing. Insufficient washing of prints is usually the cause of deterioration. The "automatic processing" types of equipment seem to have been the worst offenders in the past. Records managers should point out these dangers also in making recommendations. File clerks should be alerted to the danger of interfiling photocopies in direct contract with other papers since there is always likelihood of migration of acids from the photocopies, just as in the case of cheap folders cited above.

Microphotography was thought fifteen years ago to offer the solution to all storage problems for records. Unfortunately, this idea was exploited by the various microfilm companies before the numerous limitations to such application became evident. Experience has proved that the process is far more expensive than represented. Although the cost of the admittedly inexpensive film is a minor item, the true cost of the filming is the overhead involved in preliminary checking of the filing, removal of rubber bands and clips, unfolding and repairing of broken papers, preparing of proper certifications and target guides, checking of completed films for retakes to be substituted for omissions and poor reproductions, plus the indexing of reels. Cost studies indicate that these overall costs of microfilming largely offset supposed savings in storage cost, particularly where the necessary retention period is short. Often a proper weeding of the files would permit storage of original records in manageable bulk. Other disadvantages of microfilm are also apparent. It is inconvenient to use, requiring reading devices. It is difficult to use microfilm effectively, if at all, where comparison of documents within the file is necessary. Despite claims as to the durability of microfilm, it tends in practice to become brittle and to break, sometimes thus destroying a vital section of a record. Improperly processed film tends to darken just as in the case of photocopy work. Too great humidity in the storage place may result in mildew. The emulsion which bears the photographic images is easily scratched, either accidentally or with malice aforethought. In case of a fire, microfilm will melt at temperatures that will merely char the edges of paper. Expensive apparatus calling for skilled operators is necessary for making enlargements of the film.

Records management surveys have often resulted in discontinuance of microfilming projects. This has understandably disturbed the microfilm companies, and some of them have been accused of attempting to undermine confidence in records managers. This, if true, is regrettable for microphotography has many legitimate applications to record work. Among these are its uses to supply copies of records and printed material for inter-institution loans, for making security copies so that vital records could be reconstituted in case of destruction of the originals through fire or other catastrophe, for transmission of copies to branch offices, for providing desk copies of active records too voluminous to be kept in easily accessible locations, and for recording of less important documents directly on film (such as the state treasurer's register of warrants issued). It is also used as a cheap publication medium, an example being the microfilm copies of federal census records sold by the National Archives. These and other applications of microphotography have a definite place in the records field.

Records managers are in a better position than archivists to advise with departments concerning microfilm applications to their problems. Under Illinois law any state official may microfilm any records of his office, but he may not destroy the originals without authorization from the State Records Commission. Most officials now confer with the commission before embarking upon an extensive microfilm project to ascertain the commission's probable reaction to destruction of the original records. In several instances the commission has indicated that it would be willing to authorize destruction without microfilming; occasionally it recommends a longer retention schedule than that suggested by the department.

Punch-card devices, electronics, and other mechanical devices promise to revolutionize office procedures just as the typewriter and various types of duplicating devices did in the recent past. The archivist frankly knows little and understands less about these mechanisms. He looks to the records manager to know when and how to apply them. He has seen cases where mechanization was uneconomical because the machines were too costly in relation to the quantity of work needed. He is conscious of the concern of both employer and employee of the sociological results from dislocation of labor. As an archivist, he is chiefly concerned over record problems created by such devices, including the fact that some materials now used are unsuitable for permanent records.

Always, the archivist is concerned over the emphasis upon elimination of records-keeping. He sympathizes fully with the objective of reducing the bulk of records because his own problem is finding space in which to house the records he receives. He deplores current indifference toward the positive side of creating records of permanent value, not because he fears becoming a displaced person, but because he subscribes to the saying that "the people that have no records have no history."

APPENDIX

NOTES

INDEX

Chronological List of Articles

"The Archives Department as an Administrative Unit in Government," National Association of State Libraries, *Papers and Proceedings, Thirty-Third Annual Convention, Los Angeles, California, June 23–27, 1930* (reprinted from *Bulletin of the American Library Association,* September 1930), pp. 44–48. See also *Bulletin of the American Library Association* 24 (September 1930): 563–67.

"Scope and Functions of a State Archives Department," National Association of State Libraries, *Papers and Proceedings, 1936–1937, Fortieth Annual Convention, New York City, June 21–25, 1937* (Springfield: n.p., 1936 [1937]), pp. 15–20. See also Society of American Archivists, *Proceedings,* Providence, R.I., December 29–30, 1936, and Washington, D.C., June 18–19, 1937 (Urbana, Ill.: n.p., n.d.), pp. 75–82; and Jerome K. Wilcox and A. F. Kuhlman, eds., *Public Documents with Archives and Libraries: Papers Presented at the 1937 Conference of the American Library Association* (Chicago: American Library Association, 1938), pp. 262–75.

"The Place of Microphotography in the Collection and Preservation of Local Archives and Historical Manuscripts," Jerome K. Wilcox and A. F. Kuhlman, eds., *Public Documents with Archives and Libraries: Papers Presented at the 1938 Conference of the American Library Association* (Chicago: American Library Association, 1938), pp. 327–34.

"Repair of Manuscripts," *Illinois Libraries* 21 (February 1939): 5–6.

"Archives and Libraries," *Illinois Libraries* 21 (March, 1939), 11–13.

"Archives and Libraries: Classification and Cataloging," *Illinois Libraries* 21 (April 1939): 2–4.

"Archives and Libraries: Inventories, Calendars, Indexes, etc.," *Illinois Libraries* 21 (May 1939): 9–11.

"Archives and Libraries: Public Documents," *Illinois Libraries* 21 (June 1939): 12–14.

"Archives and Libraries: Reference Work," *Illinois Libraries* 21 (August 1939): 26–28.

"Classification in the Archives of Illinois," A. F. Kuhlman, ed., *Archives and Libraries: Papers Presented at the 1940 Conference of the American Library Association Representing the Joint Program of the Committee on Archives and Libraries of the A.L.A., the Conference on Historical Societies, the Midwest Members of the Society of American Archivists, the Historical Records Survey, and the Committee on Bibliography of the A.L.A.* (Chicago: American Library Association, 1940), pp. 78–92.

"What the State Archives Can Do for the Business Man," *Chicago Filing Association Official Bulletin* 9 (November 1940): 17–21.

"Archives and War," *Illinois Libraries* 23 (February 1941): 17–19.

"Establishing Priorities for State Records: Illinois Experience," *American Archivist* 5 (January 1942): 18–27.

"County Records and the War," *Illinois Libraries* 24 (March 1942): 41–43. See also *American Archivist* 5 (October 1942): 274–77.

"Archives and Historical Manuscripts," *Illinois Libraries* 25 (December 1943): 399–402.

"Disposal of Records," *Illinois Libraries* 26 (March 1944): 120–24.

"Reduction of Records," *Illinois Libraries* 26 (April 1944): 152–57.

"Microphotography and County Records," *Illinois Libraries* 26 (December 1944): 505–9.

"Some Legal Aspects of Archives," *American Archivist* 8 (January 1945): 1–11.

"Record Making," *Illinois Libraries* 27 (February 1945): 127–33.

"Control of Administrative Records," *Illinois Libraries* 27 (March 1945): 182–89.

"Record Materials: Paper," *Illinois Libraries* 27 (May 1945): 270–74.

"Record Materials: Ink," *Illinois Libraries* 27 (October 1945): 438–44.

"Photography for State Records [pts. 1 and 2]," *Illinois Libraries* 28 (February and March 1946): 151–55, 180–87.

"Name Indexes," *Illinois Libraries* 28 (April 1946): 217–25.

"Organizing a New State Archives Department," *Illinois Libraries* 28 (December 1946): 496–503.

"What Does an Archivist Do?" *Illinois Libraries* 29 (May 1947): 211–20.

"Handling Fragile Manuscripts [pts. 1 and 2]," *Illinois Libraries* 29 (November and December 1947): 410–13, 460–64.

"The Place of Archives in Government," *Illinois Libraries* 34 (April 1952): 153–60.

"The Archivist Looks at Records Management," *Illinois Libraries* 38 (October 1956): 222–33.

INTRODUCTION

1. *Laws of the State of Illinois Enacted by the Seventieth General Assembly at the Regular Biennial Session, Begun and Held at the Capitol, in the City of Springfield, on the Ninth Day of January A.D., 1957, and Adjourned on the Twenty-ninth Day of June, A.D., 1957,* p. 1293. Hereinafter cited as *Laws of Illinois,* with appropriate date.

1 / THE SCOPE AND FUNCTION OF ARCHIVES

1. This paper was also published in *Bulletin of the American Library Association* 24 (September 1930): 563–67.

2. This paper was earlier presented to the Society of American Archivists and appears in its *Proceedings,* Providence, R.I., December 29–30, 1936, and Washington, D.C., June 18–19, 1937 (Urbana, Ill.: n.p., n.d.), pp. 75–82. This paper was also published in Jerome K. Wilcox and A. F. Kuhlman, eds., *Public Documents with Archives and Libraries: Papers Presented at the 1937 Conference of the American Library Association* (Chicago: American Library Association, 1937), pp. 262–75.

3. "Archives Division—Illinois State Library: Report for the Biennium Ending September 30, 1936," *Biennial Report of the Secretary of State of the State of Illinois, Edward J. Hughes, Secretary of State: Fiscal Years Beginning October 1, 1934, and Ending September 30, 1936* (Springfield: n.p., 1936), p. 26.

2 / The Purpose and Nature of Archives

1. John Henry Wigmore, A Treatise on the Anglo-American System of Evidence in Trials of Common Law Including the Statutes and Judicial Decisions of all Jurisdictions of the United States and Canada, 3d ed., 10 vols. (Boston: Little, Brown and Company, 1940; updating supplements), 7: 562–665. Hereinafter cited as Wigmore, Evidence.

2. Ibid., p. 626.

3. Hilary Jenkinson, A Manual of Archive Administration, rev. ed. (London: Percy Lund, Humphries & Co., Ltd., 1937), pp. 10–11. Hereinafter cited as Jenkinson, Manual.

4. Ibid., p. 11.

5. This article was Miss Norton's presidential address to the Society of American Archivists, delivered at Harrisburg, Pennsylvania, November 8, 1944. The principal part of the address is preceded by four pages of comments on the archival profession which are not here reproduced.

6. Wigmore, Evidence, 7: 626.

7. Wigmore, Evidence, 7: 627.

3 / The Organization and Operation of an Archives

1. "The Proposed Uniform State Public Records Act," American Archivist 3 (April 1940): 107–15.

2. "Model Bill for a State Archives Department," American Archivist 10 (January 1947): 47–49.

3. Albert Ray Newsome, "Uniform State Archival Legislation," American Archivist 2 (January 1939): 1–16.

4. Manual of the Survey of Historical Records, January 1936. See also supp. 6, "The Preparation of Guides to Manuscripts," September 1937; and supp. 8, "Instruction for the Preparation of Individual Manuscripts Form, WPA Form 19HR," 1937. These were combined into and replaced by Preparation of Inventories of Manuscripts: A Circular of Instructions for the Use of the Historical Records Survey Projects (Washington, D.C.: Federal Works Agency, Work Projects Administration, 1940).

5. Theodore R. Schellenberg (1903–70) joined the staff of the National Archives in 1935, becoming chief of the Division of Agriculture

Department Archives in 1938. He became records officer of the Office of Price Administration in 1945, returning to the National Archives as program adviser in 1948. Three years later, he became assistant archivist of the United States for the National Archives, a position he held for eleven years. At the beginning of 1962, he became assistant archivist in charge of a new Office of Records Appraisal, a position he held until he retired at the end of 1962. He was well known as the author of *Modern Archives* (Chicago: University of Chicago Press, 1956) and *The Management of Archives* (New York and London: Columbia University Press, 1965). See *American Archivist* 33 (April 1970): 190–202.

6. "Minutes of Meeting of Open Conference on Administration," The National Archives, April 23, 1945. Reprinted in *Illinois Libraries* 29 (April 1947): 170.

7. National Archives Act, 48 Stat. 1122.

4 / SERVICES AND RESOURCES OF AN ARCHIVES

1. *Illinois Revised Statutes*, chap. 38, sec..401 (1941).

2. *Laws of Illinois*, 1951, p. 1619. The definition of "records" was further clarified in the State Records Act of 1957, *Laws of Illinois*, 1957, pp. 1687–93.

3. Commission to Study State Government (Walter V. Schaefer, chairman), *Organization and Functioning of the State Government: Report to the General Assembly—December, 1950* (Springfield: State of Illinois, 1950), p. 114.

4. *Laws of Illinois*, 1951, pp. 1618–19.

5 / THE COMPARISON OF ARCHIVAL AND LIBRARY TECHNIQUES

1. Roscoe R. Hill (1880–1960) served in the Library of Congress, 1926–35, and then in the National Archives, 1935–46. In the National Archives he served first as chief of the Division of Classification (1935–41) and then as chief, Division of State Department Archives, until his retirement in 1946. See *American Archivist* 24 (January 1961): 83–84.

2. Illinois State Library, *Catalog Rules: Series for Archives Material* (Springfield, Ill.: Secretary of State and State Librarian, 1938).

6 / Classification and Description of Archives

1. S. Muller, J. A. Feith, and R. Fruin, *Manual for the Arrangement and Description of Archives*, translated by Arthur H. Leavitt from the French 1910 edition (H. W. Wilson Co., 1940), pp. 52–59.

2. David W. Parker, "Some Problems in the Classification of Departmental Archives," *Annual Report of the American Historical Association for the Year 1922* (Washington, D.C.: Government Printing Office, 1926), 1: 164–72.

3. Luther H. Evans and Edythe Weiner, "The Analysis of County Records," *American Archivist* 1 (October 1938): 186–200.

4. Paul Lewinson, "Problems of Archives Classification," *American Archivist* 2 (July 1939): 179–90.

5. *Lineage Book, National Society of the Daughters of the American Revolution*, 166 vols. (Washington, D.C.: Daughters of the American Revolution, 1908–39).

6. *The New England Historical and Genealogical Register*, published quarterly by the New England Historical Genealogical Society, began publication with vol. 1 in 1847 and has published continuously since that date. Vol. 128 was published in 1974.

7. *Guide to Similar Surnames: For Use in The Adjutant General's Office, War Department* (Washington, D.C.: Government Printing Office, 1920).

8. General Table 111, "Nomenclature, Dealing with Names Represented by at Least 100 White Persons, By States and Territories, at the First Census: 1790," Department of Commerce and Labor, Bureau of the Census, *A Century of Population Growth from the First Census of the United States to the Twelfth*, 1790–1900 (Washington, D.C.: Government Printing Office, 1909), pp. 227–70.

9. Charles A. Cutter's *Rules for a Printed Dictionary Catalog* (Washington, D.C.: Government Printing Office) appeared initially in 1876. These rules provide for arranging the library catalog by the first words on the card in a single alphabetical file. The dictionary catalog intermingles entries for authors, subjects, and titles. In addition, Cutter developed alphabetic order tables so that the second line on the catalog entry number would represent the name of the author. Thelma Eaton, *Cataloging and Classification: An Introductory Manual*, 3d ed. (Urbana, Ill.: n.p., 1963), pp. 3–6.

7 / Making and Control of Administrative Records

1. *Laws of Illinois,* 1943, pp. 385–86.
2. Henry Campbell Black, *Black's Law Dictionary,* 3d ed. (St. Paul, Minn.: West Publishing Co., 1933), p. 1516.
3. U.S. Department of Agriculture, Office of Plant and Operations, *Disposition of Official Records* (O.P.O. Pub. No. 1 [Rev.]), September 1944, p. 2.
4. Ladson Butler and O. R. Johnson, *Management Control through Business Forms* (New York and London: Harper Brothers, 1930). Hereinafter cited as Butler and Johnson, *Business Forms.*
5. Willard F. McCormick, "The Control of Records," *American Archivist* 6 (July 1943): 164–69. Hereinafter cited as McCormick, "The Control of Records."
6. Butler and Johnson, *Business Forms,* pp. 69–70.
7. Ibid., pp. 70–71.
8. McCormick, "The Control of Records," p. 166.
9. Butler and Johnson, *Business Forms,* p. 51.
10. McCormick, "The Control of Records," p. 165.
11. Ibid., pp. 165–66.
12. Butler and Johnson, *Business Forms,* pp. 196–97.
13. McCormick, "The Control of Records," p. 166.
14. Butler and Johnson, *Business Forms,* pp. 197–98.
15. *Paper and Printing Digest for the Allied Industries* 5 (April 1939): 11.

8 / Physical Properties of Archives

1. Julius Grant, *Books & Documents: Dating, Permanence and Preservation* (London: Grafton and Co., 1937). Hereinafter cited as Grant, *Books & Documents.*
2. William Bond Wheelwright, *Printing Papers* (Chicago: University of Chicago Press, 1936).
3. Dard Hunter, *Papermaking: The History and Technique of an Ancient Craft,* 2d ed., rev. and enl. (New York: Alfred A. Knopf, 1947).
4. Grant, *Books & Documents,* p. 100.
5. William Bond Wheelwright, *Paper Trade Terms: A Glossary for*

the Allied Trades Printing and Paper (Chicago: Bradner Smith & Company, 1938).

6. *Facts about Paper Values* (L. L. Brown Paper Company, ca. 1933), p. 34.

7. This article is based on Grant, *Books & Documents,* pp. 112–40 and 165–84; and on C. E. Waters, *Inks,* Circular of the National Bureau of Standards C426 (Washington, D.C.: Government Printing Office, 1940). The latter is hereinafter cited as Waters, *Inks* (1940).

8. Reginald B. Haselden, *Scientific Aids for the Study of Manuscripts* (Oxford: Oxford University Press for the Bibliographical Society, 1935).

9. Grant, *Books & Documents,* pp. 118–23.

10. C. E. Waters, *Typewriter Ribbons and Carbon Paper,* Circular of the National Bureau of Standards C431 (Washington, D.C.: Government Printing Office, 1941), p. 20. Hereinafter cited as Waters, *Typewriter Ribbons and Carbon Paper.*

11. Waters, *Inks (1940),* pp. 48, 69. See also C. E. Waters, *Inks,* Circular of the National Bureau of Standards C413 (Washington, D.C.: Government Printing Office, 1936), pp. 32–33, 45.

12. Waters, *Typewriter Ribbons and Carbon Paper,* p. 24.

9 / The Handling and Repair of Fragile Documents

1. Adelaid E. Minogue, "The Repair and Preservation of Records," *Bulletins of the National Archives,* no. 5 (September 1943), p. 16.

2. Ibid., p. 21.

3. Ibid., pp. 21–22.

10 / The Protection of Records from Disaster

1. *Laws of Illinois, 1935–1936,* p. 56.

2. *Illinois Revised Statutes 1941,* chap. 15, sec. 9.

3. Ibid., chap. 124, sec. 5.

4. Ibid., chap. 129, sec. 41–42.

5. Jenkinson, *Manual,* pp. 147–52.

6. This article was also printed in *American Archivist* 5 (October 1942): 274–77.

11 / PHOTOGRAPHIC AND MICROPHOTOGRAPHIC REPRODUCTION OF
     RECORDS

1. This article was an address before the Illinois Circuit Clerks' and
County Recorders' Association before the end of World War II.

2. *Laws of Illinois, 1943,* pp. 1055–57.

3. Ibid., p. 1056.

4. H. W. Greenwood, *Document Photography: Individual Copying
and Mass Recording,* 2d ed. (London and New York: The Focal Press,
1943).

5. Ibid., p. 81.

6. Ibid., p. 39.

7. Bertha E. Josephson, "The Ninth Annual Meeting of the Society
of American Archivists," *American Archivist* 9 (April 1946): 108.

12 / RECORDS DISPOSAL

1. *Eighth Annual Report of the Archivist of the United States for the
Fiscal Year Ending June 30, 1942* (Washington, D.C.: Government
Printing Office, 1943), p. 3.

2. 48 Stat. 1122.

3. McCormick, "The Control of Records," 167.

4. Philip C. Brooks, "The Selection of Records for Preservation,"
American Archivist 3 (October 1940), p. 231. Hereinafter cited as
Brooks, "Selection of Records." Philip C. Brooks (1906–), served on
the staff of the National Archives, 1935–48 and 1950–53 as examiner,
records appraisal officer, and special assistant to the archivist of the
United States. He also served as records officer, National Security Re-
sources Board, 1948–50, and as director of the Federal Records Center,
San Francisco, 1953–57. He served as director of the Harry S. Truman
Library, 1957–71. He served as secretary of the Society of American
Archivists, 1936–42, and as president, 1949–51. See *Who's Who in
America* (1970–71), 36: 273; *Directory of Individual and Institutional
Members,* Society of American Archivists, 1970, pp. 11–12.

5. Brooks, "Selection of Records," 233.

6. *Laws of Illinois, 1943,* 1: 1056.

7. Ibid., 2: 385–86.

8. Ibid., 1: 1056. "The county records microfilm act approved July 16, 1943 was extended [in 1951] to include any 'municipal corporation or political subdivision of the State of Illinois' in the scope of the act and the title amended to read 'An Act in relation to the reproduction on film of public records of counties, municipal corporations, political subdivisions and courts, and the destruction of the original records so reproduced.' . . . In brief, any county, municipality, or other political subdivision in the state may destroy original records after microfilming or otherwise photographing the same, after due notice and a public hearing at which objections may be presented." "Recent Illinois Records Legislation," *Illinois Libraries* 33 (December 1951): 472. The amendment is found in *Laws of Illinois, 1951,* 1377–78.

13 / The Archivist and Records Management

1. Morris L. Radoff, "What Should Bind Us Together," *American Archivist* 19 (January 1956): 3–9. Morris L. Radoff (1905–), was editor, Maryland Historical Records Survey, 1936–38, and regional editor, Historical Records Survey, 1938–39. He became Maryland state archivist in 1939 and subsequently was designated archivist and records administrator. He was vice-president of the Society of American Archivists, 1946, and served as president, 1955. See *Directory of American Scholars,* vol. 1, *History,* p. 416; *Directory of Individual and Institutional Members,* Society of American Archivists, 1970, p. 61.

2. Margaret C. Norton, "The Illinois Records Management Survey," *American Archivist* 19 (January 1956): 51–57; Thornton W. Mitchell, "The Illinois Record[s] Management Survey," *American Archivist* 20 (April 1957): 119–30.

3. Robert Beeman, "Tools of the Office: Duplicating Equipment," *Office Management* 17 (March 1956): 51–80.